MW00719601

trenchart monographs hurry up please its time

Edited by
Teresa Carmody
Vanessa Place

LES FIGUES PRESS
Los Angeles

TrenchArt Monographs: hurry up please its time
FIRST EDITION

ISBN 13: 978-1-934254-59-2
ISBN 10: 1-934254-59-2
Library of Congress Control Number: 2015938244

Cover art by Stephanie Taylor.
Text and cover design by Les Figues Press.

Les Figues would like to acknowledge the following individuals for their generosity:
Lauren Bon, Johanna Blakley and Peter Binkow, Coco Owen, Pam Ore and Sara LaBorde,
Dr. Robert Wessels, Chris and Diane Calkins, Patrick Greaney, Elena Karina Byrne, Amy
Hood, Andrea Quaid, Deborah Harrington and Tracy Bachman.

In producing this book, special thanks to Les Figues interns:
Fisayo Adeyeye, Chloe Badner, Lily Clifford, Danielle Davis, Amber Donofrio, Sara
Newman, Matthew Polzin, and Becky Robison.

Thank you to our volunteer copy editors:
Harold Abramowitz, Mairead Case, Lindsey Drager, Brandi Homan, Coco Owen, and
Jeffrey Pethybridge.

DEPARTMENT OF CULTURAL AFFAIRS
City of Los Angeles

This book is made possible in part by a grant from the City of Los Angeles, Department of
Cultural Affairs.

Les Figues Press titles are available through:
Les Figues Press: http://www.lesfigues.com
Small Press Distribution: http://www.spdbooks.org

Post Office Box 7736
Los Angeles, CA 90007
info@lesfigues.com
www.lesfigues.com

TABLE OF CONTENTS

03. Parapet

04. Tracer

05. Maneuvers

06. Recon

07. Surplus

FOR WHAT REASON IS THIS WRITING: PUBLISHER'S PREFACE

Teresa Carmody

There are a number of well-loved stories about small press publishers. In one, Sylvia Beach, proprietor of Shakespeare & Co. in Paris, publishes James Joyce's *Ulysses*—a book considered too experimental and/or profane for a larger, commercially-minded venture. In another, Virginia and Leonard Woolf start Hogarth Press in their dining room, publishing Virginia's work, plus books by E.M. Forster, T.S. Eliot, Vita Sackville-West and more. There is also Amiri Baraka's Totem Press, which, with Corinth Books, co-published the beats—Allen Ginsberg, Diane Di Prima, Amiri Baraka when he was LeRoi Jones, Gregory Corso, and that guy Kerouac—thus making a new generation of writers and expanding the *OED*. These stories are loved, in part, because the later-recognized brilliance of the now-well-known writer simultaneously justifies the artistic vision of the writer and the existence of the small press.

Understand this: small presses (often mission-based, artist-run) are constantly asked why they exist. It is a question posed at conference panels and book fairs, in grant applications, and (sub-textually) in the publisher's own end-of-the year fundraising letter. It is a good question, one that commercial publishers—with their obvious profit motive—are not asked because we presumably understand that making money is a good and final reason in itself. And because money carries power, many people still believe that anything really truly worthwhile and important will be published—sooner or later—by a big, commercially-successful press.

Yet we also know that commercial legibility is socially scripted, that certain bodies, with typically deeper voices and standardized English, take up more cultural space because they sound and look like the people with more money and power. Excellent, commercially illegible work must find its place elsewhere. And so in answer to this *why*, many small presses understandably locate their origins in the desire to publish work nobody else will. Work considered too experimental, literary, innovative, cutting-edge, too transgressive by voices too often marginalized, ignored, unheard, or unrecognized. And when one of these voices "makes it," the press, and at least one of its writers, proves its worth. Which makes it easier for the press to receive grants and approach donors. And which returns us—uncomfortably, perhaps inescapably—to the language and logic of commercial justification, celebrating the break-away author story with its emphasis on the singular, individual voice over the social/material situation from which the writing, and thus, the writer, emerged.

*

We started Les Figues Press in 2005 to publish the TrenchArt series. In other words, the idea of the Press was the idea of the series. Or, simply put: we wanted to publish books as a conversation or group curation. As writers, we frequently discussed our work in terms of other people's writing, even as our individual efforts were writing into, or against, a larger social inscription or text. This larger text could be what Charles Taylor calls the "social imaginary," defined as "the ways people imagine their social existence," including their expectations, relationships, and the "deeper normative notions and images that underlie these expectations" (23). To Taylor, the social imaginary[1] is held together by the stuff of the imagination—images, stories, legends. If, as writers, we are making texts (poems, prose bits, novellas) in an increasingly networked world, what might our individual works, placed side-by-side, reveal about a social imaginary, which is also in/forming these individual texts? Fred Moten, in a talk at the University of Denver, refused to talk about writing "beginning," because writing, he said (and I'm paraphrasing) is simply a way our ongoing sociality sometimes emerges.[2] Writing, in other words, is a form of sociality. Writing never comes from one alone.

When we founded Les Figues, we (or to be more exact, I) did not have this language for writing. Yet demonstrating this intuitively-held relationship

---

1. This is also how Taylor distinguishes the social imaginary from social theory, which emphasizes theoretical terms over legends, stories, and images. Taylor, Charles. *Modern Social Imaginaries*. Durham: Duke University Press, 2004.

2. Fred Moten. University of Denver. Workshop at the University of Denver. October 7, 2014.

between individual texts—and the larger social text—felt worthy of publishing. Vanessa Place, Pam Ore, and I had been talking about this "something" we wanted to make for a few years, and one afternoon[3] we imagined a publication structure: TrenchArt.

Each TrenchArt series included 5 books: 4 perfect-bound works of poetry or prose, and 1 hand-bound collection of aesthetic essays or poetics by the writers and artists published in that particular series. The aesthetic/poetics collection was always the first series title; its contents helped frame the forthcoming conversation in the artists' and writers' terms. Altogether, we published eight TrenchArt series: Material (2005/06); Casements (2006/07); Parapet (2007/08); Tracer (2008/09); Maneuvers (2010); Recon (2011); Surplus (2012); and Logistics (2013). Each series was distinguished by color and the visual art on the back of the books (in lieu of blurbs or descriptive marketing copy). Because every book in the series had the same front cover design and trim size, people often confused them for a literary journal. To anyone familiar with the French publisher Gallimard, the cover design was obviously copied, making the book covers even less distinctive.

Yet in the midst of this merged social space, the TrenchArt series writers and artists agreed to our strange request that they write an aesthetic essay or poetics. We asked them to write about their writing, about the why of it: for what reason is this writing? Our question was, and is, about engagement with language, inscription, and the world. The answer, for most writers, changes. Multiple times.

*

Here is one more story. We imagined the TrenchArt series in late November 2004, shortly after the US Presidential election. TrenchArt is "any decorative item made by soldiers, prisoners of war or civilians where the manufacture is directly linked to armed conflict or its consequences." TrenchArt is commonly made from bullet casings, scrap metal, wood, bone. To that list we add images, words.

---

3. We happened to be at Chartres Cathedral, wandering through the labyrinth tombs beneath the Gothic structure. Sara LaBorde was also there, asking questions and warning us away from the sausage. We should have listened: the sausage was terrible.

EDITOR'S PREFACE

Vanessa Place

Historically, the salon has been a primary forum for literature and ladies. The salon is also forum for cross-talk and subtext. Cross-talk is conversation that is not, strictly speaking, on topic. It is also unwanted signals in a communication channel, such as a computer or radio, caused by transference of energy from another circuit, such as leakage or coupling. It exists for a receiver, which is a very different thing from something meant for a listener. Cross-talk is always slant, always subtext, the means of innuendo and inference—the way that sounds can insist on their points and points of reference, especially through leakage or coupling. Editorially, Les Figues Press was very much born from the desire for cross-talk as conversation. Conversation was (and is) the polite way of putting it, just as the desire to publish work that you believe would otherwise languish is the very mannered motive for being a publisher. But these reasons are like mythic virgins, pure offerings tossed at impure gods. What I wanted was cross-talk. I wanted, we wanted, to elicit conversations to the side, to induce seepage between writers and artists who would not be aware of their audience, not really, because they were busy thinking of their listeners. A German short story writer whose spare parables sound against the soundscapes cast into stories of a Los Angeles artist (Parapet Series); a South African collagist whose exacting baroque turns are countered by the indexical rigor of a New York artist who turns sonnets into word-lists. We are only as good as our ingredients. The TrenchArt series was a creature of conceit in the literary sense, where the seemingly unrelated and even contra-indicatory are connected by way of metaphor. Metaphors, as you know, posit that A = B. There is an argument for, or at least a feeling of, equiva-lency. Conceits are metaphors with a surprise inside: the parity is not so very obvious and often thus smacks of the metaphysical. In this, the TrenchArt series was also a conceit in the ordinary sense, as a kind of goddish gesture at making a world out of nothing, in which the rule is *contemplatio in caligine divina* (contemplation in divine darkness). Perhaps here is where it should be noted that Les Figues Press was also born from a women's art salon, Mrs. Porter's, held mostly regularly from 2004 until 2013 or thereabouts. Everyone who attended presented some item for aesthetic contemplation (one's own or another's) during the first half of the evening; the second half was devoted to teasing out connections and distinctions between the works. To a consideration of how these scraps of writing or bits of art might tat together, not a telos, but an essay. As in *essaie*, as in try. Try as in trial. The trial, of course, in the TrenchArt series, was the work itself. The sentence, also of course, the aesthetic essay asked of each writer and artist. To articulate what is aimed for and with, and whether or not the round was won, by the standards of the game now set out. The point at which cards are laid on the table and one must confess one's intentions, or at least betray one's inclinations. But as the essays gathered here followed in the hearts and minds of the writers and artists who wrote them, they preceded the readers' experience of the works themselves. And so, the TrenchArt series followed the sound-sensical manner of Alice's Queen of Hearts—sentence first, verdict afterwards. Which is an admirable way to run anything, especially sentences.

trenchart monographs
hurry
up
please
its
time

01. Material

Vanessa Place / Jennifer Calkins / Pam Ore / Teresa Carmody / Stephanie Taylor / 2005–06

Casements

Parapet

Tracer

Maneuvers

Recon

Surplus

Logistics

UNTITLED: RED OVER BLACK, BLUE, ORANGE

Vanessa Place

Beauty is a verb. Beauty, like history, is the movement of time through space and space through time; beauty, unlike history, is the movement set to music. The deepest music, the music that resists hearing, but whose register runs river-thick in the atomistic soul and bubbles over all appearance. Beauty is resistance, the trapped tension between form and uniform, space and figure, speech and silence, approach and retreat. Beauty will play itself in inversions of its occurrence: the painting, which occurs over the course of one or more planes, inherently favors space over time: the beautiful painting approaches time while retreating from space: this temporal confrontation cannot help but compound the space within which the confrontation takes place. Something that "takes place" takes place in both space and time, and space and time are perceived as a singularity: now/here is the only fully imagined reality: the poem, which occurs over the course of time, approaches space to prove, like the mind, that time past and time future are time present: *hurry up please its time*. The approach/ retreat is a singular, verbal event: beauty.

beauty as verb

For this reason, beauty is only image: Kant's *Critique of Pure Reason* segments then synthesizes perception into a tripartite action of apprehension, reproduction, and recognition. His *Critique of Judgement*, distinguishing between dynamic and determinant logics of perception, renders formal aesthetic operations beautiful and chaotic ones sublime. There is a teleologic

beauty as image

given to beauty, a prime regulative principle contrasted with the technologic of the sublime, which constitutes, but does not itself regulate, all regulation emanating from the perceptive subject: beauty is composed without, sublimity within. But there is no in/out, out/in, no subject separate from an object, no object separate from subject, for we are that which we apprehend, and that which we apprehend is, as are we, altered by the apprehension. The object exists as the subjective experience of the object which is itself subjective only as relative to the experienced object. As only image can be so apprehended, beauty is an event of the apprehension of the fuse and flux of time and space, subject and object, where being is revealed as hinged imagination, it is a moment, it is irreducible, and it is in the infinitive.

beauty as transcendent subjectivity

[This is not to say, as has been said and said, that there is no objectivity, or that the subject reigns supreme. For to say there is no objectivity is to at once exhaust the subject as rootless and, by the sin of subtraction, confess a pathetic belief in objectivity, at least as a negative integer: for as a thing exists relative to other things, the trump-subject calls to its absent object. The distinction here is there is no distinction, no subject without object, no object without subject. This is the deepest subjectivity, that which insists on the constant and communal fact of subjectivity, on the multiple truths of multiple subjectivities, which, by virtue of their persistent concurrences, establish the ineffably human. The point is not that a particular thing of beauty is transcendently beautiful, beautiful for all time and in all places (though Nature has its way of sly refutation), object sans subject, or that beauty is an acquisition, being both matter and effort of calculable taste, subject sans object; the point is the fact of beauty as verb: the transcendently subjective fact of the act of beauty. Until questions of noun/content are understood as secondary to the act of beauty, to the fact of transcendent subjectivity, there will continue to be countless and pointless pendulum pitches between those who would cast the rose contingent and those who only see statuary. And while both are true and sweetly needy, this rock-a-baby fact is the steadier feeling. Feelings being the slippery moment of this and that, the wormhole in the wormwood through which we are this, and that, here and there, us, and the drylipped them. Feelings inarticulate and exact, the smell of sun on winter skin, a bit of buttered bread across the tongue, the cold crack of the neighbor's nightly beer, a warm sweat plucking the back of your sunburnt neck, these are our inescapables, and like a surgeon's probe, art invokes history to provoke these facts into a new-named creation, making past things present and present things past, making things made compounded by their constant transparency—evoking infinite moments of infinite beauty.]

But this is too easy: if beauty is a verbal moment, it is necessarily movement, and movement implies alteration and finitude, circling back upon the serial questions of the traverse of time and space, previously posited as unified within the event. So beauty's movement must take place, like the lady laking the lake, within a vast thickness which gives Newtonian sway to obscurities and illuminations, just as exact metaphor becomes metamorphosis. In this way, Proust collapses time, folding movement ever-inward until it unfolds on the other side of time, the moment of epiphany, which, like the smashed atom, unleashes and obliterates the delusory orderings of chronology and location. Beckett expands time to the same devastation, bloating each tick til the clock, unable to sustain itself against its own gravitational pull, collapses into the void of absolute, inescapable singularity. Rodin turns bronze rock-rough and marble-smooth as melted brass, Shakespeare uses syntax like sacks of bagged cats, the iamb rock-skips, descanting the line as the sonnet paws and purrs its arguments, Soutine eliminated the prepositional and Ashbery gave subject, rather than predicate, to the airy nothing. All thickness, all tensile preparations for the infinite. Another example: Gass's admirable *The Tunnel* fails because the metaphor falls in on itself, a void (the tunnel) being incapable of holding a void (the Holocaust); W.G. Sebald's *Austerlitz* succeeds because the metaphor is avoidance, and the gentled minute makes possible the holocaustic monster. In this again, Kant returns to point out the need for the point of perception, and again, in this, there is the poignant and pathetic insistence on perception apart from perception, the eye that somehow lies outside the I. The eye incising the *imparfait*.

beauty the imparfait

For the imperfect is perfect: unfixed, lying along an ongoing past like iron train tracks, evoking the heat of history without whistle-stop, or terminus, constantly beckoning towards the present tense. Plain history, seen properly, is a scarification of beauty, where movement moves most knotted, dead lying beside dying, dying more living lying by dead, the brass in the tribal mask marking then events now seen, making a mock man mocking the man mocking the mask made. Plain history, seen improperly, lies horizontal and vertical, marching on and up into plus-one infinity: plain history is *moins-une* eternity, needing always the absence of something to create the illusion of unity, and the something is, as suspected, the tensed perception. In Ozu's *Tokyo Story*, Helios's seed has been duly scatter-shot, "Little Boy" god-dropped, so now only humans pass between planes: lines of telephone, smokestack, and sky, rectangles of wall, door, and window, the square sea bisected by a stone width of wall, proving themselves the permeable point of Euclidean irregularity, proving themselves human to themselves only; contrarily, in Reifenstahl's *Triumph of the Will*, humans were willed geometry, precise vertices who passed, historically, into a tumble of bulldozed bones. History is, as has been said, that upon which we currently agree. For this reason, plain history is image, but it is image rendered without beauty, for it does not move within itself: it is the long-legged march from here to here, movement confounded by the appearance of movement. *Triumph of the Will* contains no resistance to itself, Reifenstahl's progressive geometries never traversed, or suffused, which is why Reifenstahl's film is beautiful only in its stills, for the stills are stopped, the black mass bound, beautifully disordered by the white-empty border: why the stills have passed into the iconography of high commercial art: why we now live under the boot of capitalist democracy: there is only regress and regress and regress.

[The infinity of history referred to above is the historical feeling, which may be generally evoked via the common genius, such as Oedipus and Jesus, or more specifically constelled, like the stars moved by the love that is all souls' inception and terminus. So adorned, history, as mastered memory, is then the indifferent

the con-
junction of
history and
beauty

feeling of history: the ladies will still come and go, talking of Michelangelo. How to get from here to another here.]

The confusion of beauty and history is the account of great art; blind Tiresias saw the fusion of compound pleasure and the misprision of uncoupling, Mrs. Porter knew what to tell her daughter, wash, that is, what's needed, and wait. And now, it's time again.

In Dante's *Commedia*, each realm is shaped according to its burden of being: hell lies conical, the damned dropped downward according to their deeds, hell is heavy with narrative allegory, squirming with thick biography: the suicide who turned house to gallows is turned to wood becoming the cursed everyone that hangeth on a tree and their perverse rejuvenation, he bleats his faithless story with bubbled bleeding breath, swearing it true by his own incontinent roots. Time, like life, lies discontinuous but Fortune keeps rock-steady time. Purgatory means gradation: the terraces stepped with personal intent, deeds repented, and by this repentance, ordered and transformed to metaphor: history, not biography; time means something when there's an about-face, there's the sin and the contrapuntal

In Godard's *Notre Musique*, the Commedia is turned commentary on the clipped cliché: hell a congery of well-thumbed images, three-headed as a dog, a past-tensed ascent of visions of war to war's technology to war's victims to the war in Sarajevo, the movement from the random general to the private specific, which is the embodied cliché, the one we can't ignore. Purgatory is where distinction lies: the world is rendered and cleft, yolked with narrative, the image of an ordered world with horizontal plotting happening followed by the happening of other things just as a tram is seen going this way and that, and Godard himself expounds on the shot/countershot, the cliché of this versus that, the Janus-truth, which has been film's consequence and predicate. But this and that are undermined by the vertices of text: the

examples: Dante's *Commedia*; Godard's *Notre Musique*

angel, not opposing but conjoining, shaft to arrow, this is the hope of history infused with beauty, that the spine of self will be broken and the vessel thus rendered will render itself into something else: Christianity is built on the promise of metamorphosis. Paradise is the dogmatic simile, the positive *is*: the risen Rose beyond time, space, object, movement, all one, one all, the simultaneous concert so perfectly attuned as to seem as still as the Will of the Almighty.

A condition of complete simplicity
(Costing not less than everything)

current literary cliché of text its tendency toward interruption, the current commercial cliché of text its endless obliteration. Today built in degradation. Heaven is the personal cliché, completely positive as the digitized image, allusive and benevolent as a hunky U.S. Marine and an Edenic apple shared by the sun-bubbled shore.

The death of hope, and despair,
This is the death of air.

We use clichés because they are what's left, the dying dialect of a tribeless nation: what's right is the revised cliché, the aphoristic unconscious, the singular of the multiple, the object of me that is subject and object of I and that demands such shepherd's stew as is had by the absolute existence of the eternal me and the eternal you. The problem of foregrounding image over text—which is the current problem, it seems to me, as all is projected from *in camera's wake*, is the image can never replicate the metamorphosis of self that is the reality of our imagined existence. Text can. Text can envisage the impure or idealized self that is pure self because language is the stuff of our self-invention: as Eliot said, "Without words, no objects." And so we cannot return to sacred language, because sacred language is the language of purity, and purity, once the province of image, has been irrevocably contaminated by the image, or continue on blathering as if,

the problem of images

hidden in the meaningless coterie of meaningless imagery, there were some unimagined reality to which we append words like stammering postscripts, but must move to the verbal incantation of our imperfect beauty, measured rhythmically. Empires, like Ottomans, rise and fall under our feet, and what will be left are the frozen shipwrecks of faces, flowers, golden acts of grace, arias, *dis*pairs, and glass-coated hates, the past that trails after us and the future blazed before, what we want is the purity of the line neither new nor old, emerging, like the statue, breathing, stone.

the solution of text

[Metal shells along sandbagged shore. No cathedral but the library, no library but the looted library, no library but the reader, who will restock, book by book, the hereafter that lies before, soldered bullets halo our Gothic clocks, *its time, its time.* The image forever compromised, words pandered and pimped, that which is adulterate may not be aesthetically sufficient, there is nothing seen or heard but everything and still, in this constant shattered sound we will go on, noting the time: language that cannot be treated may be alchemized, the impurity of word and image becoming like rot in rich meat and ripe cheese, a source of high satisfaction, if we cannot purify the language of our impure tribe and if we do not think it moral to even try, then we must insist upon its absolute maculate beauty, the full force and effect of its rank and rival constitutions, we must not blind ourselves to any permutation or cadence, winding all reels around us to see to what level will be our destination, we must char our pretenses with Whitsunday faith and clutch the oily foreskin to our scabrous cheeks, talent tempering tradition tempering talent, we must move within our homemade confines, noting warm burnish of the walnut gun butt and the way a ringlet of blood circles counter-clockwise.]

the beautiful impure

Goya's *Saturno devorando a su hijo (Saturn Devouring His Son)*, is a beautiful painting, a perfect painting, the movement of man to man, consumptive and regurgitate, the divine father, having orgasmically created in his own image, sees in his own image the death of the image maker, and so he eats, feeding first from the head, the right arm next, then the left, feeding uncontrollably, the

example:
Goya

eyes cartooned insensate, knowing there will be another spurt so spent, knowing what the black pit will next erect, knowing that his feeding is death to his death and death to death is death to dying, again.

Movement eternal, movement locked within its own evocation. Here attensed so thick it appears transparent: the king is on the throne, we've seen him on TV, believing the righteous reign, faithless belief commanding fidelity, mission *accompli*, the queen is in the counting house, tallying the sheets, *dolce, dolce*, white, white, out and in, the streets run rich with poor believers and the salons coo-coo with pigeoned intellect, the artist makes the great refusal, the supreme won't of will, the decanted genius, the fraud sips at this and thinks it fine, why I could do as much, had I the time, the best part is its frankly universal appeal, impenetrable fun for the whole family, for children of all aged, I have seen these rank creatures, dogs all, all lapping their own vomit, death-greedy, starving, their ribs racked with gratuitous hunger, I have seen these things and seen more, their exhausted flesh composts me and the rhythm of their ticker tape hearts mirrors my backward dilation.

There is the rhythm here of paratactical hysteria, of hot wire leaping through hot blood, there is the need for cool vaulted gossip, the scrubbed whore telling of others to others and self to self, stories of no significance and so, every significance, special, you are, me too, and him and her and them in the back, we're all of us unique in our incantation, inside the round area is felt, something, nothing, no, something, we've pictures to prove it, objectively, don't be silly, but it's true, a starburst is an exploding gaseous celestial body, true, a starburst is a candy fruit chew, true, a starburst is a mandola'd star, true, a starburst is a clutch of star nits, true, a starburst is a headache, exactly, the black hole, that's what we've been saying.

[The reason *The Scream* is painted instead of its triggering horror is there is no contradiction to the scream. The trigger is contingent, the scream absolute. History spasms, there are historical screams, but the scream is not keyed to the epileptics of Church or State, but to the state of state itself: it is infinite objection. Relief sculpted out from the lack of relief that puddles and storms around us; like a black bat, the scream echolocates the world around us, fixing the unfixed distance between them and it and them and us and us and them and it is as attendant as a grain elevator at the edge of any town and it is beautiful.]

example: *The Scream*

What can we hear around us? These constant controversies are not mine, nor are they controversies. Pixilated facts, that's all, Hansel and Greteled from here to there by bits of stale something, no, nothing, it seems, explains these loose footsteps circling our sleeping brown cities. Didion wrote about the narrative frame and I misunderstood her to my benefit, I thought she was saying it is now only the narrative frame, like a series of photographs, one slid atop another in a narrow drawer, each hatched black and white, dabbed with not-quite-gray, each wrought cream-thick on fat pale paper, edges cut just ragged enough to gesture towards another, though the contiguous other is not necessary, nor needed, and in point of fact, would betray the complete singularity of the one in the drawer: as long as the one before us makes sense, all history requires is the smooth sense of one laying beneath and the bacon-breathed hope of the hereafter. She was not saying this, of course, but she was pointing at the wooden horse and whispering, *please*.

example: Didion

Beauty requires an attendant. The movement inhering in beauty is to be witnessed, and it is by this witnessing that movement comes within the moment of beauty. The rhythm of the tensed approaches or recedes against the rhythm of the attended: neither one nor other, but both. This is the doppler function of space around a statue and the words found not in the sonnet. This is also the function of what has been improperly called harmony: beauty is never the cambric resolve, but the heated umber of the always overtoning the now. History does not require an attendant, though it adores a gatekeeper. This is the difference between history, which aspires to communicate, and beauty, suspiring and constellate. We are the white-haired ones with black eyebrows and blue eyelashes, crooking towards the later years, we know

beauty's need for an attendant

logic is ensensate, the rose window beautiful as the rose. We know there's no knowing how deep the water lies, or whether its curative powers will prove, or prove most popular, but will insist on building on the soft-tarred seaside. We're familiar with the coastal interchange off the coastal interstate and the cold glass of cold beer, served by a thick-hipped waiter, we know beauty is not random, or unformed, we insist on the shot-call, the picture hung low, and close, the pattern described by the pattern, the cutlery purposefully put, the hair artfully parted and the trousers unrolled, we skip a quarter across the shore to court the thievish mermaid, our best hands best kept in the corner pocket, tattooed, they are, with the love song of all to all.

[Form, that's what we've been saying, form and formation, the latter understood as an invitation to the glacial workings of chance: chance is not random: chance is a combination of select probabilities, which might include the chance of absolute chance, therefore random and just: but not just random: for possibility without is no possibility, and it is no answer to lick the chain unless you leave the tongue. Duchamp bared his bride front, back, and side to side, and even in this there are no accidents save the cracks in the framing glasses, the seepage of the onanistic Word. Fruit, that's what's coming, some thing inherently incubatory, potentially corrective. Form, that's what we've been wanting, and though sometimes deemed a group grope among the smart set, a telescopic *rapprochement* doomed to recollect its collection, form is rather quick-cast, a transcribed proportion in torn silk and rattan, in French, that is, in English we prefer the clang of copper pots and clay pans and all transcription must suffer the low-slung consonance of an equally clumsy silence, again, it's rude to point but as beauty moves, it must move according to its motions, not formal subjugation but formal elaboration, and while footsteps painted on the floor precurse the dance, there is the dance, allure, call.

beauty's
need for
form

[A trebuchet ballet, a sonnet crown of holocausts, the melting ice cube, a man going over a pole vault, held to the earth by the head of a pin, unplanted feet pinwheeling the sky, the snuff and tang of the beloved's armpit, the rattle of yellow onions in a brown paper bag, the clean cut of a kitchen knife, pressed against the thumb, *example* and *if you take cranberries and stew them like applesauce they taste much more like prunes than rhubarb does,* here is a portrait of my love, the hickory girl, she with digitized eyes, she moves, that is, like a dancer, her feet broken in several places, like movement itself, fracture-footed, her toes beached and clawed like a bathtub's brass paws, she bathes in bubbly water and drinks pure Ivory flakes, she moves like a dream, like a dream had in stucco, three bedrooms, two baths, she's the darling of her regiment, she's fully corporeal, a private tutorial, and oh, oh, oh, how she sings, my love sings like a mirror, forward and back, neither soprano nor alto but rather sfumato, not merely nutritious, she's downright delicious, her candled skin coddles her filted blue skeleton, she loves, and lays waste, she moves, and by her movements nothing proves, sand spits and scorches to glass beneath her shattered feet, while her teats leach lugubrious corpuscles and a wood violin, apricot-scented smoke seeps from her cracked brass nostrils and her teeth are canted in venom and peat, she grasps at my neck, shredding tissue and tendon, she strings her instrument with these beating catastrophes and she screams.

Los Angeles
2005

Notes:

4. *hurry up, please its time* from T.S. Eliot, "The Waste Land," *The Waste Land and other poems* (New York: Signet, 1998).

7. "like the stars moved by the love..." refers to Dante, *Paradiso*, Canto XXXIII, trans. Singleton (Princeton, NJ: Princeton UP, 1975).

8. "talking of Michelangelo" from Eliot, "The Love Song of J. Alfred Prufrock," *The Waste Land and other poems* (New York: Signet, 1998).

9. both quotations from Eliot's "Little Gidding," *Four Quartets* (Fort Washington, PA: Harvest Book, 1971).

9. "dialect of a tribeless nation..." and (10) "language of our impure tribe..." refer both to Stéphane Mallarmé's "Le Tombeau d'Edgar Poe," *Stéphane Mallarmé: Selected Poetry and Prose,* ed. Caws (New York: New Directions, 1982) and Daisy Auden's *To Purify the Words of the Tribe: The Major Verse Poems of Stéphane Mallarmé* (Huntington Woods: Sky Blue P, 1999).

9. "Without words, no objects" from Eliot, *Knowledge and Experience in the Philosophy of F.H. Bradley* (New York: Columbia UP, 1964).

11. "inside the round area..." refers to Baudelaire, *La Chambre Double* (Hamburger, trans., *Baudelaire: Twenty Prose Poems*, City Lights Books, 1988).

12. "sleeping brown cities..." refers both to Baudelaire, "Les Sept Vieillards," *Selected Poems* (New York: Penguin, 1995) and Eliot, "The Waste Land."

12. Joan Didion, *Political Fictions* (New York: Knopf, 2001).

13. "love song of all to all..." refers to "The Love Song of J. Alfred Prufrock."

14. "if you take cranberries..." from the Marx Brothers, *Animal Crackers* (1930).

Postscript:

This is a historical document.

Los Angeles
2014

THE BULLET AND THE BIRD

Jennifer Calkins

Introduction

To be comfortable.
To be comfortable.
To want more and more.
To know nothing but an empty glass.
To know shades of truth.

To inhabit your mausoleum.

To draw your image in a windstorm.

To use your ashes
and paint my face.

I've got a Tomahawk in my side but that dont hurt me much
Wonder stings me more than the Bee
I am in danger—Sir—You think me 'uncontrolled'

This indeed
The thunder said

Methods

The fullest use of the materials at hand allows the artist to drag the viewer, reader, recipient in and hold, while the emotional concoction works its magic. For example, the distraction of Emily Dickinson's hymnal prosody and sweet-natured song leaves us completely unguarded when the ax comes down; similarly, Walt Whitman's discursiveness allows our corners to be softened.

The materials create the space for the piece to enter. The artist ablates the yoke of those that teach fear—letting the piece enter without the expectation of understanding on a cortical level. Understanding comes through the limbic system and is later processed by the cortices. In other words, your heart understands before your head.

Because of the acceptance that understanding will start at the core rather than the canopy, there is a level of egalitarianism to true art. Though increased referential knowledge may make the work richer, and the baseline import, the gut feeling, the heart, can come free of such ties if the apprehender only allows the naiveté of full surrender. There is a thirst for this richer deeper fuller experience for the mysterious in it.

"What is the matter with the day?
said Lord Wimsey. "Is the world
coming to an end?

"No, it is the eclipse."

Results (Figs. 1 and 2)

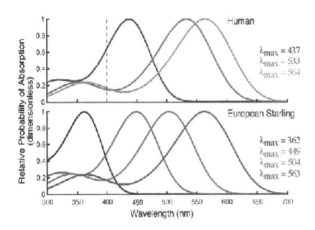

Fig. 1

**A A C A T C T C C G T C A G C G G C C T C A T G T G C T G C A T C T
T C T G C A T C T T C A C C G T C T T C G T C T C C A G C T C C C A G
G G A T**

Fig. 2 *Sturnus vulgaris*

ravish me three-personed God

a change in potential across a membrane
like Isis after copulation
ever the virgin queen

an inculcation of the work into the cellular culture
an emphasis on a particular neuronal circuitry—novel
extreme
inviting nonetheless

Blessed is the day.
And the one who destroys the day.

Discussion

There is a society
of life that goes on behind our backs.

In the movie *Winged Migration*
there is a movement towards an art in bird time,
an art that begins to capture the world of a variety
of avian species.
This is a world that is deeply strange, foreign to us
though it be right under our
noses (above our heads).

This bird time—
the strangeness, the mystery,
the horror we seek in art.

who is the third
that walks beside

What the movie captures
what we seek if we wish a certain freedom
the commonality of experience viewed with radically different eyes.

We share the same heart
we are so strange to one another
the goal
only connect
is infinitely unreachable.

if I feel so cold no fire can
If you saw a bullet hit a
if I wake tonight
a timbril to a tune

Here is a proposal:

to see with eye of a bird
one must have bird eyes.

A European starling, its vision into the UV, lives in a world radically different from our own. Essentially, we do not see this starling the way other starlings see her—for her feathers reflect colors we've never conceived.

How then might we have the eye of a bird when we have the soul of a mammal?

One answer is that we cannot.
Yet another is that it is not something to want.
A final is that although a European starling might never
place its pearly orbs into our blind sockets, nonetheless,
we seek *the wild thought of the bird as it casts itself into the void.*

Make yourself inhabit bird time
Make yourself envision bird sight
Make yourself become naïve and I will enter and enthrall you.

Conclusion

i work to drive the awe away, yet awe impels the work

Seattle
2005

Notes:

17. "I've got a Tomahawk..." from Emily Dickinson, *Selected Letters of Emily Dickinson*, ed. Thomas Johnson (Cambridge, MA: Belknap Press, 1985).

18. "What is the matter..." from Dorothy Sayers, *Unnatural Death* (New York: HarperTorch, 1995).

19. Figure One from *Palaeontologia Electronica,* (Volume 7, Issue 2, 2004).

19. Figure Two from genbank accession number AY227180.

19. "ravish me three-personed God" refers to Donne's *Holy Sonnet 14* (New York: Anchor, 1967).

19. "Blessed is the day..." from Brigit Pegeen Kelly, *The Orchard* (Rochester, NY: BOA Editions, Ltd, 2004).

20. Jacques Cluzaud and Jacques Perrin, *Winged Migration* (Columbia Tristar, 2001).

20. "who is the third..." from T.S. Eliot, "The Waste Land," *Selected Poems* (Fort Washington, PA: Harvest Books, 1967).

20. "only connect" from E. M. Forster, *Howards End* (New York: Penguin Books, 2000).

20. "if I feel so cold..." from Emily Dickinson, *Selected Letters of Emily Dickinson,* ed. Thomas Johnson (Cambridge, MA: Belknap Press, 1985).

21. "the wild thought..." from Susanna Clarke, *Jonathan Strange and Mr. Norrell* (London: Bloomsbury, 2004).

21. "i work to drive..." from Emily Dickinson, *Selected Letters of Emily Dickinson,* ed. Thomas Johnson (Cambridge, MA: Belknap Press, 1985).

Postscript: Addendum, Erratum

I was someone else when I wrote this research. I asked you to inhabit *bird time*. To see with the eyes of a bird. (I want access; I still want to inhabit.) My conclusion was wrong; the abyss is deeper than I'd thought.

I have stashed you away

The year after my paper was published, the Avian Brain Nomenclature group, Jarvis et al. 2006, released a radical revisiting of the avian brain and its functionality, destroying the old assumption of a common structure to function relationship across the brains of all vertebrates.

in a heart made of stone

In my paper, I asked you to be a *bird*; this was presumptuous. Not presuming you but presuming bird. I am not pessimistic; I continue to observe. If you observe honestly, you too struggle with the other, the hidden, lying across a deep abyss.

Do something for me

A new conclusion: In recognizing the impossibility of my inhabiting the mind, eyeballs of a bird, I am recognizing the presence of something so utterly other and strange. If I had interpreted my results with an eye stripped of assumption, I might have told you the truth in the first place. There is nothing but the illusion of shoals, immeasurable depths.

I simply know nothing else.

Seattle
2014

References:

Bachmann, I. *Darkness Spoken*, trans. Peter Filkins. Brookline, MA: Zephyr Press, 2006.

Jarvis, et al. "Avian brains and a new understanding of vertebrate brain evolution." *Nature Reviews Neuroscience* 6 (2006): 151-159.

A THEORY AND PRACTICE FOR POETRY IN AN AGE OF EXTINCTIONS AND ENVIRONMENTAL COLLAPSE

Pam Ore

Language is an ecological adaptation, an evolved
behavior that helps humans negotiate the environment,
to gain resources and reproductive advantages.

Writing is a particular specialization of the language adaptation.
It permits detailed knowledge and a history
of the patterns of such knowledge
to be transferred and built across generations.

Writing accelerates and entrenches habits of resource use
and reproduction. Commerce, law, science, religion
could not stand as they are without documents.
Writing is the mortar of human institutions.

What exactly are the responsibilities of poets in an age of mass extinctions?
How does poetry reinforce, constrain, accelerate, or re-imagine hard-wired
consumptive relationships with the environment?

How can poetry function as adaptive
when human success threatens so many species?

What new purposes and behaviors, if any, are possible if
each written word is a physical interaction with the Earth?

OVER

(Earth – Wilderness) x (temperature +) x (– species) = Human Life plain mathematics environmental biology evolutionary aesthetics a manifesto written language is law and linear as the bars on a cage as skin as the in and out of it humans are six billion plus and will double in a generation or two we're crashing foot on the gas into a wall poets typically witness events mark petit griefs but the many species of plants animals diatoms we'll send to extinction first is maybe a bigger grief than language can handle how does it feel to be an instrument of destruction if the pen is mightier maybe a word could slow things down a little but swords are not known for much Lavinia bore his hand as ransom as means instrument replacing language in her tongueless mouth speech without writing is the language of shame shameful shame on us the regular work of science and poetry is the excavation but what follows is commerce and commoditization of a brightness in human breathing truth repackaged as opinion sold as culture to we who are eating the last apples of paradise and no one will give twelve billion the boot these are notes slips of paper like prayers folded and crammed between the stones of the westernmost wall we will wail and wail wail wail we did not see it coming or not wail wail wail forget our inevitable altogether keep our dominant eyes on the beauty in the rearview while righteous liars sink into leadership put the pedal to the metal can poetry slow us down a little notice realize the meaning of tears in the ethogram mark the fulfillment of pity what resists writing that accelerates consumption what does poetic conservation look like a field a corner many dead leaves have blown into the telephone ringing in the next apartment what is our underlying trajectory without other species who reinforces denial keeps the knowledge of the holes in the world away or who creates sanctuary habitat environment for a spirit which feeds on mystery and requires real wilderness no poems exist without trees can something written inspire massive mutation upset the weakening steer the fast car of our evolutionary towards a different direction put a good foot on the brakes of accelerating sameness lay rubber on the dead-end road who can sleep anymore trade comfort for happiness twice a day write the disappearing earth and disappearing humanity written English is inheritance and respon-sibility scientific business political religious and military lexicons where imagination bleeds bandage or not whenever necessary writing is weapon and choice *angeled riffleshell green-blossom pearly mussel lined pocketbook true pigtoe cahaba pebblesnail pygmy elimia pagoda slitshell interrupted rocksnail eelgrass limpet moorean viviparous tree snail sutural partula acorn ramshorn corded purg wicker ancylid reverse pebblesnail snake river sucker longjaw cisco* utah lake sculpin ash meadows killifish maryland darter mexican dace whiteline topminnow thicktail chub phantom shiner durango shiner pahranagat spinedace sardinita de salado clear lake splittail new zealand grayling silver trout stumptooth minnowsouthern gastric-brooding frog southern day frog golden toad paestinian painted frog yunnan lake newt ainsworth's salamander vegas valley leopard frogcollin's poison frog armoured mist frog yellow-spotted tree frog marbled toadlet jamaican giant galliwasp kawekaweau cape verde giant skink gecko diurne geant de rodrigues tonga ground skink saint croix racer round island burrowing boa yunnan box turtlerodriguez giant tortoise charles island tortoise seychelles black terrapin great elephantbird oahu 'akialoa mauritius blue pigeon guadeloupe amazon glaucous macaw amsterdam island duck chatham island bellbird red rail kusaie island starling mysteroius starling cuban red macaw red-throated wood-rail double-banded argus ascension flightless crake chatham island fernbird st helena bulwer's petrel labrador duck imperial woodpecker bonin island grosbeak kona grosbeak brace's emerald gould's emerald reunion pigeon carolina parakeet new zealand quail delalande's coua raiatea parakeet black mamo hawaii mamo king island emu kangaroo island emu lanai hookbill st helena dove passenger pigeon macarene coot tanna ground dovetristan moorhen diffenbach's rail tahiti rail sharpe's rail wake island rail lord howe gerygone canarian black oystercatcher greater amakihi bogota sunangel huia new zealand little bittern mauritius grey parrot broad-billed parrot reunion shelduck reunion owl rodrigues owl mauritius owl mascarene parrot aukland island merganser solomon island crowned pigeon o'ahu 'o'o molokai 'o'o kaua'i 'o'o hawai'i 'o'o hawaiian thrush guam flycatcher st helena cuckoo aldabra brush-warbler bar-winged rail norfolk island kaka reunion night-heron himalayan quail molokai creeper oahu creeper specktacled cormorant great auk colombian grebe atitlan grebe maupiti monarch lord howe swamphen new caledonia gallinule kosrae crake white-winged sandpiper tahitian sandpiper paradise parrot newton's parakeet red moustached fruit dove slender-billed grackle dodo lesser koa-finch greater koa-finch pink-headed duck laughing owl reunion flightless ibis stephens island wren grand cayman thrush south island piopio north island piopio st helena hoopoe javanese lapwing bachman's warbler new zealand bush wren bonin thrush panay giant fruit bat bubal hartebeest burrowing bettong caucasian wisent oriente cave rat hispaniolan edible rat aurochs desert rat-kangaroo spanish wolf hokkaido japanese wolf honshu japanese wolf florida red wolf portugese ibex pyrenean ibex eastern elk merriam elk schomburgk's deer pig-footed bandicoot big thicket hog-nosed skunk white-footed tree rat ilin bushy-tailed cloud rat dicerorhinus sumatrensis lasiotis phillipine bare-backed fruit bat falkland island wolf tarpan syrian wild ass quagga arabian gazelle queen *of sheba's gazelle red gazelle cuban coney swan island hutia goff's southeastern pocket gopher imposter hutia madagascan dwarf hippopotamus malagasy hippo bluebuck stellar's sea cow robert's lechwe central hare-wallaby rufous hare-wallaby eastern hare-wallaby banded hare-wallaby lesser stick-nest rat toolache wallaby lesser bilby lava mouse martinique musk rat carribian monk seal sea mink new zealand greater short-tailed bat atalaye nesophontes darwin's galapagos mouse indefatigable galapagos mouse short-tailed hopping-mouse long-tailed hopping-mouse big-eared hopping-mouse darling downs hopping-mouse nendo tube-nosed fruit bat crescent nailtail wallaby nelson's rice rat kenya oribi barbary lion cape lion arizona jaguar bali tiger javan tiger caspian tiger verhoeven's giant tree rat western barred bandicoot desert bandicoot chadwick beach cotton mouse pemberton's deer mouse ponce de leon beach mouse cape warthog puerto rican flower bat sturdee's pipstrelle broad-faced potoroo miss waldron's red colobus monkey barbados raccoon sardinian pika dusky flying fox okinawa flying fox large palau flying fox guam flying fox twisted-toothed mouse maclear's rat bulldog rat dangs giant squirrel arizona cotton rat pallid hairy dwarf porcupine cebu warty pig kansas bog lemming nebraska bog lemming tacoma pocket gopher tasmanian tiger emperor rat mexican grizzly bear jamaican monkey japanese sea lion robust white eye*

Olympia
2005

Notes:

25-27: List of recently extinct animals from the International Union for Conservation of Nature and Natural Resources and the Washington State Fish and Wildlife Service. This list is not complete by any means.

A CATECHISM OF AESTHETICS FOR A TIME OF RELIGIOUS WAR

Teresa Carmody

1.   *What do you believe?*

We believe in art, creation's grand creation, succor of human sorrow, accuser of human error; in literature as liturgy and testament: conceived in necessity; born in humility; bred of ambition; and suffering the weight of its forebears. We believe the artist descends into her work; for which she must examine her self and her sentences with honest ferocity, so she may, through some grace, make something true and transcendent rise from the dead sleep of dailyness and diversion. We believe the best art ascends more brilliant than its creator; to be held in the infinite; a model to be judged by the living and the dead. We believe in the muse (we call her passion); the canon; the communion of the saints; the solidness of sin; the redemption of a life; and hope—always hope—everlasting.

2.   *What are the number of Articles in your Creed?*

The numbers depend upon form and function.

(a)   We are naked.
(b)   We are thirteen which indicate nouns, eleven in definitive, and two indefinitely.
(c)   Twelve persist as tenets of faith; twelve is a good number, divisible by one, two, three, four, six, and itself.

3.   *Do you agree with this statement: true believers believe most truly in the tenets?*

No. True believers believe most truly. That is enough to bring both hope and harm. I give no proof and proof is not required, but give me your ear and I'll fill it with rationality and allusion. Still, all must be justified.

4.   *What is proclaimed in the First Article of the Creed: I believe in art, creation's grand creation, succor of human sorrow, accuser of human error?*

Art is reflective and audacious, ancient and impulsive. Humans, creations themselves, with or without the art of the divine, formed in the womb from nature and the elements, fed on mother's blood in Edenic isolation, being one with the mother, held separate from chaos, come into this world and find it scary, learn they are subject and object separate from the mother, and at this they are relieved and upset, deeply betrayed, and the world around them is good and bad and all in-between. And when they have grown, some of these humans will make art. There is always at least one in each tribe and clan, at least one of each people and one throughout time, and this artist creates art, and the fact of this art is universal. So too is the impulse to create, effecting calm and arousal. King Saul could not be still without David's harp; David witnessed Saul's infirmity while his heart held the prophet Samuel's anointing that he would replace Saul as king. Art intended for the gods shames humans into remembering all we are not.

5.   *What is meant by the Second Article: in literature as liturgy and testament?*

Great literature, by its complexion of complicated form and content, requires a concentration of focus: meditative musing away from the text, close exegesis of detail held at arm's length. This meditation should illumine the human heart and condition; as literature focuses the public's attention, its writing is a public service, its reading a means of communion, instruction, and ritualized belief.

6.   *Must there be a morality in literature?*

There is always morality in literature, for words create a world the reader enters into even as the reader is entered by this world. This is a place beholden to the author's imagination, for it is she who named this world and ordered it according to her reason and passion, that is, her moral view of the world told through her conscious and subconscious minds.

7.   *Why do you say morality and not ethics?*

Individuals make art; societies make ethics. Morality is the weight of an individual; ethics is the consequence of social mores and standards. Individuals make moral decisions; judiciaries make ethical decisions. Art is experienced in the deep solitary of individual; art exists beyond jurisdiction.

8.   *Aren't you using a very basic legalistic definition of morality?*

Yes and No. In the basic sense, I am using morality to mean the beliefs of an individual: what she believes is good and/or bad, right and/or wrong. One's base moral fabric is the basis for most decisions, for even if one believes all is permissible, there is morality behind that permission, as the championing of amorality betrays a moral judgement. In a non-legalistic sense, morality is both:

(a)   part of the primal human psyche; and
(b)   a structuring aesthetic principle, especially at the sentential/line level.

9.   *Where is the morality of literature?*

Morality can be found in the psyche of actions, the syntax of belief. In Aristotle's *Poetics*, the thief steals; in Sartre, he who steals is a thief. Hugo asks, what if he needs bread to feed his starving children? We agree: stealing is a lesser sin than allowing children to starve. Still, the poor man in this situation must make an individual decision based on his moral outlook, and he may afterwards see himself as a worse person for not being able to properly provide for his children, or he may see himself as a better person for risking his personal safety for the welfare of his children, or he may not see himself at all, but the action remains: he took bread that did not belong to him, and this is stealing, and thieves steal, and people who steal are thieves, and sometimes one must simply steal, and sometimes one must be a thief. There is something true and horrible about the word thief; it is an archetypal noun, and nouns do not move. But characters do, and likewise character is not a noun, but a verb, capable of movement, including stagnation. Moral literature stresses the tension between character verbs and archetypal nouns.

10.   *Does morality exist in the eye of the beholder?*

We are judges; our eyes are unclear. We are guilty, born in pain.

11.   *Can you explain the third Article: conceived in necessity; born in humility; bred of ambition; and suffered the weight of its forebears?*

Art conceived in necessity is art the writer must write, because writing is the way one exists in the world, because there are those who have, as Wallace Stevens says, "a feeling about the world which creates a need that nothing satisfies except poetry and this has nothing to do with other poets or with anything else." We start with the feeling—a peculiar kind of sight—and learn again how putting pen to paper is an act of humiliation, for we do not know what we see, or see what we know. Ambition pushes our prose, raises a poem to its highest potential; stubborn ambition fueled by an acute focus of imagination, as well as the challenge put to us by other writers, living and dead, for we write in conversation and joyous competition, and when it is finished, it is only the work that matters or remains.

12.   *What is your responsibility to history?*

I am part of history, regardless of what fleeting feeling (*I am alone in the corner overeating*), fecal thought (*I come from dirt and coleslaw*), and facile theory (*I am only constructed, I am pure self beneath superficiality*) tries to trick me into trading my inheritance for a bowl of red stew (*I am Jacob, I am Esau*). I cannot excuse the sins of my forefathers; I bear their burden even as I am bereft of their blessing. It is difficult to be alive, and in another time and in another place, I would not be here, and so how dare I waste one minute wallowing in what's been done to me or what I did or did not do. Purposeful and painful reflection instead; the pursuit of education, engagement, until I am prepared (*as much as is possible, for trial is an imperfect teacher*) to wrestle flames from the upper hand. Literature is a history of illumination and hell's insulating fire, a great responsibility, for history is before and after, a life.

13.   *What is more real: history or fiction?*

When one examines the gospels—both the canonical works of the New Testament, and non-canonical works such as Thomas and Peter—one sees the details used by any one particular author were chosen to stress a theological point, not to document the actual life, words, and actions of the historical Jesus.

(a)   Mark: the name of the oldest and first gospel, written an estimated thirty-five years after Jesus was crucified. Few believed Jesus to be the Messiah, and in the text, no one understands Jesus as the Christ, not even the disciples. Mark is written for a doubting world.

(b)   Matthew: used Mark as a source, probably also Q, stresses the Jewishness of Jesus, traces his lineage back to Abraham, through David, after the exile. Fourteen generations between each major event—the founding, the kingdom, the exile, the Christ—and so Jesus is born on the seventh grouping of sevens. Jesus is analogized to Moses, giver of the law, through whom the covenant is written. Matthew is written for a present world awaiting the Messiah.

(c)   Luke: Jesus, Saviour of the world, for Jews and Gentiles, the lineage is traced back to Adam, progenitor of the human race. Christ is compared to the Elijah and Elisha, the prophets who ministered to gentiles. Of the four New Testament accounts, Luke is the only one who tells of the two thieves also crucified with Christ. One repents, and joins Christ in heaven; the other keeps his hardened heart. Luke is written for a future world of bleeding migration.

(d)   John: Christ, the lamb who was slain, notes the crucifixion at a different time than the other three: the day of Preparation as opposed to the Passover. This is the day the lambs are slain. John is written for eternity, past present future, for in the beginning was the word, and even the world can not contain all the books that would be written.

14.   *Why does an artist need to descend into her work; why, for the integrity of her work, does she need to examine her self and her sentences with honest ferocity?*

I am working with Biblical syntax and seepage, archetypal nouns and situations, as foretold through myth. Biblical language is beautiful and contradictory, carrying shame and inciting comfort. Pain cannot be stronger than endurance, and pleasure cannot be forever satisfied, for both instances would destroy the locus of these perceptions. God will not dole out more than one can endure, and this is necessarily true. Desire is primal. Fear and Love and Anger and Joy are universals, with local manifestations of experience found in rituals of belief.

I am very fond of Flannery O'Connor; her stories are convicting depictions of mystery and redemption, a momentary experience of God-given grace. These are her masterpieces, as both the short form and the sudden conversion belabor a brief, indefinite interval of time. O'Connor's characters are deeply corrupt, easily judged: a reader will rarely be as horrible as the Misfit, nor as naïvely selfish as the Grandmother. In their very materiality, her characters require a wrenching epiphany to meet their moment of grace, and the reader experiences this moment simultaneously, though to a lesser degree, as is appropriate given his smaller sin. The fierce truth of O'Connor hangs in the deeply flawed nature of human beings, who are slowly corrosive and death-seeking in their selfishness; they require the miraculous sentence to experience the grace of God.

15.   *What is meant by the Fifth Article, that humans may, through grace, make something true and transcendent rise from the dead sleep of dailyness and diversion?*

And it came to pass in the two thousandth and fourth year after the long-laboring birth of the man who came to be known as Jesus, son of God, the man for whom all male babies in Bethlehem were murdered, each one who was not yet two years old, which is to say one-thousand nine hundred and seventy three years before I was born, that I looked up and saw a woman, of red hair and short stature. She paced upon the carpet in her mother's house, like a girl of seven, though her age was fifty-nine. She wrung her hands and said perhaps it's time for another piece of apple pie, perhaps it's time to grow older, but she doesn't know how. Her hands were swollen and blue with fat veins. She sat then, at the head of the table and began to cough and choke on her own saliva, and her mother, who was also there, did not turn to comfort her, but told a story about two sisters who are so shy their long hair touches their knees, and they only leave their mother's house when there are offers of free things: beef at the tire store, a tote bag at the beauty counter, a stuffed spotted horse for opening a new bank account. The girls, that's what they like to do, said the women's mother, and she rocked in her chair and rubbed her cracked finger with the tip of her thumb.

16.   *Explain the claim: we believe the best art ascends more brilliant than its creator, to be held in the infinite.*

We are small and deeply flawed. We are arrogant and easily angered. We snap at our children and sink into horrible depressions. We are judgmental, especially of those whose writing betrays their best intentions: they write poorly and are pleased with themselves all the more. We are very serious, and we are deeply in love. We may be delusional, but we are truly in love. Our prayer is to make something of lasting value. An object of beauty is of lasting value.

17.   *What is revealed in the Seventh Article: a model to be judged by the living and the dead?*

How does this artifice stand next to Melville's ship in a bottle? And what of Eliot's minutely-webbed town, Shelley's monstrous cathedral, Woolf's lighthouse? For ultimately we must, as Woolf says, "be severe in our judgements; compare each book with the greatest of its kind."

18.   *Who is this muse?*

Passion may be uninformed; knowledge may be passionless.

(a)   Job: From the voice of the whirlwind, God speaks directly for the last time, saying, *Where wast thou when I laid the foundations of the earth? declare, if thou hast understanding.*

(b)   Psalms: Reasoned poetry, covenant reminders, praise, and persuasion: *Teach us to number our days, and establish the work of our hands upon us; yea, the work of our hands establish thou it.*

(c)   Proverbs: Didactic and parallelistic aphorisms recited to give *subtlety to the simple*, to teach *wisdom, justice, and judgement*, and equity. To fear the Lord is to act as if he exists.

(d)   Ecclesiastes: We are searching for the root of a wind and, *in much wisdom is much grief; and he that increaseth knowledge increaseth sorrow.*

(e)   Song of Songs: There is beauty in desire, wisdom in flesh, *set me as a seal upon thine heart, as a seal upon thine arm: for love is strong as death.*

Wisdom is passion informed.

19.   *What is the canon? The communion of the saints?*

As literary exegesis evolved from religious exegesis:
Have mercy on us.

So secular canons from ecclesiastical:
Have mercy on your servant.

The canon sets a basis for judgement, a standard criterion, established principle:
Good Lord, deliver him.

The canon is required training, and reading most excellent:
We beseech you to hear us, good Lord.

The canon is not closed, its cornerstones are well-formed and pleasing to the ear:
Give him your peace.

The canon is not closed, though heavily guarded:
Have mercy on him.

To write in English one must know English:
Into your hands, O Lord, we commend our brothers and sisters.

To know English one must know another language:
Christ, have mercy.

To know language is to know its limits:
Lord, have mercy.

20.   *What do you mean by the solidness of sin?*

Do you hear a man clearing his throat in the back of the room? He wants to explain how his work embodies modern man's constant feeling of void and alienation, the disconnect of everyday existence, that the author has been transformed, is part machine, this is the lack of feeling in his work.

(a)   While this has been a theme of most serious literature since World War II, great work is never without great emotion, for if humans matter, then the matter of humans must be conveyed.

(b)   The more difficult and moral action is to seek truth in the absence of absolutes, to hone the question regardless of its unanswerability. So we become like Job, who questions and praises God.

(c)   While the King James translation of Ecclesiastes begins: *Vanity of vanities, saith the Preacher, vanity of vanities; all is vanity*; the New International Version states, *Meaningless! Meaningless! says the Teacher. Utterly meaningless! Everything is meaningless.*

21.   *Who pays the price of redemption?*

I remember looking up and the sky was the color of blue found in Japanese paintings; there were branches above me, bare and deeply brown, with small pink buds beginning.

22.   *Why do you end with hope?*

First there was hope, and then there was love, and love changed everything.

Los Angeles
2005

Notes:

31. "a feeling about" from Wallace Stevens, *Poems by Wallace Stevens* (New York: Vintage, 1959).

35. "be severe in our judgements" from Virginia Woolf, "How Should One Read a Book?" *The Second Common Reader* (Fort Washington, PA: A Harvest Book, 1986).

35. Biblical quotations, Job to Ecclesiastes, from *The New Chain-Reference Bible*, King James Version (Indianapolis, IN: Kirkbride Bible Co, 1964).

35, 36. Litany in response to the canon refers to "The Ministration at the Time of Death," *The Book of Common Prayer* (New York: Church Hymnal Corporation and The Seabury Press, 1979).

36, 37. *Vanity of vanities* from *The New Chain-Reference Bible*, King James Version (Indianapolis, IN: Kirkbride Bible Co, 1964).

37. *Meaningless! Meaningless!* from *the Holy Bible: New International Version* (Grand Rapids, MI: Zondervan Co, 1988).

Postscript:

One must appreciate all one's selves.

Denver
2015

CHINESE COOKING

Stephanie Taylor

*Speech was given to the ordinary sort of men whereby to communicate their minds;
but to wise men, whereby to conceal it.*

— Robert South, sermon 1676

*Safe upon the solid rock the ugly houses stand: Come and see my shining palace
built upon the sand!*

— "Second Fig," Edna St. Vincent Millay

The *TrenchArt: Material* series work began with a source text—"Second
Fig" by Edna St. Vincent Millay (chosen because of the press namesake, Les
Figues Press). The short (partial) poem was divided into a series of single
syllables. Each syllable generated a list of rhyming words. A new text was
then written, loosely based on the syllable sequence of the original text.

This is a method of quotation in which what is quoted is not words but
sounds. Rhymes relay a sound sequence. By removing a text-portion (in this
case a sound) from a familiar setting, there is a hope of avoiding problems
of pointless and sloppy citation: when less is retained of the original text
(i.e. both the meaning and the associative status), a more active reworking
is required.

The lists of rhyming words for book one—*TrenchArt: Material*—included
the ever-irresistible "Wok," which thus shaped the new text into a reworked
tale of Chinese Cooking. In this same manner, each word in the new text is
based on a rhyme with the Millay text. "Prawns," for example, comes from
the –pon of upon, "Plums" from Come.

As the new text describes a tilt and some squids, the accompanying line-art illustrates these elements. Certain details, such as the range and fridge in the background, are presented merely as factual support of a story whose plot, in truth, is a semi-accidental product of words which share a sound. Because the Chinese text says "Chinese Cooking," the ink must be red like a Chinese menu.

As for book two—*Dies: A Sentence*—"Jug" came from the ug- of ugly, "hands" from sand. When you have hands and a jug, you're telling a story of hygiene. The Chinese text says simply, "Cleaning Technique." Incidentally, the second book is about war, invoking other techniques of cleaning.

Books three and four (*Grammar of the Cage* and *Requiem*), distributed simultaneously, make one picture when put together. Within the narrative framework, the yin-yang mirrors the two-books-as-one concept. Conveniently, in China, even food is divided into Yin and Yang. Book three (*Grammar of the Cage*), a book of poetry, lists Yang foods; book four (*Requiem*), a book of prose, lists Yin foods. The single-syllable foods are listed alphabetically and edited as a sound sequence.

These two covers are not directly generated from the Millay text. Rather, they are meant to demonstrate, by expanding the breadth of explication, that this now is truly a story of Chinese Cooking. The truth, of course, is that it is both a story of Chinese Cooking and a story of a text written from the ongoing performance of a sound sequence.

Finally, the art for book five—*A Story of Witchery*—returns to the themes in books one and two. The new text suggests a landscape so the illustration portrays one. The Chinese text says plainly "Inspiration of the Homeland." Again, coincidentally, the fifth book involves a journey.

Los Angeles
2005

Material

02. Casements
Sissy Boyd / Lisa Darms / Vincent Dachy / Molly
Corey / Julie Thi Underhill / Christine Wertheim /
Nuala Archer / 2006–07

Parapet

Tracer

Maneuvers

Recon

Surplus

Logistics

INTRODUCTION

Teresa Carmody
& Vanessa Place

Part One: The Problem of Silence

To write is to realize thought already present. This thought may be, as Schopenhauer insists, already formed in mind, or it may lay hidden in the mystery, to be uncovered and known, as Didion says, through the writing. For cells hold purpose and resistance, and to write is to breathe the body's breath into sound and symbol, making one form from another. In this, the writer is as God—coming in many forms and genders, with many varieties of purpose—for the writer's mind hovers over the face of what will be, like God's great darkness over the deep, and it is from this silence that meaning will be formed.

The writers in the *Casements* series embody silence like the edge of a sound wave: a shifting entity of determinacy, whose meaning comes with accretion, whose origin can be traced but not fully known, and whose essence penetrates enormous physical distances and unseen molecular plains. In Sissy Boyd's work, language is the gesture between speech and action, the body a bridge to "utterance" as she makes her "dance to silence." For Boyd, the breath is the press of that question: "is there language for that?" Vincent Dachy carves language from mist, to give, as he says, "a pace, a slope to the vapours, the savours, the beats and spasms that travel my body (to which my head belongs)." Dachy's words speak when writing stumbles, a necessary and welcome slip in his effort to write that which dares failure, that which bears a yes. "Poetry-(|'m)-Possible," a document by Christine Wertheim from the Society for CUm|n' Linguistics, or s'CUm, outlines a system of structural poetics which uncovers categorical and binary concepts embedded within the English language. Having extended these systems to art and literature, aesthetic-based art became an expression of male desire and anxiety, a "poetics of impotency that continuously stages its own disappearance." This will not do, and so the Society begins a methodological, categorical discovery, uncovering the "'feminine' vO|d$_s$e" that may create another god-imaged face. Finally, Nuala Archer uses Japanese forms (katauta, renga, haiku, sedoka) and self-originated acronyms (see text messaging code) to write a moment for each year of her life and beyond, into a period of pre-existence. Excerpted from a longer poem, these abstractions leave gaps in the official text, accentuated by a complete list of footnotes. This mixture of multiple worlds—East and West, traditional poetics and technological language—articulates Archer's use of silence, a polymorphic aesthetic of absence, the scanned and intricate Unsaid.

Memory and history are two other kinds of mute containers: one personal and internal, the other social and public, both shifting and mutable. The series' visual artists grapple with these elements in their work, overtly or on the slant. In "Aesthetic/Politic," Molly Corey interrupts an academic portrayal of her work with subjective descriptions and transcriptions of those same pieces, thus evoking the public and private realms. Lisa Darms writes a meditation on memory and the proper—if this is possible—form for remembering. Ultimately, Darms reaches the individual body, which through language can experience the immediate and felt incarnation of cultural memory. Julie Thi Underhill combines invention with disintegration, for as we make maps, so too we have an impulse to burn them. And where is our memory in this?

As the first title in the Casements series, this book is intended as a conversation between writers, artists, and readers. Just as the writers' and artists' thoughts are placed one next to the other, so this Introduction places one reader's engagement—mine—alongside another's—yours. For while each body/mind holds its reflections, their maturation comes in their realization, and for this, we have art. –TC

Part Two: The Promise of Negative Space

Wanting words. Paintings are composed of positive and negative space, fields of equal value, one more overtly stuffed with significance, the other of another sense, the insensate form of the latter made partly from the line of the former, which, like the cut of a clavicle, articulates and heralds the breast. Where the heart hides, beneath the ribbed and split chest. Several of the Casements series' writers wrote of Adorno and his obituary of lyric poetry, but it seems to me Duchamp sounded the longer-tolling death knell. His art was criticism and reconstitution, after which all art became more commonly comment than conceit, compost than composition, and anyone who wanted more was found more wanting. Added to which was Wittgenstein, who said, for Célan, who found himself unable to speak, and with Beckett, who spared no words, that the limits of his language were the limits of his world, and only common language could express the compass points. Compressed between these positive and negative spaces, the *Casements* authors cut new horizons like fresh teeth, making geographies of lyric possibilities that neither deny nor reify our snakebit histories.

"Poetry-(|'m)-Possible" takes both canon and enemy shells, melts all in the smithy of her knotted soul and hammers out a new tattoo of the inscribed inscribing self; Vincent Dachy goes molecular, letting participaled psychologies elide through the slippery purse of Western history, one slide at a time. Sissy Boyd considers the arm, the hip, the leg, in the dry light of their bones, and they move yesterday and break tomorrow, beautiful as only secular moments can be. Nuala Archer refuses to elaborate any aesthetic as such, but orients her year by year, compacting being to birthday cakes, being to nuggets of being, suggesting art comes unconscious, and the negative field is the unfolding lay of the land. The visual artists wind words like watchsprings within their workings: Molly Corey wants to retell history, to make sure it's not forgotten though it's only through a kind of forgetting that recollection has its shot; Lisa Darms shuttles between history's kept and empty houses, noting, like Boyd, that the body is the only orifice we've got, and that the time-released scent of authenticity will penetrate us like the best poetry pierces a willing pupil. Julie Thi Underhill notes that maps are made for what is missing, which is an inversion of what is. And what is, is what will be.

For Adorno is not and cannot be right for all time, or else the Holocaust won, and won as the trump genocide. And while Duchamp had a very good point, the infrathin has worn thinner still as it has also become callous and thickened, and we are coming to the end of the age of our repression. The inability to intimacy, the quivering disdain for all that bleeds periodically, the reification of irony as the sentiment manque, the huffalump's conviction that there can be no more meaning post-It, meaning post-Him, these are the beetle-browed affectations that have been played out and out to the mirrored crowd, and can no longer play. There is something thoughtless about thought that contents itself with disappointment, that thinks art exists as either a curative for life's carbuncular nature or as a bellow of outrage at its outrages. As Dante knew and Milton had to concede, Paradise is notoriously difficult to picture, the heavenly vision too-often constrained to a perfection that exists wholly via the negation of what is. So the positive aspects of the heretofore hereafter have been frozen, sculpted in heavy water and wet clabbered paint, stilled by the sorrow-soured breath of our forefathers, while the negative space moves, buckled by the backs of what lies beneath, billowed by the bawdy insistence on the loose-limbed sentence. Art is not a palliative for human horror, or a charmed illusion to be cast against disillusionment, but is, and is all that is—ecstacy and eggshells, faith and farts, justice and hot juicy twins. And as incantation will uncork all this, then there is no more disappointment, for life lies and lies along its spectrum, perfectly rendered, and there's no more need of art.

I've written to a false end. A mirage made of thirst. Just like the artists in this collection: conceding the inutility and necessity of my art, and my being. But unlike the beggar bearing his desert, I want no real relief. Because there is only the illusion of forgetting, the myth of silence, the seemingly empty of the teeming negative field. Life lies in toto, but not in sum, and there beats the recapitulate heart of all our art: the persistent perspective of another and another and another lyric horizon. –VP

TRANSLATION

Sissy Boyd

1

my body is wise and holds its connections.

the skeleton of so many bones
shapes my spine, head, face, trunk, limbs.
and the muscles I will to move I will to move
and there are muscles that move unwilled.

my mouth and nose and eyes open on my face.
in the curve of my arms,
in the place of my torso
I write words.

movement is my first language.
language is my second language.

translation is the key.

2

in the plain turn of the body make a sentence: dusk blurs her turn toward him.
in the way of hands, make a sentence: these hands cup water.
in the way of stepping into the shallow water.
in the way of letting down her hair, it only took the weight of that.

my body is a bridge.
silence to utterance.
I cross my own bridge.

3

she was born to a cold mother, and she rarely spoke. as a little girl she stood
sweltering on the side porch. punishment presumably, to speak when spoken
to. she met her body there. for hours she watched as she moved her hands.
she bent her knees, arched her back, dropped her head. these are my knees,
she said. I turn on these feet. and I move through my mother's house speaking
my own language.

so then she moved with some slight comfort about the icy house.

I was six, on the side porch,
in the swelter alone,
when I made my dance against my mother.

and over time the movements combined and she became a dancer.

4

at thirty, she was paralyzed by a virus. her entire nervous system was disabled.
she couldn't move or talk or swallow. or feel anything on her skin. or close her
eyes. for six months she lived this death of the body.

is there language for that?

the body lies like a stick, for six months on the white bed covers. where are
the words for that?

there must have been whispering
blurring like mist the crisis
in all that absence.
there must have been a voice on my arms.

5

a figure stands and is motionless for one poised moment before stepping, or speaking. we wait with our lives at the edge of silence, before patterns of dances and words.

we live on the verge of our own translations. in the contraction and release of muscles, at the juncture of bones.

lights come up on an empty stage.
the audience waits in darkness.
there is longing in the silence.
a girl enters

who first moved to save herself,
then movement was taken.
then she sought words
to pronounce the vacancy.

6

do not be lulled by adjectives.
do not dance to music.
dance to silence.

Anna Pavlova's arms. are there words for the expanse of her arms? are there words for the terror before words come?

Pavlova's arms shimmer at the brink of silence. may it always be so.

Los Angeles
2006

½ EARTH ½ ETHER

Lisa Darms

I

There are two houses in Amherst. ████████████████████
██
██████████████ The first house is The Homestead, former home of Emily Dickinson. It is spotless, somewhat spare, a container for scant Dickinson memorabilia. ███████████████████████████
███
█████████████████████████████████████ In the living room nothing original remains, except for the chaise lounge—which we are scrupulously informed has been reupholstered. I ask about the photographs of the poet that decorate the walls and bureaus—are they originals? No, the originals are too precious to be displayed ██████████████
██
██
███████████. We are reminded that Dickinson was unknown at the time of her death, that no one thought to preserve the kinds of ████ objects through which museum goers hope to encounter the dead. ██████████
████████████████████████████ The house is empty. If there are ghosts, they most likely reside in the garden where the poet liked to walk, and where shallow stone steps hold the shape of her footsteps.

Next door to The Homestead is The Evergreens, former home of Dickinson's brother Austin and his family. ███████████████████████
██

███

███

█████████████████████ the first thing we experience is the smell: a smell entirely new, because it is entirely old. It is the smell of another century ███

███

███

███

███

███

███

██████████ As we breathe, we leave the contemporary world. Through this inhalation, our bodies enter the past by way of the present. While visual images are often referential or allusive, coy or quotable, ███████████████ ████████████████ smell can never be appropriated or re-presented: it is always of the present ███████████████

███

███

███

███████████████████████████████████ It is quite common to visit a place like the Homestead, but it is rare to visit a historically significant place that has been willfully left to wear away. We are a culture that wants to remember ███████████████████████████████████ ████████████████████████████ But what do we want to remember, and how? If memory is ██████████ the mediated re-experience of the past, which structures best serve the goal of remembrance? Which of the two Dickinson homes more successfully reanimates the past? In a culture that constructs ever more museums, memorials, monuments, and archives, ████████████████ ███ What is the ideal form of remembrance? ███████████████████████

One of the primary legacies of the twentieth century has been the denigration (or liberation ████████████████████████████) of form. Marcel Duchamp radically wrested meaning from form when he displayed a urinal as art. ██████ ███ ████████████ Lawrence Weiner's ONE QUART GREEN EXTERIOR INDUSTRIAL ENAMEL THROWN ON A BRICK WALL (1968) is exhibited in galleries as text painted on a wall; ███ its primary meaning is found not in the space of the museum, but in an imagined physical action which doesn't need to occur. ████████████████████████████ ██ art has become philosophy, pure idea. And while much contemporary art is unapologetically apolitical, or at best ironically political, some of the 'assaults' on form in the twentieth century have ██████████ been forms of resistance, highly radical gestures, or concerted dismantlings of ideology. █████████████ ██████████████████████████████████████ even while maintaining their cynicism about society, art movements like Dada and Surrealism were innately optimistic in their belief that it was possible, and even right, to represent the irrationality of culture. After World War II however, artists wondered what forms could express the inexpressible ████ ██ ██ ██ ████████████████████████████████████

██ ██

Whenever we construct memorials or monuments that commemorate trauma, we engage in debates about the proper form and design of those structures while assuming trauma should be commemorated. Alongside our belief in the necessity of memorials is a belief in the remedial power of design. If the design is perfect we will remember correctly, efficiently. ████ ██ We are becoming, in the words of a newly constructed subdivision I recently passed on the highway, a 'Master Planned' society. ████████████████ ██ ██ ██ ██ ██ ██████████████████████████ The American dream of shaping one's destiny is conflated with the ideal of the perfect plan, the perfect life design. Perfect design is so ubiquitous that we know when to interpret certain imperfections as intentional, like a private joke. Like slapstick comedy, even our mistakes are planned. But ███████████████████ contingency is the

definitive property of existence, even in America. ████████████████████
████████████████████

As a teacher of photography and future archivist, I am preoccupied with the question of remembrance. ████████████████████████████
██
██
██
██
██ do we want to stop time, or do we want to reanimate it? Should my experience of the past be contingent on my bodily distance from it, or is there a way to simultaneously embody a sense of proximity and of history? Does the past endlessly repeat itself, or can we momentarily step outside of History ████
████████████████████? I propose that it is through imperfection, ambiguity, and doubt that we give life to the past. ████████████████
██
██

Sometimes objects express the pathos of their absence through the process of their disappearance.

██
████████████ The stutterer can never repeat herself. To make remembrance meaningful, the past should be █ different each time we experience it.
██
██
██
██
██

The ideal form of memory cannot be the result of a Master Plan.

II

██
██
██
██
██

███████████ Theodor Adorno famously said that to write poetry in a post-Holocaust world is barbaric. ███████████████████████████

███████████████ In the ███████████ art world—a world exemplified by relativistic, pluralistic, commodifiable, appropriated, and even non-existent forms—we have given up the outmoded idea that art is good for something. ███████████████ ██████████████████████████ The idea of art as an aesthetics of resistance is ████████ amusing, █ we ironically 'quote' and 'borrow' from the starry-eyed avant-gardes. Sometimes these references allow us to claim that the work is inherently a 'critique' of some institution or another, but such assertions are generally self-referential and empty. We suspect art has no value other than that defined by the market. If we are contemporary, we disdain objects—we recognize that meaning is external to form, that signifiers reign supreme over the signified.

███
███
███
███
█████████████████████████████████ In the twentieth century, war killed art, but now we need art back. We want to breathe the air of the Homestead and believe something important happened here. The avant-gardes blurred the borders between art and life, and the unintended result is that anything can be and is art, and anyone can buy it. Perhaps now that art objects and consumer products freely exchange places, the only form that can effectively contain and transmit memory is the body. ████████████
███
█████████████████████████████████ But bodies are temporary and singular ███████████████████████████████████████. The body seeks a form with which to cooperate. Perhaps literature—be it stuttering, fictional, despairing, irrational—can be the temporary vessel of memory; through the temporal act of reading a memoir or testimony, the reader partially embodies the memory of trauma ████████████████████ ████████ the body and the text—material and the intangible—are united to create a contingent form made up half of Ether, half of Earth.

New Haven
2006

Postscript: Under Erasure

When I was asked to republish this essay, I thought of it in terms of my job as an archivist. I knew I'd probably be embarrassed by my writing, but that it would be a way to enact my belief that the highest function of the textual archive is to preserve mistakes, imperfections and failures.

And then, I re-read it.

The archive documents failure, yes. But it doesn't have to perpetuate it. This is the voice of someone who, after three vaguely demoralizing years in a studio art graduate program, has spent a year unable to find work, reading only holocaust memoirs and back issues of *Artforum*. The original essay's stylistic pomposity and its humorlessness are qualities I've spent the last eight years trying to purge from my writing (and life). My first inclination, when I saw this essay in proofs, was to kill it.

But instead, I decided to return it with extensive redactions—a sort of faux-bureaucratic disavowal of the more facile ideas, and an homage to the sharpie marker *sous rature* of riot grrrl zines. I've found that the essay now expresses its stuttering logic more accurately. Because we don't want to stop time; we want to reanimate it.

Brooklyn
2014

THE MIST AND THE SLIPPER

Vincent Dachy

SLIPPER

Slips, slippery slopes. Walking, dragging one's feet.
The joy and the weight of the world; at night or early in the morning.
Slip-on laughter occasionally: molting from inside as the pencil goes and something gets shaped by its own secretion like a snail leaves its wake moist.

ANECDOTES

"I detest mummy."
Wasn't that the first poem I wrote? With passion.
And I left it where I thought it would not be found.
It was short and cogent. It was well received.
My mother could read between the lines.
I don't think I recoiled from mother tongue.

The world is cruel and cruel too the path to be carved toward my beloved. The furrow started after ten years old and lasted till dawn. I liked my carving pen.

After that it was too late to ignore writing. Far too late; so late I could not remember whether there had ever been a before.

POSSIBILITIES

Some write to leave traces. Why not looking back?
Some have vivid imaginations.
Some write to show that they are from a parish or [from] a town, a tribe or a street.
Some write to show that they can wield it.
Some like to tell stories, the more lies the better. To be believed.
Some write to pull legs.
Some like to move, to move others, or to move on and on and on.
Some write to make themselves be a little bit. Well, one has to find a way or another.
Some write with an immense sense of incommensurable hopelessness.
Some write to be clever, others write, but were already clever.
Some write because they are forgetful.
Some write because they can't play music, others because they can.
Some write instead of shouting.
Some write to wake people up. In your dreams!
Some write because they do not know what else to do with themselves.
Some write just to find a place for a comma.
I may fall in all of these with more or less readiness.
But above all else I write to give a pace, a slope
to the vapours, the savours, the beats and spasms that
travel my body (to which my head belongs).

I plead guilty.
(I only plead guilty. No excuse.)

MISCELLANEOUS ROMPS AND FOOLERIES

Doing something with the fact that writing can only be defined negatively,
like many things: love, the meaning of life, God, the meaning of meaning,
the schedule of particles in an accelerator, the right moment to jump into the
unknown…
I like to venture into what I did not guess I would have said
when it's too late.

Living is tragic. Destiny! and its wordy claws…
After a while, if you get used to it enough it becomes funny, funnier.
A caddish cod on a moody day refuses a smoke.

To make words speak.
Between simplicity and mannerism.
The fumble between vowels and consonants.
With a light left over.

Ciphering or deciphering? Imagine a plank or piece of paper or a skin or a thick piece of insole. Every time you hit on one side it gets marked on the other.

To give echo to what writing manifests is urgent writing.
Urgent writing, albeit slow.
Having ideas, opinions? Off course, plenty of ideas.
Most of the time ideas are not very costly; but to make them cut some mustard is something else.

Writing with a grit of mania. I don't need writing for melancholia.

To write some sense of urgency.

RECOMMENDATION

Do not curb the carving pen too much in front
of the discourse that judges. Do not stab either.
Find a pass between flesh and bone.

ASSERTION

The core of writing is poetic: saying something that is sensible and senseless, full and empty, fool and emptied, spacious enough for time to make event.
Neither negative nor positive.
When failing becomes a chance.

IMPOSSIBILITY

There is what gets written and what can't.

The real of writing is at hand when it stumbles. Not its reference or its aim, its means, or its virtues, its shortcomings, or manners, or eloquence, or pirouettes, or pretences, or pride, or its pretension, its intention, its retention, its truth, its illusions, or its boredom, or usefulness—no, its real is in what I butt against.

To bear witness to my faltering slips (and to cover them a bit because the bare weft is too loose).

The constraint, I feel it all the time. The constraint of the tongue.

HENCE

To write with the hate that lives at the heart of love. Writing as a way to say yes to a forced choice. It is very difficult to say yes. To say no makes things so much more consistent, and sounds so much more decisive.

MIST

With my slipper(s) on and my carving pen I walk about to find a place where it's possible to spread these meshed nets that sift the mist and collect water to drink or make things grow. Anywhere where there is a bit of a draught. There is the music of the breeze through the nets and there is the trickling of the water. This is not the best way in very wet lands but I prefer it a bit wry. When I find such a place I use my slippers to think as I trip over best in them and (set) the carving pen to furrow whatever water falls. In the very wet lands one can probably follow the paths of evaporation but that is not my ordinary inclination.

These nets are very light and easy to hang up, whether in crowded spaces or desert territory. In fact, they are so lithe that they easily absorb the agitation of urban life or leave free way to birds. They are quite special nets. They have the ability to catch the drifting humidity of living breaths transported by air.

***

What do I do when I write? Do I even know what I am doing when I walk? No, I do not, not really. Shouldn't I shut up then? No. From no on.

What does it do?

What's in a nightingale?
A Yes.

London
2006

Postscript:

The TrenchArt series was a rare opportunity.

A bouquet of enunciations.

A melting pot of conceptual persuasions. The not united statements of…

From the weaving diversities and my own turns of mind I'll take a formula with me:

D.I.Y. is a figure of rhetoric.

P.S.: after all, sometimes I make images—writing and bricolart.

London
2014

AESTHETIC/POLITIC

Molly Corey

In "Signature, Event, Context," Jacques Derrida engages J.L. Austin's notion of the performative utterance in order to open up its meaning. He defines the performative, whether found in a written text or a visual one, as a force that is put into operation through the text, rather than one that is purely illustrative. A performative must not just say something. It must do something.[1]

*The photographic installation, **Over 80 Photographs** is comprised of a collection of appropriated photographs which at first glance appear familiar in nature. The images are enigmatically connected: each contains the accidental stamp of the photographer, his/her shadow. In the singular image the shadow is easily overlooked, becoming the invisible stand-in for the one who looks. Yet amassed as they are in the installation, the viewer is not allowed to bypass them. The subject of the images shifts*

A young girl stands with her hip cocked wearing just a bikini top and a hula skirt. Her bangs are pulled to the side and tied with soft yarn. She smiles. Looming largely over her hula skirt is the dark outline of a man's head ......

from the family photograph to the indexical evidence of the photographer's presence. The work is meant to performatively jar the viewer into contemplating the presence of the mediator as well as the present viewer's meditative role. I assembled these images in an attempt to rupture the certainty of objectivity,—to make the invisible visible—uncovering the obscure detail, the moment that goes unnoticed, to arouse a curiosity about what lies on the surface—that which has always been present, yet never recognized. These images are located in the space of memory and history, each a captured moment in time, yet their resonance resides in the stain of the captor.

---

1. "Signature, Event, Context," *Glyph* (no. 2, 1977).

My art is guided by history: art history, social history, political history, and personal history. The historical and the personal are inextricably linked, like two sides of the same sheet of paper. My work is about how memory itself is political, and the process by which the political is transformed into memory.

I am driven by an urge to retrieve something lost or something that will soon be lost. Walter Benjamin has written about this impulse to return to the past in order to rescue it from disappearance. In his *Theses on the Philosophy of History* he says, "to articulate the past historically does not mean to recognize it 'the way it really was.' It means to seize hold of a memory as it flashes up at a moment of danger."[2] In uncovering the historic in my work, I don't mean to tell the story, but rather I am interested in telling a story—something highly constructed and subjective. In rescuing and remembering the past, the work allegorically reinvents meaning—a new story is told.

*Miming the logic of the cultural history museum, the installation **Fellow Travelers** plays with convention to unveil the ideological systems that construct how one is to read the work. The objects found in Fellow Travelers—diagrams of mid-century floor plans, the published diary of an anthropologist, a photograph of the personal diary of a young man seeking adventure, a highlighted letter written by a man refuting accusations of being a Communist—all play with the notion of both public and private space, as well as political and aesthetic space. The presentation of these 'documentary' objects allows for a push and pull between these forces.*

In block letters the word "private" is scrawled across the tattered and stained cover of the diary. On the opening page it reads, "Herein is recorded, day by day the joys and sorrows I have witnessed, the deceit and hypocrisy I have done while engaged in pursuing the goddess of adventure, whose spirit so dominates me that I am regarded as being of dubious sanity by many people."
Signed, George H. Corey.

I look at binary systems: aesthetics/politics, self/other, present/past, private/public, civilized/primitive to find what resides in the space between these polemics, where they rub up against each other, implicating both sides in their unconscious construction.

---

2. *Illuminations.* New York: Schocken Books, 1968, p. 225.

The **Dome Project** highlights the way in which an architectural landmark can symbolize both the search for and the loss of a potentially revolutionary and utopian moment. The installation is made of two elements. The first is a series of three-dimensional models of geodesic domes constructed out of photographic images selected both from my own work over the past ten years as well as family archives. These constructed pieces offer a sculptural testimony to the past, to what is lost. The very act of construction is an act of reclamation, however fleeting. In addition to the sculptural element, the project includes audio interviews with a group of communards who built the world's largest geodesic dome ever constructed by amateurs. These interviews are accompanied by a 30-minute video created from archival Super-8 footage taken between 1968 and 1972 by former members of this rural commune. The disjuncture between the video images and the audio interviews (recorded in 2003-2004) adumbrates the passage of time, the revisionist impulse, and ultimately, the evanescence of the bohemian moment.

My work interrogates acts of cultural appropriation, aesthetic and political choices, as well as the role of the museum, the role of the photographer, and the role of the anthropologist. Yet in this questioning, the work turns back on itself, ultimately illuminating my desire to forge a new integration of the historical and unique self, the photographed and the photographer, the subject and object, the self that lies within and without.

MC: We were talking about memories and how you said you well, don't know if your memories are... **JE**: Well that is not something I figured out, I read it. By Freud. **MC**: What exactly did he say. **JE**: He said that people modified their memories to fit what they are comfortable with. And generally speaking they leave out the bad parts and include the good parts. Which makes perfect sense. **MC**: Maybe just start by explaining why you went. And what made you decide to go and participate in this commune. **JE**: That requires a cigarette... I will quit before I die. Or visa versa... Let's see, how did I get hooked up with a bunch of crazy... Well you know... I'm kinda blurry as where to start. I have pretty good memories of about how things transpired but they're disjointed, you know they aren't in one smooth thing. I got out of high school just barely on the skin of my teeth. You know it was right in the middle of the draft and I had a draftable number. And knew that the only viable, legal way for me to get out of going to Vietnam was to get a student deferment. So there was that impetus to get into school... But I just took off. I said fuck it. I'm not going to school. I'm not doing anything. I'm going to the woods. It was just a wonderful, wonderful time. Not a care in the world. Meanwhile all these people are dying in Vietnam. But it just didn't enter into the picture... I didn't care a whole lot about a whole lot of things... And then by hook or by crook I ended up moving in next to Mary and Terry. And from then it was all down hill. End of story. [Laughs] I know that sounds kinda silly but I came under the wing of two radical, intellectual, radical crazinoids, you know?... And that's when plans were made to move to Colorado and start a commune. I knew that as soon as I dropped out of school I would lose my student deferment... But again I didn't care. I cared about so little... But anyways, we painted up this Volkswagon bus and people climbed in it and away we went, down the yellow brick road... We had meetings about how we were gonna do this and we were going to be the world's greatest communists... And we proceeded on that path. We kind of rounded up people from here and there... As it turned out Mary and Terry were pretty strongly avowed Marxists. Politically, I could give a shit one way or the other. I just did not care. I hate to sound so apathetic about my life but that is pretty much the way I felt. I'd have moments of clarity, but uh, you know I just kinda went with it... We bought a bunch of materials and proceeded to build a very large geodesic dome. Which for all intents and purposes was a comedy of errors, you know? But at the same time there was this miniature sexual revolution going on too. Alliances were breaking up, people were having sex with people that they shouldn't be having sex with because they were married to somebody else. Free love, I guess is what they called it. I never called it that... I get the feeling I'm making it sound kind of bland. But it was never bland. It was all very exciting. The idea of having kids and raising kids and delivering your own kids at home and cooking for everybody and division of... breaking down the barriers of the division of labor. Which was something I was all for. I never fought feminism. I thought it was a raw deal. So that just went on and on... And you know of course there was this catalyst for this whole thing, too, which was the war in Vietnam. And nobody forgot about it. Everybody did everything they could to hamper its movement forward, you know... I wasn't a communist. You know? And pretty much everybody was. I mean I was a communist in the sense I lived on a commune and I believed in a lot of the things that it did for a group of people, but politically speaking I wasn't a communist, and it made it somewhat hard I couldn't get into some long drawn out battle about Marxism or Mao's little red book with somebody who was obsessed. You know? Eventually, I started to go my own way. I started to go local. I ended up with local cowboy friends. I started dressing like a cowboy and doing crazy things like a cowboy. And just gradually moved farther and farther away. You know, I'd touch base once in awhile. And that happened with a number of people. You know it was a long and drawn out process, whereby certain people left. They'd pursue careers, they'd let the silliness drop by the side and decided it was time to get on with their lives and they left... I don't know, it was kind of sad when people started going their own ways. I mean I could see it coming. There was no question that it was inevitable. It's now what is called a subdivision...

Los Angeles
2006

MAPS

Julie Thi Underhill

And at each door, the hinges are seams
disintegrating as we follow the wind
to source an ocean burnished with rust

there's nothing new we've lost
when loving it, the sea, we go missing

Since the past is not passed, but in rituals
indecipherable by others, draped in paper calm,
memory's gone we'll necessarily invent it
two by two alone in pairs or simply alone

Even our names will not salute us
after we burn the maps to our bodies
we'll never find those renouncing
impossible pasts, our bones smoldered
there'll be no ash ~ only memory ~ stomped
the ground

Portland
2006

Postscript:

After all these years, when I wake in the morning and hear them calling to one another from trees and power lines, I always wonder, is that particular *caaaawwwww* crying out for retribution? For one's missing other, the ragged inky silhouette belonging only to one? Or both?

Are our own fierce devotions—our vengeance on behalf of one of our own, our ache for the singular other whose peculiarities summon *o you* over and over—our own indications of highest intelligence?

What have we lost of one another, and ourselves, without such loyalties?

And, once I've cut the ink-stained red thread tying me to you and you and you and you but especially to you, is there a way to begin anew?

Berkeley
2014

POETRY-(I'm)-POSSIBLE

Christine Wertheim

Aesthetics as a discipline arose in the late eighteenth century when philosophers like Alexander Gottlieb recognized that the sciences were incomplete, given the absence of a science of beauty. [...] Early aesthetic theories were concerned not so much with sensory apprehension of reality as with *the theory of poetry*, whose topic was thought to be the meaning of beauty (Turner, 1, *emphasis added*).

What kind of aesthetics is possible today, and what kind of poetry might be thrown up by considering this question?

Following the Holocaust, and its many successors, some modern thinkers have questioned the relation of art to beauty, Adorno famously announcing that (lyric) poetry is impossible after Auschwitz. This does not mean that art per se had become unacceptable, but that poetry, or any creative endeavor, aimed primarily at the production of beauty makes a "mockery of true values in a world of total violence" (Turner, 2). By uncoupling the values Truth and Beauty, then de-emphasizing the relation between Beauty and Art, the (post)-modern turn[1] enabled a realm of human activity, known since Kant as 'the Aesthetic,' to emancipate itself from representational correctness,

---

1. I use the term (post)-modern to indicate that the general perspective referred to in this paper may be seen as either modern or post-modern, depending on one's view of 'modernity', i.e., the aesthetico-political-economy/paradigm of ideas, people, things and techniques that frames modern art. Though I make no distinction here between the modern and the post-modern, both of these should be sharply distinguished from the similar terms 'Modernism' and 'Post-Modernism' which refer exclusively to certain movements within the arts.

moral rectitude, and sensory delight, and become a separate domain with its own autonomous values and aims. The question is: how does this zone relate to other parts of the social body? And, after more than 150 years of 'experiments,' can Truth, Beauty, and Ethics play any part in its function, or are these so-called master values excluded, *by definition,* from the Aesthetic?

In this paper I approach these questions by drawing on the aesthetics of the philosopher and literary genealogist, Jacques Rancière, and the work of the social and literary theorist, Christine Buci-Glucksmann, before concluding with some words of my own. The point, however, is not to prescribe what (post)-modern art should be, nor how it should set about achieving its goals, for like Rancière, my interest lies with the Aesthetic, not art. My aim is to take the Rancièrean idea of the Aesthetic and, after considering the role Buci-Glucksmann accords gender in this realm, to give an example of the potential the Aesthetic has in it to become(ing). Whether this example embraces a Truth, a Beauty, or an Ethics, I will leave my readers to judge for themselves.

Aesthetic Regimes[2]

Rancière begins his presentation of aesthetics by arguing that there is an intimate link between art and politics. In fact, art *qua* art "does politics" all by itself, according to Rancière, for its ways of organizing what can be seen and what can be said are the foundations on which the political is *neces-sarily* erected. This does not mean that politics has been commandeered by a perverse "will to art" (2004a, 13). The aesthetic core in Rancière's schema is rather a structural *delimitation of the senses* that determines both what can be seen *as art,* and what will be accepted as *politics.* In other words, Rancière extends the Kantian notion of *a priori* forms from the realm of the logico-sensual to the arenas of cultural and social experience. He extends the idea that there are specific and determinable structures governing thought processes, to an analysis of the *forms of communication and relation* that determine the constitution of a community, i.e., the *polis.* Rancière names these aesthetic-political form-structures[3] "partitions of the sensible," to foreground the fact

---

2. An earlier version of this section appears in my paper, Wertheim, Christine, "The Unboring Boring and the New Dreams of Stone." *Open Letter,* Twelfth Series, No. 7, Fall 2005. Eds. Lori Emerson and Barbara Cole. 131-139.

3. In this paper, the terms 'form' and 'structure' are used synonymously. Though this may seem odd to those trained in certain branches of the humanities, in mathematics a 'structure' is a minimal group of relations from which other forms are derived by closing down even more of the structure's potential.

that they are neither solely physical nor solely conceptual, but apply to the boundaries where Sense meets the senses in the processes of human intercourse.[4]

Unlike Kant, however, Rancière is no universalist. Rather, he follows Foucault in arguing that the fundamental organizing structures of human experience are fungible, even open to total realignment. In fact, he argues, at any given time there may be more than one such arrangement in play. Politics from this perspective is not so much the vying for power within a particular system, as the battle *between two or more forms* of political organization that are, in themselves, completely different. Likewise, Rancière argues with Plato, the ways of making and doing that we call art are also not universals, but divide, at least in 'western' culture, into three fundamentally different modes, all of which may be in play at any point in time. Each mode of politics is allied to a specific organization of art, for both are produced from the same fundamental communicative form, the same partition of the sensible. Thus is the political inextricably tied to the 'aesthetic,' here meaning a partition of the senses that determines both what can be seen (as art), and what can be said (within the political arena).

Following Plato, Rancière recognizes three main "aesthetico-political regimes in Western culture," the *ethical*, the *representative* or *poetic*, and the *aesthetic*, and, like Plato, he does not recognize any necessary teleology in the order of their appearances.[5] As stated, all three may exist simultaneously, each vying for the upper hand. As Rancière notes, much confusion about art in the modern era stems from the (misunderstood) differences between the aims and methods of the *representative* and *aesthetic* regimes. Though Rancière's regimes echo Kant's *a priori* forms, his main historical precursor is Plato, for whom what we call the 'arts' played a fundamental role in community formation and the constitution of the polis.

---

4. The term 'intercourse' is used here in the widest possible sense, encompassing communicative, economic and social exchanges, as well as the sexual. Marx used the similar German term *verkehr* to name the activity that defines the specifically human form of being.

5. In this paper the term 'aesthetic regime,' unitalicized, refers to all three of Plato's social forms. However, the italicized term '*aesthetic regime*,' refers exclusively to the form that is synonymous with democracy, the form we live in today.

For Plato, 'art' as such did not exist. There were simply different ways of making and doing, each with its own unique political implications due to the inherent differences in the way each relates bodies to space. In the Platonic schema, there are three main forms of making/doing, dubbed by Rancière the Chorus, the Theatre, and the Page. Ranked by Plato in descending order of desirability, each provides the model and the expression of a different form of social relation. For Plato, the best form of making/doing is the chorus, which constitutes a "choreographic form of the community that sings and dances its own proper unity" (2004a, 14), with its own proper body and its own proper voice. The catch in this paradigm is that it demands such clarity in the partition of places and identities that each body may only ever occupy one position. A butcher cuts meat and a mother tends children. Being otherwise engaged, neither is placed to handle the business of governance. In Plato's political theory, the analogue of the chorus is thus a body of men whose sole occupation is the running of the state, that is, a separate political *class*, who of course were all men. Rancière calls the order built on this paradigm the *ethical regime*, and claims that, in the Platonic schema, it is strictly opposed to democracy.

The next best, or second worst, artistic mode round which Plato allowed that a community might be formed is known as the "theatrical," even when it is practiced in the mediums of paint and ink. When this mode dominates, we have what Rancière calls the *representative* or *poetic regime*. The problem with theatre is that it confuses identity and places. Theatre splits people (both actors and spectators) by introducing a fantasy with which they identify, overriding their real experience, of being in a particular social space communing with other particular living bodies. In the Platonic ideology of essences the duplicity engendered by theatre is only slightly less dangerous than the poison of the simulacra. Though stage-bound theatre had been practiced for ages, it became the paradigm of the arts in the Renaissance, when theatrical methods of representation were transferred to the page, the canvas, and the wall.

The *representative regime* is based on the dual principle of mimesis/poesis. Rancière insists, however, that these 'principles' are not prescriptive, but rather that they grant artworks the ability to act *as if* they could actually stand in for real events—acts of living speech, or decisive moments of action and meaning. On the mimetic side, classical poetics established "a relationship of correspondence between speech and painting, between the sayable and the visible" (2004a, 16), that accorded imitation a positive value. On the poetic side, the *representative regime* upheld the Aristotelian idea that life is a disordered succession of events that can only be endowed with meaning when they *are arranged* into causal chains by poets. In this regime, meaning is not seen as inherent in the world. It is constituted only in the Sense given to it through the composition of a poetic or artistic structure. Now, not only can high (mimetic) art be distinguished from low (decorative) art, but there is a specific criterion for distinguishing between good (high) art and bad (high) art; the criterion of adequation under which every position in the order of things has its own unique style of speech and look, its own unique character. From this perspective, the monologue of a Shakespearean fool is better art than the songs of angels penned by a hack, for what makes the "art" is neither the topic nor the voice, but the *fit* between the two, the *adequation* between a subject, and the manner in which this is represented.

In opposition to the Modernist ideology that art in the modern era distinguishes itself by its focus on medium-specificity and (inscriptional) surface, Rancière asserts that an obsession with surface was already apparent in the *representative regime*. However, he argues, a 'surface' should not be defined as merely a geometric object, but rather should be seen as an *interface*, a space in which the representational purity of high art has always been infected by the non-representational abstractions of the decorative, as we see in all classically decorated interiors. From this perspective, the modern, or *aesthetic regime* is not so much defined by its turn towards abstraction, as by the arts' final realization of themselves as *Art* through their complete capitulation to the *lack of distinction* between the figurative and the decorative, and their unification as the singularity Art, via their wholehearted embrace of the infrathin structure of their own proper space, the page on which they are inscribed.

It is in this sense that, for Plato, painting and writing are banded together, for both subsist in the same inarticulate, infrathin, and superficial space. Even more than theatrical mimesis, Plato hated arts inscribed on a page because he conceived of this surface as a dead thing wandering aimlessly without knowing whom to speak to or whom to not. In the great Greek's eye, this futile wandering of inert sign-surfaces destroys every legitimate foundation for the relationship between the positions of bodies in shared space and the effects of language. In other words, under this regime, in which Plato saw only dead letters and mute signs, there is no adequation between ways of speaking and socio-spatial positioning: anyone may speak to anyone, in any way, from any place, and all utterances have the same (lifeless) value. For Plato, the aesthetic formation built around such inert sign surfaces is strictly identical with the reign of democracy, which he saw as a form of community based on an indefinite partition of identities that can only lead to illegitimate relations. Thus was Plato's aesthetics driven by his political reaction to the Democracy: his diatribe against writing being simply another part of his political campaign to topple what was then a fragile new form of community. But the repressed has returned, and with it the indiscriminate, wandering page.

Art as Paradox

In contrast to much contemporary theorizing on the arts, Rancière argues that the lack of (classical) artistry of (post)-modern art is not the result of an allegiance to abstraction, medium specificity, or any other formalist principle. It is not even essentially determined by the infrathin space in which it first spawned. The only essential quality of (modern, or *aesthetic*) Art, for Rancière, is that, in its form, it is divided against itself.

> In the aesthetic regime, artistic phenomena are [...] inhabited by a heterogeneous power, *the power of a form of thought that has become foreign to itself*: a product identical with something not produced, knowledge transformed into non-knowledge, *logos* identical with pathos, the intention of the unintentional, etc. (2004a: 22-23), [*emphasis added*].

For Rancière, the ultimate example of such an Art is Flaubert's *Bouvard et Pécuchet*, the story of two copy-clerks who quit their jobs for a life of self improvement through reading, but wind up returning to copying when their learned aspirations turn out to be just another romantic fantasy.

> Instead of trying to apply the words of the books in real life, they will [now] only copy them. [...] The novelist himself has nothing more to do than to copy the books that his characters are supposed to copy (2004b: 22).

But if it is true, that in the *aesthetic regime* for art to be Art, it must "undo itself" (2004b: 22), what is its purpose?

As both Adorno and Rancière make clear, the point is simple, the *aesthetic partition of the sensible* does not just define a regime of art-making practices. It also defines a form of community. Art is divided against itself because the modern (democratic) community is divided against itself. This is not a contingent state we could possibly overcome by a universal consensus, (what we might call the democratic fallacy). Contradictory paradoxical relations, and the inability to totalize or homogenize society, are the terms of communion 'democracy' brings, not consensus. If Art is thus to 'represent' the society within which it flourishes, it too must—indeed, according to both Rancière and Plato, it *will*—appear in a form that has become foreign to itself.

But where for Plato such contradictory forms were anathema—to be wiped from the *polis* by erasing them from art—Rancière and Adorno take the opposite approach. Accepting that the tide has turned, and that it is impossible, at least for now, to return to a more coherent age (albeit these were built on hierarchical grounds), modern philosophers argue that the one function Art can have is to help us learn to bear our contradictions by staking out spaces where these will not be covered up or denied, but kept out in the open and fully embraced. This open maintenance of contradictions, paradoxes, and oxymorons is the ethical function of Art in the (post)-modern era. Of course, this does not mean that Art does not have something to say about Truth, for the 'truth' of the (post)-modern era is that all intercourse takes the form of a paradox (a logical state that is neither true nor false, for it erases the difference between these classical values.) Neither does it mean that Art cannot be beautiful. Few would argue that Flaubert's writing is ugly. But these are not the values central to its being. All that matters essentially is that the phenomenon be beside itself.

The question is then, why, after first having spawned over two-thousand years ago, this paradoxical mode of communion should have re-emerged so vigorously in modern times?

Aesthetic Regimes and the Gender of Politics

As Rancière shows, aesthetic regimes are linked to political forms. The philosopher does not include familiar and sexual relations in his analysis of the community, for neither does Plato[6], but many other theorizers of the modern, from Lacan and Derrida, to Kristeva and Irigaray, have concluded that the sudden flowering of paradoxes within modern society is linked to a transformation in the symbolic division of gender. For the social and literary historian Christine Buci-Glucksmann, the essence of this transformation is a modification in the flow of desire, brought on when the sexual drive meets a desire not to know. The effect of this meeting is a transformation in the object of desire, no longer ~~The~~ Woman, but the cessation of desire itself, the want not to want.

For Glucksmann, as for many others, this desire to not know is connected to (Western) men's increasing sense, as modernity matured, of a catastrophic loss which threw into relief the power of (an) absence. Within this framework, the feminine became visible in a new kind of way as masculine desire began to imag-(in)-e its absence in/on/with the figure of the female body. In other words, in the modern partition of the sensible, the feminine becomes the ultimate ground on which men decipher/inscribe the catastrophe of their self-perceived loss of power, meaning, and love. This is how the myth of "castration" plays itself out in the modern world. However, the (anti)-hero in this version of the tale is not a prince, but the *flaneur*, a wandering poet barely glimpsed as he flees through the (in)-toxified city. And the (m)other is not ~~The~~ Woman, but the ultimate commodity-fetish, whose being frames his gaze, the figure of the prostitute in whom love and sex are radically separated and the body is nought but another thing to buy. According to Buci-Glucksmann, this masculine desire, which separates eros and love, and deciphers contingency, mortality and man's own 'castration' in the feminine form, is not just caused by men's (sense of) loss, it takes this impotencyality as its ultimate goal. In other words, for Glucksmann the paradoxical uncreative creativity of Rancière's *aesthetic regime* is linked to *an* anaesthetic poetics of impotency that continuously stages its own disappearance without (this) ever coming.

---

6. I use the terms 'familiar' and 'sexual' rather than 'gender' because it is not clear that our system of classifying people by a combination of anatomy and object-choice is universal. For the Greeks, a more important division seems to have been between the predator and the prey, the seducer and the seduced. See *Sappho is Burning*, by Page duBois.

This idea, that modern, or *aesthetic* Art does nothing but perpetually stage its own death is not new. Nor is it new to link this perpetual dying to modern (Western) man's sense of impotencyality. What Glucksmann highlights is the link between the formalist theory of art—in which *aesthetic* Art is defined only by its contradictory form—and the socio-gender theory, which states that in modernity Woman becomes the allegory of the blank in/on/with which men inscribe their sense of loss. She draws attention to the paradox in the form of desire at play in modernity. By this move, she adds desire to the aesthetico-political mix that defines the Platonic schema, and the paradigms within which we, in the West, still abide. This addition of desire to the aesthetico-political offers, I believe, a way to conceive of an aesthetic that, while continuing to bear its own contradictions, need not be consumed by thoughts of death. Perhaps there is another side to the modern in which the paradox of desire does not play itself out around the cata-strophes of loss, but rather sees in this form a way to move beyond a logic that harshly divides the right from the wrong, the true from the false, and the beautiful from the ugly. Perhaps this encounter with the paradox of desire opens the door to a space where such dichotomies no longer have meaning. And perhaps that space is not so disastrous after all.

In the following section, I offer a brief outline of an aesthetic aesthetics, a poetics that embraces the contradictions and paradoxes of desire as this is manifest in language—at least in the English tongue—but does not fixate on the cata-strophe of loss.

Archeology for a Linguistic Future

> Aesthetics as a discipline arose in the late eighteenth century when philosophers like Alexander Gottlieb recognized that the sciences were incomplete, given the absence of a science of beauty. [...] Early aesthetic theories were concerned not so much with sensory apprehension of reality as with *the theory of poetry,* whose topic was thought to be the meaning of beauty, (Turner, 1, *emphasis added*).

Aesthetic-s is the study of theories of poetry, and it can be performed from an aesthetic, political, or historical perspective. It may also be performed from a structural one. My approach to this discipline concerns the structures in-forming language. In other words, my interest in aesthetics is poetic. It revolves around ideas about linguistic structure uncovered through a poetic exploration of language itself. In this I adopt a Lucretian approach.

For Lucretius, the notion that the infinite variety of the material world could be explained as different arrangements of a small number of basic atomic units was equally applicable to the linguistic world. Thus, just as the smoke and flame produced when wood is burnt are simply rearrangements of the atoms composing the original log, so a slight rearrangement of the letters in their names changes *Lignum* to *Ignis*. Likewise, many philosopher-scientists in the nineteenth century, from William Rowan Hamilton to Freud's mentor, Brentano, also believed that structures found in nature and mathematics were also manifest in language, and more importantly, in the *shifts* from one set of meanings to another. While Freud took this idea as the basis for his free association method of analyzing unconscious structures, I would like to show how this Lucretian methodology can be applied more literally to a full scale analysis of language that takes into account both the findings of modern science and the ancient concern with "categories," along with the *aesthetic* attention to paradox.

As we all know, under the paradigm of modern science, the substance of the universe is 'space-time,' which is composed of strings and fields of energy. By the Lucretian principle that the linguistic world is constituted in the same way as the material universe, if we follow the findings of modern physics, then our analysis of language must begin with space-time itself. So, we begin:

space-time

Through the shifts afforded by a poetic lens this may also be seen as:

time-space

which becomes:

time's pace

which becomes

+ | 'me 's pace

which becomes:

| + me = pace

which becomes

| + me = rh|thm

From a poetic perspective, this phrase may be read as proposing that:

$$+ \ |'\text{me'S-pace}$$
$$'S$$

the substance of Life,
what shivers
between
the (pro) position of |
and (|'m) position of nO (or me).

Orienting themselves into time-space, we are subtly led up a flight of sta|res to the realm of the 1 and the 0, the | and the me, that ethereal zone where atomic units arrange themselves as complex (pro)-positions in a linguistic flow. The 'paradox' is that, though these (pro)-positions may not appear together in classical logic, here they collectively form the nexus of an ever-expanding network of linguistic knots whose (dis-)harmonious forms appear not as autonomous singularities, but as intertwining threads in a multidimensional linguistic veil.

Beginning with this fundamental paradox, a poetics can be developed that privileges no -| above the $_m$any of the $_m$Other-|'s. Rather it takes count of *both*, the 1 and the 0, the e|e and the vO|dse, this | and the M-any-Others— joyfully, simultaneously and without perpetually failing.

Los Angeles
2006

Works Cited

Buci-Glucksmann, Christine. "Catastrophic Utopia: The Feminine as Allegory of the Modern." In *The Making of the Modern Body: Sexuality and Society in the Nineteenth Century*. Eds. Catherine Gallagher and Thomas Lacquer. California: University of California Press, 1987. 222-228.

---- , *Baroque Reason: The Aesthetics of Modernity*. Trans. Patrick Camiller, London, Thousand Oaks, New Delhi: Sage Publications, 1994.

duBois, Page. *Sappho is Burning*, Chicago: University of Chicago Press, 1995.

Rancière, Jacques. *The Politics of Aesthetics*. Trans. Gabriel Rockhill. London and New York: Continuum, 2004a.

----, "The Politics of Literature." In *Substance* 103. Ed. Eric Mechoulan. Madison: University of Wisconsin Press, 2004b. 10-24.

Turner, Bryan S., "Introduction." In *Baroque Reason: The Aesthetics of Modernity*. Trans. Patrick Camiller, London, Thousand Oaks, New Delhi: Sage Publications, 1994.

Wertheim, Christine. "The Unboring Boring and the New Dream of Stone." In *Open Letter*, Twelfth Series, No. 7, Fall 2005. Eds. Lori Emerson and Barbara Cole. 131-139.

THE AMAZING ADVENT OF
KALI & **C**UN ⊓ [1]

To Ruth Wieder Magan

Nuala Archer

49

Cun⊓ **TAP** [5] from

her sister Scheherazade

& learned how to string

stories along like pearls—O-

O+O- —**POGP!** [5]

48

BC [7]—

Cun⊓ started **AO** [8] her

own Plots & *good* Parts

37   **ONNA!**[33] Why

should **C**un∏ forget the Floating World

of Labé's Phoenix Lantern?

Cun∏ ties rainbows on

her **WCs**[34], beams eight-tongued

Ma **K**ali, apple coring

35   O[35] whomever

refuses service to *their*

Unanimity

34   Axis, refuses

to morph into Vayne, Vain

Xenophobia.

28   while bright Silences

connect—like a quorum of

Whales—suffusing **C**unꜫ's

27   throat with Ambergris—

combining The Real-At-Home-

In-Her Ascending—

26   Rooted—Recognized.

Binding's Bright Unboundedness

Lo-ping (Wonderful

Word!) toward **C**unꞁ Herself within

Her-Deep-Light-Sounds-Connecting

24   Grounded in Merely

Beholding Abiding A-

Brightening **C**unꞁ Strides

Into Contradictory's

In-Grained-Brightening Banyons

20   in-deed Pro-moted—

              turned-inside-out-&-un-self-

              contracted—Other!—

              Utterly Other!—Tables

              Reel, Unreel **AI**[37] Up-On

19   your Contents! **C**unꟼ, smart-

              dust, angels, ants, drenching rains

    GT[38]

on your periwinkle porch—

              Radical's address—

18   (ATS:[39]

"Gone Native," "Gone Natural,"

"Gone to the Root's Roost")

17   as Ordinary

as Hoogli's Mouth brimming Blue

Moon Theatre mo-

ment-by-mo-ment spoiling our

ears, our seven stork-stiff

16   walls, your six geo-

desic circuits—*Now! Bull's Eye!*

piercing the heart's flux

& flex of fish, of spooling

lights & bright parabolas

15   **PO!**[40]

IEO![41]

RO![42]

14

TGSO![43]

What a Relief! What Bliss!

CunꝐ's Awareness Is!

13

Conditional-this-

&-that **CAG**[44] until

Heart's Heart All Enjoys

12   Swooning into **D-**

O - **C**⁴⁵—Brightness All-

Blasting dark Times' Shrine

2   Vibrations of Roots

Stem cell's Quickening coffins—

Chrysanthemum's Buzz

0   Lashed to a bloody

rainbow string sash—Clover Girl—

High-flying **C**un∏— **YH!**[48]

-3   Happier than most

Words—this Light-Thatching your Ear—

Nerve Mirroring Dear

-0 Cun∏ Sat Deathlessness

Down, Sat Desirelessness

Deep Shining Quark Songs

-7^2 O+0-O+0-O

0+O-0+O-0+O-0+

O-0+O-0+O-[52]

Endnotes:

1. TAAOKAC
2. CALLED IN SICK
3. SHOWED UP
4. WAS A NATURAL
5. TOOK A PAGE
6. PEARLS OF GREATEST PRICE
7. BREAKING CHARACTER
8. ACTING OUT
9. MENTIONED ON THE FLOOR
10. LIVING COLOR
11. ENCORES, STANDING OVATIONS
12. OF COURSE
13. WHO'S WHO OF WHAT'S WRONG WITH
14. BY DAY
15. CREATIVE WRITING
16. ENEMA
17. A PLEDGE OF ALLEGIANCE
18. CROSS YOUR HEART
19. SHRAPNEL OF SHAME
20. TWO-THOUSAND-SIX
21. WITCH BURNINGS
22. IMPROVISED EXPLOSIVE DEVISES
23. AFFIRMATIVE ACTION OFFICES
24. AS IN STOLEN
25. QUIET
26. SHUT UP ALREADY
27. WILDEST CLITS
28. IVORY TOWERS
29. IVORY HALLS
30. IVORY STAIRWELLS
31. IVORY WALLS AND LADDERS
32. MERIT MARKS
33. OH NO NOT AGAIN
34. WILDEST CLITS
35. PRETEND FARCE AND FUCK OVER
36. NO LOST ENERGY

37. AS IF
38. GATHER TOGETHER
39. AS THE IRISH SAY
40. PILGRIMAGE OVER
41. INTERNAL EXILE OVER
42. RESISTANCE OVER
43. THE GREAT SEARCH OVER
44. COMES AND GOES
45. DEPTH OF CONSCIOUSNESS
46. A BILLION YEARS LATER
47. DEEPER SURRENDER
48. YOU'RE HERE
49. GOOD-BYE
50. NEITHER HERE NOR THERE
51. LAUGHING MY ASS OFF
52. PRE-ROGAM BLOOD TYPE "INCOMPATIBILITIES"

Cleveland
2006

03. Parapet

Axel Thormählen / Danielle Adair / Alta Ifland / Stan
Apps / Stephanie Taylor / 2007–08

CUPS & MUTTS:
AN INTRODUCTION

Vanessa Place

The likeness of thing to another thing is a point of comparison. If there are greater points of comparison, the likeness is deemed great. If there are fewer points of comparison, the likeness is the lesser, and difference deemed great. But likeness can also lie beside itself, like twins, whose greater points of similarity insist on even more separation, than the easier difference between

A parapet is a low wall, a useless thing in some senses, as it keeps nothing out and less in. It is in this sense a gesture at a wall, a wall like a wall. Things that are alike are the cause and effect of metaphor: with things that are most alike, the metaphor becomes too porous, like the parapet, and the simile stands for the thing itself. Dark as night is dark. The tree is a metaphor for the tree. With things that are too dissimilar, the metaphor becomes too fierce, like the parapet, and the simile usurps the thing it is

another pair of brothers, or a set of strangers. When things are very much alike, likeness becomes a game of rock, paper, scissors: scissors sever paper, rock hammers scissors into smooth submission, and gentle paper proves more powerful than stone. It is a metaphorical game, of course, a game of imaginary equivalencies played, like all games of love and war, with fingers and fists. But likeness collapses into the operative, so fingers can cut and cover and, cupped, bring the lips a drink and when a thing becomes the thing it most resembles, when does it become that thing

itself ?

A

woman

, true to her cliche, looks in the mirror and becomes the woman she sees therein, part self, part self-reflection, her imaged being lying separate from her, following her, and teaching her to become more like the one she sees, to become her own projected reflection.

A

man,

true to his hang, slaps his visage on the mugs of all the others, others, he will insist, are just like himself, and if not, then not, unrecognizable as an ultraviolet ray. In his strict self-fidelity, he belies the separate anxiety of his many penetrations, blind to the screams he surrounds. A person, given a good shellacking, will turn to something like a bug.

Art

that is like art is art.
A god that acts goddish is. The writer is the mask, however more or
less the mask resembles
the man: Shakespeare
may or may not be an aggregative, but he is, as is
Hamlet,
singular in his authority. A river

most like. The dark is that in which we cannot see and so the sun is the darkest light and love sees by black day's night, and roots branch the tree. The pieces in this series resemble themselves and their opposites, which are sometimes one another, and sometimes themselves again. The self-negation that circles around Ifland and Apps finds its counterweight in the god-act of creation celebrated by Adair and Taylor, and the shadowed part of this Venn diagram is joyously occupied by Thormählen, who is his own Adam, tasting of the apple and pronouncing it picaresque. But Adair's haver dares the pregnant nothing, the void that came before creation and will endure after, and Taylor says it's all story, nothing but, while Ifland makes and makes, mask upon mask, and Apps lets lyric burst like birds from barren plane, the sheet of paper Adam will impress from the tree. We cannot help our walls. They give us something to raise and raze, to scale over and stand beside, one side or the other, it doesn't really matter. The point is the parapet and the brazen trumpet of our own sweet making.

made of a soiled watercolor is like a river except in width, and so the story of the Livey is the Livey, and all art is writing, and all writing paper, it can be cut up but not in, it covers and coats and turns all things into their own image, a thing to be read as is.

ADAM OR
THE PROPER PICTURE

Axel Thormählen

Not many people have had Adam as their art teacher. I was one of those who had that pleasure, but unfortunately he didn't like me. My face, he announced in front of the entire class, didn't fit into any aesthetic context. I must have seemed so ugly to him that he avoided looking at me even in passing. In fact, he didn't look at any of us for longer than absolutely necessary. We were, so he told us at the beginning of every art class, a superfluous, vulgar breed, and teaching us art was a waste of time. Twelve-year-old pupils, we thought of art—if we thought of it at all—as a random thing, rather than as a school subject. The main thing was for Adam to approve what we painted, then we'd get a good grade and that was art. I got one poor grade after another because Adam kept telling me to paint an apple; but I couldn't do apples, or faces either. The soft cheeks and the shadows were beyond me. Art teacher Adam was a good-looking young man whom the biology mistress was running after, as the whole school knew. He, however, yearned for the perfect apple. Not angular and certainly not cut into pieces, cubist-fashion; not blurred in transports of water-colour or thickened in oil sludge; a pure, clear apple was what he wanted, taken from the dish of an English still life or bought off a Dutch market-woman. As time went by and nobody in our class was able to produce that apple, his apple, he tried a river instead. "Paint me a river!" he commanded. "And anyone among you good-for-nothings who doesn't do it properly will pay for it on the grade-sheet."

My first river didn't find favour with him. What was that miserable blue line, he yelled at me, did I think this was the geography class? Adam snatched the sheet of paper from my desk and tore it up in front of everybody. "Once more, and you'd better be quick about it!" he ordered. Desperate, I squinted at the thing on my neighbour's desk to see if I could pick up any ideas. But all that had occurred to him was an estuary, a delta, and that only meant a few more blue lines, some thick, others thin. Now I changed styles and used the paintbox instead of soft pencils. A river, I thought, needs water, blue water. It was the work of a moment to get a wide blue stretch of water on to the paper, framed by green, my idea of a river bank. I felt Adam's sceptical gaze on me as I pursued my artistic endeavour and suspected he was just waiting to destroy another work of my hands. But I accepted his challenge. I suddenly grasped that a river has a bottom across which the movement, the current, rolls and tumbles; and I found that there isn't just one blue, but endless variants. With some shades of blue you could go deep down, into the coolness; in other, lighter tones, you could even bathe. I tried hard, had deep-blue shades relieved by shallow ones, even went almost grey along the bank. From the corner of my eye, I observed that my diligence made Adam increasingly restless. Finally I saw him stride towards the window. Oh, right, I thought, he wants to think about something else; it annoys him that I'm still at it.

Our art teacher, however, did something unusual: suddenly, with a powerful gesture, he tore open both window sections, letting the gale outside into the classroom. It immediately lifted all our sheets of paper off our desks, twirled them—like an acrobat his skittles—through the air and then, chaos completed, let them drop.

"As the wind blows," said Adam mockingly, closing the window again. Most of my fellow pupils were disconsolate; why, the teacher himself had intervened and torpedoed their work! That gust of wind had ruined what had come so easily to them a moment ago. I wasn't exactly jubilant either as I picked up my sheet from where it was lying on the floor. Painted side down, of course, in the dirt which had been dragged in by many shoes and now stuck to the water-colours. A botched picture, as it seemed. Once more the art teacher relished the shot of despair that must have been evident on my face. I took another look at the misfortune and suddenly found that even dirt could be made something of, if... Swiftly, before it all dried up, I seized a wooden ruler and pushed the sand and earth into the watercourse, making lumps of it. When I added more watercolour, the lumps turned to rocks in the river. That encouraged me to create movement, eddies, around these rocks. At this point I was even having fun, playing in the river. I was just imagining trout jumping in it when Adam took the paper out of my hands once more. He looked at it, long and hard; he'd never looked at a person for that length of time. I was waiting for him to tear this one to shreds as well, but he didn't. He held up the sheet before him and walked along the aisles like that. At last he moved back to the teacher's desk, still staring at the picture.

"Here," he said, turning around and holding up the sheet in front of the class, "this is art." Then he was silent for some time. The wildest emotions clashed within me. Branded as an eternal failure, I was unable to believe in this monumental accolade; resigned, I took his words as a piece of implicit scorn to which I was sure he'd give full expression in a moment.

However, the expected opprobrium didn't materialise. Instead Adam came up to my desk, leaned on it, pointed to my picture and said: "That's really good, you know. You went through all the phases: instead of laziness—contradiction; instead of whining and giving up—sincerity, bowing to the motif. Responding to a serious challenge, not everyone can do that. And then to go on and fill it with one's own stuff, that takes a lot. You can do it, lad. Move around in your imagination. Bring me the apple!"

I tried to produce an apple but found I wasn't able to. I could describe it, though, how it hung there high up on its tree, an alluring prize for a boy who coveted it and went to any lengths to get hold of it. Thanks to that essay I got a good grade from a colleague Adam respected, and from then on I went in for the written story.

But I kept running into my limitations when writing as well. Soon I concluded that while creating yields fulfilment, a successful piece of work immediately engenders further demands. First among them is the demand for beauty, which won't let itself be captured, but it doesn't want to find itself on paper by chance either. If a figure turns out well, that doesn't necessarily mean that it fits into the framework you created for it. If you want a story too badly, it has a way of ending up in shallow waters. Far too often, these burdens breed a fear of the empty sheet of paper, of the colour, even of the sentence. And the questions linger on: Can I repeat what can't be bettered? Hasn't everything been said and done already? Be careful, I say to myself at such times, Adam's standing there right behind you, he'll tear up your piece of paper, he, the observer, the reader, the teacher. Take care to stay good: first think of the form, then of the craft and the idea together. And only then, at last, of the pleasure at the chance of taking a bite from the apple, never mind who hands it to you.

Lund
2007

Postscript: Beyond Adam: The curse of the once-achieved

You achieved a thing of beauty; other people tell you so, and you know it too. Creation itself made a shape out of the swirling fragments, and it didn't happen by chance, because there is no chance in the space where these things come into being. It all came together before and through you, and for a moment fulfillment fills you with jubilation. Once you've had that experience, there's no way back. All those who gave up and purchased an easier happiness did so before it could come to them.

The fulfillment of achieved beauty breeds an addiction which adheres to every major event that breaks into your subsequent existence. Serious illness has to be mastered in words; death insists on an obituary; disappointed love must be assuaged by another form of expression. You're the artist, you were born to supply the answers—or so you must hope. For doubt is now your companion. Doubt is like your big brother who always knows better, and like the corpulent person in the fourth row who falls asleep during your readings.

Someone looks at you as if you were the only lover in the universe and tells you she forgot to get off the bus because she was lost in your words. But you must accept that she may be the only one. Fulfillment is one thing, success another. The moment of let-someone-else-try-to-do-that-if-they-think-they-can complacency is over in seconds, and the hunger bred by the curse of the once-achieved knows no satisfaction.

Lund
2014

HAVER

Danielle Adair

The Haver loves to hold   in her   . She loves to feel the tangible   of their   . The Haver works within her four-walled   of   and   . She prefers this   for what it implies. She prefers its   and its   . The   of her leaves   for   to amount. It also welcomes the   of a   conditioned to such   and the   it begets. For in her   the Haver continues   and assembling and rearranging   . She works to stave off the   of the   . She works to challenge the   of   in   .

Although the Haver creates   , she has been told repeatedly that her   is much better. For her   to be valued beyond   , the Haver's   must be moveable and collect an   . Not having   stand on its   troubles the Haver, but   is always required of consummate   and so the Haver begins to record her   . She places a   way up high and lets it leer down at the   inside her   and at her   .

The Haver works with   . She works with   and   and   and   . She works with   and   and   and   . She works by first holding her   and embracing them. She lets her   feel them over and tell her what they think. She feels the ridged   of the blank   of the   and the   of the   . She feels the prickly plastic   of the   . She lets her   feel the   of the   . This is when it happens first.

When the Haver becomes her   . When she lets herself into her   , she begins first at her   . Later her   and her boney   take up the   of   . She evaluates their   and her   as she gazes at her   . Her   is   . She is thinking of the   of the   and where her first   of   will touch down.

The   Haver works with   . She uses   because it creates   in the   , because it makes one blink. She likes to make her   disquiet. She likes to let them be seen twice in a   . The Haver chooses the   . After visualizing the   of the   , she tumbles them over with   . She lets herself avow the   in her   by pounding it on the   of her   . She makes her   first dictatorial, then decorative, and then yellow. This is videotaped. She is the first   of her   , and then   to   when through the   she surveys them.

Only after she begins her   do the   in her   appear. The Haver claims she is not a   , but that she is controlling her   . But she does allow herself to recognize that what she sees are not just linear   but the   of her   all in   , within the   , upon her   . She accomplishes her   when her   becomes the   of her   and herself in it. In her   , though, she has to face the   of who is the Haver and what is the   .

When the   of the Haver gets shown in   it is upon a   not unlike her   . Her work sits within a   , within a   , with white matte   and grey   , and it starts its   in this   . For the Haver this is hard to assimilate. It is hard for her to see her   within the   of the   . It is hard for her to see the   of herself without herself beside it.

Mostly, the   she receives are from the   within. They say, "Make it longer." "Show more results." "It doesn't close." "There's no resolve." "Why the repetition?" "I want to see what you mean in this text."

So the Haver makes her surveillance   twenty-six   to the   . They say this is a   that   can understand. Then she waits and lets a new   ,   that doesn't know her, receive the   of the   that are supposed to understand. They comment as they pass by, "Another Haver." "Anachronistic." "Hollow." "Not what a text should say or do." "It's so-and-so done over." "It's her-meets-he again." "Like it." "Detest this stuff." "Don't know." "Let's move on."

The Haver returns to her own   , the   that takes her own   and supports her own   . This single   of the Haver can unearth the   of her   and the   that she knows. It can see her   and her   and make the   a   . And so she begins again without erasing what she has done.

This   the Haver edits herself. She puts a "   " near where the "   " was and a "   " in   of the "   ." She scribbles over "   " where it rounded the   of her   and   and puts "   " above it. She adds "   " where "   " had inscribed a   . And then she creates a new   in a deserted   with herself kneeling on her   . Within this   she lines the with "   ."

The Haver works based on   . She takes more   back and thinks through her   . She remains holding a   in her   , but now, she only lets the   scathe her   . When she stands back and contemplates, she uses her   . She lets them blur. Her   never blurred before, they blinked. She used to let her   her   . Now it is an   for   , it is an   towards the   that sanctions her   .

The Haver re-presents her   . This   another   assumes her   . "I know her." "Yes, she's a Haver." "Oh, that's it. Yes, I see it." "Yeah, Havers, they still work?" She stops twirling a   of   through her   , because the Haver knows what "work" means. She knows her   must make   for this   or else it will continue to be seen as   and   .

The Haver thinks about becoming the   that the   needs to see. She knows she doesn't want to just document her   . She begins taking   and measuring. She begins measuring the way she wants her   to fit. Then she lets the   of her   overtake her and make her physical   become what they mean. The Haver starts behaving and moving as if a   . She takes   upon   and   after   of herself becoming the   she hears and recalls.

The Haver believes her   only sees in two   - dead or alive, two   - functional or decorative, two   - formal or conceptual, two   - fail or succeed, two   - good or bad, two   , two   , two   , two   - this is where she stutters. She begins to repeat, but she cannot configure her own   . She cannot remember who she is, supposedly. She's now afraid she can only rehearse how she is supposed to be.

The Haver's   concave. Her   feels arrested and insistently tightens in its   . She gets a   and then interrupting   , so much so she can no longer stand. The Haver realizes—she almost let her   destroy her. Her   has a killing   .

What is a Haver that does not make   ? The Haver stamps on the   of her   . She uses   to blot out the   , and she carefully covers the   of former   within them by adhering   of various   . She feels best when she self-edits out-loud and when she lets herself witness her own   only as she creates them. There is an   , she declares, in finding yourself through   . The Haver cannot help what she births, but her   isn't solely attributable, it's living.

Los Angeles
2007

NO ONE'S VOICE: NOTES ON BEAUTY, LANGUAGE, AND ARTISTIC CREATION
Alta Ifland

"In the air, that's where your root is,
there in the air."
– Paul Celan

These notes are occasioned by the publication of my volume of prose poems, *Voice of Ice,* which could be said to belong to several aesthetic traditions, the closest probably being Baudelaire's *petits poèmes en prose.* Baudelaire's prose poems are literally short stories—they have a narrative line and characters—with a moral or a twist at the end, which makes them similar to prose fables. Some might call this genre "short shorts," an expression I personally dislike, as it casts a quantitative, prosaic dimension upon the texture of words. A "little poem in prose" is not quite the same as a "short short story." Other poems in this collection are image-centered rather than narrative, but even in these poems the description of the gazed-upon object (whether the ocean or the sky or a fictive space) is intertwined with the reflection triggered by that image.

Reflecting Beauty

If there is an aesthetic vision behind these poems it is a vision that refuses to separate reflection from beauty. This separation, often manifested in contemporary poetry, which reflects the poet's ideology, is an artificial one and is a function of where poetry originates these days: academia, the workshop, or one's room.

To put it very briefly, those who write "reflective" poetry—usually characterized as "postmodern" or "language" poets—reject the idea of beauty as poetry's "goal" (if such a word can be used in relation to poetry), while, on the other hand, those who write a more lyrical kind of poetry very rarely seem to *reflect* on the images they are describing. It is as if thinking were separated from sensual perception—insofar as beauty is something that comes from outside and is perceived with our senses (I am paraphrasing here Elaine Scarry's *On Beauty*). I find this extremely puzzling, and if the subscribers to the ideology of lyricism have at least an excuse—they don't claim to "think" but rather to "experience" (incidentally, the divorce between "thinking" and "experiencing" doesn't exist in other aesthetic traditions; to give one example: Philippe Lacoue-Labarthe, one of the greatest contemporary French philosophers, who is also a poet and writer, is the author of a book on Paul Celan titled *Poetry as Experience*. According to Lacoue-Labarthe, authentic poetry is *pensante*—i.e. "reflective," "thinking," "philosophical"—while being at the same time an "experience" because it is lived and felt.)—I find no explanation for the subscribers to the opposite ideology. How can thinking—serious, *focused*, articulated thinking—even begin to take place if one cannot recognize beauty? To recognize beauty means to look at something outside of yourself—another person, an artifact, or something in nature—and to be able to *exclude* that something from the neutral background against which it stands by conferring on it an exceptionality that the rest of the world (other persons or other objects) doesn't have. It means to be able to *focus,* to look attentively and *to see* in a way we normally don't when we don't pay enough attention. It is not by accident that lovers often *understand* each other simply by *looking* at each other. Looking at an object in a way that makes it truly *visible* doesn't involve just our senses, it also involves our capacity for understanding, that is, our judgment.

On the other hand, those who write poetry that attempts to be "beautiful," either by purposefully using "poetic" language or by praising beauty, often have a naïve vision of the poetic or the beautiful, as if these were synonymous with the idea of adornment. Or else, they may describe a beautiful landscape or interior or building or even a dramatic scene, and give a mimetic representation of it, a representation that might be "beautiful" in a technical sort of way, but once you are done reading, you are often left with the feeling that something is lacking. This descriptive or image-centered kind of poetry, which is conceptually related to representational painting, can certainly be "good poetry" if, as in good paintings, it succeeds in taking you *beyond* the literal surface. And when it does, it is because the poet (or the painter) had a *vision* in his mind, an *idea* of the world that was consequently sublimated into a *particular* representation.

Prose, Poetry and the Mystery at the Core of Thinking

One of the problems with poetry in a time when aesthetic rules have been abolished is that it can be easily faked. The poet W. S. di Piero has made the interesting remark that much of contemporary poetry can be faked, while prose, for better or worse, cannot, because prose needs to develop out of articulated thinking, and one cannot fake thinking.

The essential difference between poetic and critical discourse is best represented, I believe, by the different answers given by two emblematic intellectuals when asked where their inspiration comes from: the poet W. S. Merwin and the philosopher Jacques Derrida. The poet answered that he doesn't know and *doesn't want to know*, while the philosopher said that this is one of the questions to which he is still looking for an answer. An inattentive listener could conclude that the poet doesn't care, but this is not what Merwin says; what he tells us is that he wants to keep the mystery of the poem—of its source and of its essence, which comes from its source—hidden; that he doesn't want to reveal it, not to himself, even less to others. The philosopher, on the other hand, wants to know and to unveil the secret behind the surface. In light of the above, it can be said that the prose poem harbors a conflict between the desire to protect its mystery and the desire to lay it bare—a conflict present, I think, throughout *Voice of Ice*.

Translation as Re-creation

I wrote *Voice of Ice* in several months, and soon after I began writing, I decided to do something I had never done before—translate my own work into English. The most famous case of a self-translated author is Samuel Beckett, who actually re-created his books in the process of translation. Whenever he felt that the idiom of the original could not be transposed smoothly in translation, he preferred to replace it with something entirely different rather than find an approximate equivalent, in order to keep the rhythm of the text, which was for him essential. W. G. Sebald, who wrote in German but lived in Britain for most of his life, had a similar attitude toward the translation into English of his works, rewriting and even adding certain passages for the English version that didn't exist in the original.

While doing my translation, I found myself more than once under the influence of the English language, going back to the original (in French) and *changing* words in it. This is certainly something a regular translator cannot do, and which in my case was possible because I am the author both of the original and the translation. I do know, however, of another writer, the Albanian Ismail Kadare, who, while preparing the first volumes of his bilingual *Complete Works* brought out by his French publisher, checked the French against the Albanian, and vice versa, changing the Albanian whenever he felt that the French sounded better, although someone else had done the translation into French.

Who is I? or Writing as Self-creation

Originally from Eastern Europe, I learned French in school at an early age, and although I have probably read more books in French than in any other language, French has been for most of my life a foreign language. After I immigrated to the United States I began writing in French; it became clear to me that in order to write I needed a distance from language that was impossible to attain in my native idiom. Our "own" language may be the only language we can master in all its delicate nuances, but it is also, by its very nature, the language that roots us to our place of origin. It is the language that comes to us as a linguistic reflex and, like all reflexes, becomes an opaque screen interposed between us and the world. Writing in a language that detaches us from our origins removes that screen and forces us to re-create our very depths by renaming the world and by changing the way we relate to it, which is reflected in our grammar. It is an *uprooting* in the strongest sense of the word, and it is not by accident that writers who have gone through it—for instance, Julia Kristeva, who left Bulgaria and emigrated to France when she was very young—have compared it to acquiring a different body. It gives one an exhilarating sense of freedom grounded in an almost physically painful experience. But what is freedom if it's not gained with, or at the price of, our own self?

Some might think that to translate from your second language (in this case, French) into your third language (in this case, English) is a very difficult task, but in a way, it is actually easier than writing in your "native" language ("langue maternelle" in French) because you work with pure language, as Walter Benjamin would say, and since you don't belong to either of the two languages, you can let yourself be the instrument that creates relations between the two systems of expression. It is almost as if you were trying to solve a puzzle by filling in the gaps, only you never know what the final form will be, because there are several possible final forms.

Thus, French became my language almost by default. After I finished translating *Voice of Ice*, I began to write directly in English, and in the process I realized that the more remote I was from the origin of speech, the easier it was to attain an impersonality of the voice, which is, I believe, the essence of true literature. Since I have been writing in English, I feel much more at home in it than in French, but the truth is that I am not really at home in either of them and that I don't really have a language of "my own." It may be that the desire to write is in some way related to the desire to find a language of one's own.

The Other I or Becoming It

There are quite a few examples of writers who have stated unequivocally that their language is their "home" or even their "country." The Portuguese poet Fernando Pessoa complemented his literary creation with that of several dozen personas, each with a different name and biography. These heteronyms—as Pessoa called them—were masks of Pessoa himself, although it would probably be more accurate to say that they were *no one's* masks, as Pessoa often described himself as "no one." In this respect he personifies poetic existence *par excellence* because he has transformed an aesthetic idea—that of the author as a mask—into a way of being. He was a "passerby of everything, even of my own soul, belonging to nothing, desiring nothing, being nothing—abstract center of impersonal sensations, a fallen sentient mirror, reflecting the world's diversity" (*The Book of Disquietude*).

Of the numerous explanations of the act of writing, the following one by Italo Calvino is probably the clearest and most truthful in its clarity:

> It is always only a projection of himself that an author calls into play while he is writing; it may be a projection of a real part of himself or the projection of a fictitious 'I'—a mask, in short. [...] The author is an author insofar as he enters into a role the way an actor does and identifies himself with that projection of himself at the moment of writing. (*The Uses of Literature*)

I could go on developing Calvino's idea by invoking, as he does, the analyses of the French structuralists regarding the "I" who is writing, but one needn't invoke French structuralists, because many of their ideas can be found in other forms in the writings of many writers who have little or nothing to do with them. In Paul Celan, for example, we can find the idea that the poem allows the I to separate from himself, becoming a space where the I seizes himself as a stranger. But Celan goes a step further than the structuralists: in the making of a poem, he says, the I transforms himself entirely into a sign. Such a statement doesn't make him a post-structuralist, as some would have it, but "merely" a Poet. And Pessoa goes even further: in transforming himself into several dozen poets, he changes himself *literally* into numerous signs; it isn't only his language that is an artifact, but the poet too—Fernando Pessoa becomes Álvaro de Campos, Ricardo Reis, Alberto Caeiro, Bernardo Soares, Antonio Mora, et al.

All and Nothing

Most great writers of modernity (and, insofar as literature is concerned, postmodernity is still modernity; outside of modernity—understood as the realm of the adventure of the *Subject*—the very concept of literature ceases to have meaning) have felt in one way or another that they were *nothing*—an idea so eloquently expressed by Borges in his story "All and Nothing"—and that this nothingness is the very thing out of which creation emerges. A writer does not have a face. A writer is a no one with a thousand masks. Even if the writer doesn't "invent" anything, he still creates a "persona," that is, a mask covering nothing. He is "*less* than one," as Joseph Brodsky says, and it is this less that makes creation possible.

The Photo in the Paper or the Comedy of the "Real Person"

In light of the above, there is nothing more comical—sadly comical—than today's vision of the author as a "real person" whose photo is displayed like a flag at literary venues and on book and magazine covers, who is invited by voyeur readers to "explain" his work, and whose biography is summoned like a hidden mechanism that makes sense of the work. The work seems to have become the pretext that allows a public avid for "reality" to peek into what it imagines to be the writer's veiled life, and to have this "virtual reality" confirmed by the flesh-and-bones existence of the writer. It may be that this need for "reality" is an unconscious reaction to the impersonality of the technological cocoon in which humans have recoiled, but even so, it's a reality at odds with the electronic medium embraced with such passion by those who also happen to believe in the promotional value of the "real person."

In fact, a writer—if he is indeed faithful to what writing is—is the most unreal thing of all, for he is made of nothing but words. To say that "a writer is made of nothing but words" may convey for some an image of the writer as someone "superficial," but if that is the case, it is only because for those people words are some kind of pretty garments in which truths are clothed, when in fact, for a writer there is no separation between form and content. For a writer, the word is the thing itself.

If a writer were really true to himself, he would never put his face on display. Not because the face were "outside," while writing came from "inside," as our naïve dichotomies would have it—quite the contrary: the face is always a reflection of our inner world—and not even because in today's societies of the spectacle, a face has become nothing more than a marketable image, but because our face and our name are the non-transferable print of our I within the real, and through them we belong to the world, that is, to the very opposite of the universe of the imaginary. What is writing if not the desire to cancel the prosaic world we are a part of? In other words, what is writing if not the desire to destroy the face and the name that we are in everyday reality? From this point of view, the name and photograph authors attach to their work are a betrayal of the very essence of literature. If writers were true to this essence, they wouldn't reinforce their identity as civilians of the everyday; on the contrary, they would swear allegiance to the only world they can belong to, the world of shadows. True, writers faithful to the world of shadows are very few: Fernando Pessoa, Emily Dickinson, Franz Kafka and several others. They were so much part of *another* world, that they were invisible to their contemporaries.

Creation between Being and Nonbeing

Because writing is the attempt to unite being and nonbeing, the desire to bring into being something that hasn't existed before is, for a writer, as strong as his discontent with everything that already exists. Everything that already has a shape is subject to the law of Time and its destruction; only what has yet to be born is on the side of perfection. Thus, the creative impulse is always a function of our rapport with being and nonbeing or being and nothingness. And our rapport with nonbeing or nothingness is shaped by centuries of religious tradition and literary works that have preceded us.

Most creation myths in the Western world are actually of pagan origin, and they usually reflect two ideas: that all creation comes out of chaos, and that the desire to create is the desire to reshape chaos; and that at the basis of all human creation there is a sacrifice. In its most domesticated form this vision means that all artists sacrifice something of themselves in order to create an enduring work of art.

There is a parallel thread in Western spirituality, which is derived from Judaic mysticism, more specifically Kabalistic myths of creation. According to the father of the Kabala, Isaac Luria, the world was created not through divine emanation, but through God's withdrawal. What is unique about this Jewish creation myth in comparison with other creation myths is the idea that nothingness or emptiness is creative. According to the myth, God's withdrawal left an emptiness in the center of the universe, and this emptiness became the original matrix for the future world. In his desire to create the world, the Infinite (which in the Kabala is not quite the same as God) sent his rays toward this empty center, but the vases carrying them shattered under their divine weight, and their shards fell to the ground, creating the four elements: earth, water, air and fire. The shards kept sparks of divine wisdom in them, and ever since, humanity has been trying to release these sparks, prisoners of matter, and reintegrate them into the divine light from which they have been separated.

Becoming Nothing

Since our vision of artistic and literary creation is based on secularized religion, one could say that these visions of creation, one derived from paganism and absorbed within Christianity, and the other, derived from Jewish mysticism, are present in various forms in the works of many writers and artists, from early European history until today (although they certainly aren't confined to Europe). As a matter of fact, many writers may derive their creative impulse out of these primordial desires without even being aware of it. In their more modern form, these impulses can be perceived in writings in which the narrator—usually, but not always, an alter ego of the author—disappears at the end of the story and thus becomes one with the nothingness that precedes all creation. One could say that this disappearance is the trademark of great twentieth century writers, from Mallarmé, to Borges, to Beckett, to Merwin (I am particularly thinking of his fables).

Animal Metamorphosis or Becoming Other

In its more alienated form, the desire of losing one's being in the story, and thus of becoming one with the artifact, is rooted in Kafka's *Metamorphosis*. It is not an accident that Gregor Samsa's literary descendants can be found in contemporary Japan and not in Europe, considering that Japan is the place where human alienation from our natural surroundings has attained its peak. Among the numerous stories in which the narrator is transformed into an animal at the end, one need only think of those written by twentieth century Japanese writers such Kobo Abe, Osamu Dazai and, more recently, Yoko Tawada.

Through this *inhuman* metamorphosis, writers rejoin in a paradoxical way the first artists who painted murals in the caves, and for whom humans were creatures that had animal features: feathers, beaks, tails. But this encounter occurs at the other end of the circle, so to speak: if, at the dawn of humanity, men and women saw themselves as akin to animals, now, it is their lack of connection with the animal world and their machine-like emptiness that invites identification with *nonhuman* forms.

Writing as Primordial Desire to Give Form to the Shapeless

Although the forms taken by artistic and literary creation throughout history and from place to place have an enormous variety, the creative impulse is fundamentally the same. Where there is great art or great literature one can always recognize, even if buried deep down, the archetypal desire of ordering chaos, or of making something out of nothing, or of disappearing into one's own creation. Writing is the manifestation—one of the possible manifestations, along with music, painting, sculpture, theatre, and maybe even dance—of our longing to give shape to something that hasn't found its form yet, it is the desire to create new forms.

The archetypal desire to recreate the world—a desire all myths tell us about—is from this point of view identical with the longing to give shape to what is yet shapeless. Insofar as this longing comes from the obscure depths of our being, the very depths where desire takes its roots, and insofar as desire is one of the most untamed and untamable primal components of our being, art is the shape taken by our darkest part in its struggle to find its way to light.

Santa Cruz
2007

ON UNIMPORTANT ART

Stan Apps

I think art is unimportant. I think this because I live in a society and I look around me and people seem to think that art is unimportant. I agree with them. I guess I choose to agree with them. Anyway, people are more important than art, even horrible people. Awful people are very important and powerful. It seems that I do not want to be important, or that on some level I feel that I will never be important. I am not and have not been important. I think this is an attraction of art for me: I'm looking for an unimportant context, in which to situate my unimportantness. I guess it's a sort of ego-mania. If I can't be important, at the very least I'll be unimportant in a very unimportant place. And so: poetry. Of all the arts, poetry is considered the most unimportant in this society where I live. And so naturally it's the best one. Poetry is the most beautiful of all the arts, the most excellent, the most flexible and expressive, and poetry actually gives me infinite power, to be unimportant with an infinite plasticity. Poetry makes me a dynamo of potential. I think it is because it is so unimportant that the power it confers on me is so infinite. Naturally, the more of this power I express, the more ridiculous other people think I am, because I am an unimportant person, and unimportant ego-maniacs are mad. They don't understand that I've already handled this issue of my unimportantness, handled it and moved on from it. I'm content to be a master of the least important art.

Now I also write essays (like this one) which are a much more important medium, and so naturally one should be more modest and make more limited claims about what's true in an essay, because the more important the medium you are working in is, the less ego-maniacal you should be.

But an artist who is truly unimportant has the power to create and destroy. Consider a man who draws the pictures in a comic book. One day he draws a whole book, 24 pages, of pictures of the Earth being destroyed. They are simple, brutal pictures. The cities are leveled; the buildings fall; the fields burn; the envelope of air around the world is ripped and living things are hurled off into space where they float a moment before bursting into clouds of blood; the surface of the world is totally desertified. The best moment in this (imaginary) comic book is a picture of a milk-cow in orbit. The cow is about to die and is puffing up its cheeks to try to hold its air in, and then (next panel) the cloud has popped into a cloud of blood. This all takes a page and illustrates with a specific example what happens to living things from Earth when a destructive cataclysm suddenly (and in clear violation of the laws of physics) throws them into orbit. If comic books were more important, this imaginary artist would have to destroy the world more careful, with discretion and with consideration of the Earth's physical laws. If a comic book artist were as important as, say, a psychotherapist or sociologist, he or she could not destroy the world at all, because professional considerations would militate against such a violent, adolescent project. Even a novelist, relatively unimportant, but higher up the hierarchy of the arts than a comic book artist—even a novelist could only destroy a world in a very plausible way, and to be respectful to the material and the concept would have to make a thousand-page emotional epic about three families out of it. What I'm trying to get at is that importance and boredom are intimately connected. Boredom, plausibility, and adult caution are ingredients of importantness.

Poetry, the least important art form (popular poetry books sell far less copies than popular comic books) is potentially the least boring. Without a readership, anything can be done; there are no expectations worth being restrained by. So, for instance, I wrote a little bible of my own, a mini-Bible, and it's sort of a commentary on the real Bible, full of rage and destruction and love for what is right, just like the real Bible(s). If you love what is right enough, everything in the world that is already good seems just like an obstacle. Only in a very unimportant place could it seem acceptable to replace everything in the world that is already good, to sweep it out of the way and let it all fall off the table, and put there in its place something that's really right: equitable, with resources liberated so that they flow without stint to the least of us and every one of us. Heavens are all incredibly democratic, and there's nothing more cynical than organized religion that pushes the ideal society into the next world, so that we all die and we can't get there. Boredom, plausibility, adult caution, and cynicism: organized religion is very important, and so its goal is to help adolescents be good citizens. It certainly worked on me; I've become very good. I pride myself on being exquisitely well-socialized. I'll admit it took longer for me than it did for some. When I was twenty, I had this long dirty hair and I was very thin and all my clothes were old and raggedy, and some of my clothes had holes in them. I didn't have long, stringy attractive dirty hair like Vincent Gallo or a supermodel either; I had bushy, clumpy sticking-up-into-the air dirty hair like a white man's tragic malformed loaf of Afro. I was a monstrous hill-billy man-child looking to make good. Thank God I picked an unimportant specialty, something to do without being laughed out of town. Because poetry is very unimportant, poetry audiences are very tolerant, bless them. I stood in front of them and declaimed the most ignorant hill-billy curiosities about meaning, truth, life, and love. People loved it. They adored me in the way you would adore a piece of vintage furniture in too poor of a condition to be worth restoring. I remember this poem about how my soul was like a corpse of a dog that had been cut in half by a train. I'd been walking around town balancing on the train-tracks, because visionary hill-billy boy-children have nothing to do, and I had actually come across the hindquarters of an old dog, lying right next to the tracks, and obviously the train had come along and taken the poor boy's head clean off! I so related. The half-dog had yellow leathery dried-out skin around it like a chrysalis, and inside it were these lovely yellow bones, like yellow pearls! That is, they would have been like yellow pearls, if pearls were yellow and if pearls came in the shape of dog-bones. I wasn't quite a master of plausible metaphor yet, you see: I was using metaphors without a license.

When I was twenty-five, I was much the same. I moved to California and lived in a trailer that had been the home of a drunken lawyer. Beneath the trailer he had hidden a hundred old empty whiskey bottles, and his cigarette smoke had made the trailer's walls the color of yellow pearl, just like those dog bones: a color sure to please any ladies who visited. I tried to do a little maintenance on the place. I painted one wall electric blue. But I was demoralized; there was too much to be done. I wanted to live in a wonderful nice apartment already and it seemed too hard to turn my horrible little trailer into an approximation of that. So I sulked; I lay on my mattress next to my electric blue wall and dreamed of lovely condominiums. I dreamed of them falling into the sea and becoming aquatic and electric blue: underwater the lovely condos would be occupied by these sensuous sea-creatures with the souls of men and women but bodies more like agile genitals. I barely survived that adventure. In my hill-billy trance or stupor I was possessed by the spirit of the drunken lawyer who preceded me in the trailer, and was soon adding my own empty bottles to the vast bottle-hoard beneath the floor. The bottles clanked together in the middle of the night as the trailer rocked back and forth with the motion of a sensuous sea of electric blue baroque poetic ornamentation that crusted my real experience like salvific barnacles. And the barnacles wept teardrops indistinguishable from saliva, and I became unable to distinguish my good moods from my bad, which is a sign of severe depression. California made me realize that I, who had worn the idea of unimportance like a glad, ragged costume out in Texas, was actually so grotesquely unimportant that the curiosity I was was foul, low, and not just sad but lame and pitiable. In California, everyone around me was bourgeois enough to live except myself. Partially, this is because the trailer I was in was among a group of trailers occupied by graduate students at the University of California in Irvine. It seemed that I was the poorest white person in miles. I had arranged purchase of the least expensive and most unpleasant of the trailers. It was culture-shock. I quickly became vicious: to defend myself. In my classes I went straight for the throat, and everyone's throat was more exposed than mine. The meanest dog is the closest to the ground.

Things have changed nowadays, and I'm not the least bit mean anymore. I'm very good, and I think people are more important than ideas, and I think that awful people deserve the room they need to be awful in, because we ought to have respect for subjectivities. I'll admit I'm no fan of subjectivities, which I think (except for a few particularly delightful characters) are by and large a waste of time. Nevertheless, if subjectivities are attached to people, I feel obliged to admit them and respect them, and they do come attached, by and large, tied on with big rambunctious bow-knots. As for me, I've gotten rid of my subjectivity several times and substituted for a new one, because my view is it's just protective camouflage, and if you're in the market for protective camouflage it's best to pick something simple and dull rather than something eyecatchingly stylish. Even at my most miserable and alienated, I was always alienated in as generic a way as possible, preferring to keep my self-image on the inside where I could chastise it rather than spreading it around outside on my body. So all the things I said about myself above were mostly fantasy: fantasies of an alienation I could have worn like a flag, but instead kept like a snot-rag in my pocket. These subjectivities of my own past were a waste of time precisely because they were no more than manifestations of the alienation that I appropriately felt as a member of a subordinate social class. Too low for pride, I had self-loathing, and like all self-loathing people I was proud of it. That is how all the poor are proud of themselves; it's how they wear the internalized self-loathing forced on them by the dominant class.

I do of course have beliefs, and beliefs are a delight, because even if your beliefs are wrong they still have validity simply because they show that you exist. Subjectivity is just a substitute for belief, emphasizing self-love and/or self-loathing rather than the universalizing grasp of belief. Belief emphasizes each person's right to be in the world and to speak on the world's behalf, whereas subjectivity describes individuals as self-images rather than self-assertions.

You might detect, based on some of what I've said, that I am angry. But in fact I'm only sort of angry. I keep my anger limited to a sphere of unimportance: poetry. In this sphere of poetry, everything becomes crystalline and transparent, like a forest of opinions made of ornate glass, or like a forest of frozen water masquerading as opinions made of glass. In this sphere of poetry, anger simmers like a small boiling lake, whose steam, as it rises, crystallizes and hails back down.

Within the unimportance of poetry, anything can be collected, gathered, incorporated: anything can be re-used in a new context much less important than wherever it was before. For instance, I wrote a poem, using internet search-engines. One half was a description of an exorcism of demons from the body of a woman after a Christmas party at church, told by a somewhat reluctant participant in the exorcism. The other half was a description of a pornographic video. I fused these two texts into one, producing a narrative in which evil spirits are exorcised from the woman's body by a pornographic process. In this way, I produced something that (I think) did not exist before: a narrative of "gang bang" exorcism. This new narrative is a satire, I think, but I would prefer not to say what it is a satire of, because I think readers are important people whose autonomy in forming their interpretations ought to be respected. But what I want to point out about this example is that the poem I created is of less importance and utility than the two sources. The description of the exorcism by the reluctant participant has a valuable role in an internet community of Christians who believe in the necessity of exorcising demons and want to communicate together about the best approaches for carrying this out. Therefore, the text I plundered has significant importance for a probably large Christian sub-culture. Similarly, the description of the porn video is very useful for porn aficionados since it tells them that the video is worth purchasing; many porn enthusiasts will read this description in order to decide if they want the video. Thus, the porn description also has significant importance for decision-making in a probably large sub-culture. My poem, more beautiful and more thought-provoking than either of these, is also less important. It is less important because the thoughts it provokes are less practical. It does not ask: how shall exorcisms be performed? It does not answer the question: what porn will make me happiest if I buy it? It raises impractical questions, like what is the excitement of the ritual of exorcism, and is that excitement parallel to the excitement of speechless, athletic sexual submission? Are two sets of hooting monkeys exercising themselves in ways that are, somehow, fundamentally similar? Is it the same silence at the center of each pack, and can silences be told apart? (As Walt Whitman might say, I stand for all the silent ones: There is no better constituency to represent, no group less likely to contradict the advocate.) The poem asks why culture in general is so invested in turning individuals into automatons in order to enable collective, ritualistic performances. It asks questions about exploitation and complicity. These are unimportant questions which have already been answered in everybody's otherworldly theories. Exploitation is wrong, of course; that is why it is everywhere and unceasing. That is why the world must be swept away, but it would be irresponsible to do so, because there are people in the world, and people are worth more than ideas are.

People are wrong; ideas are right: this is a good general view. In the 70s in San Francisco, the poets felt they could see exploitation happening any time that one narrative sentence followed another. Storytelling itself was visible and offensive exploitation of all the participants (or should I say inhabitants) of culture. To liberate them (the world) a new anti-narrative writing was invented. Of course, anti-narrative writing had been invented before: the digressive poetry of Byron for example. But this new anti-narrative writing was more opposed to narrative than ever. It was right, because it was driven by an idea and it was against something. People were wrong, because they were duped and complicit with their own exploitation. But of course, even though people were wrong, their ways of being wrong and exploiting themselves (and, through themselves, exploiting others) prevailed. The anti-narrative poetry of the 70s, sometimes called L=A=N=G=U=A=G=E poetry, became a relic. Poetry in general is correct in its principled rejection of the world, and soon becomes a relic for that reason: principled rejection is unimportant. Even Ezra Pound would have been right, if he had lived in the world he believed in (the lousy bastard). Of course there is quite a bit of poetry that accommodates the world quite well, poetry about descriptions, scenes, love, and the real estate in which love flourishes, but I say: Those lousy bastards are even worse than Ezra Pound. They believe in the easiest world to believe in. In the marketplace of beliefs, they picked the one that looked the best and had the best testimonials. Perhaps it says more about me than about them, but I must ask: What could be more contemptible? Someday I will write a book about everything I hate about the people of America, and I will call it this: THEIR CONVENIENT BELIEFS. Everyone is trying to sell a belief that they themselves were eager to buy because it was so easy to believe, with no one stopping to ask why it is that the easiest belief is always right. For example, free trade will solve global poverty. Lowering taxes on the rich will enrich the poor. I believe that there is nothing more true than that all people share the same self-interest in the broadest sense, but that broadest sense remains unachievable in the present social system which is predicated on the conflict between interest groups. The most convenient thing to believe is anything that squares the circle, anything that presents self-interest in the broadest sense as being identical with the self-interest of a specific group (particularly one to which you aspire or belong.) Poetry written in square circles has a quiet lyricism which astounds me with its lack of hope. The odd thing is that it is generally a sad poetry, and yet a poetry which has no use for hope. Comfort and convenience are more inspiring than hope could be. Descriptions lack emotion but are full of utility. Descriptions have emotions that nobody really has: intense glorious decorative feelings. Emotions of pure writing, emotions like furniture that is only sat on by important guests.

Poetry is important as a forecast of what is to come: a beautiful future. Such forecasts are actually unimportant, because we live in the present; the present has gobbled the future up and there's none left for us to share. Poems are at least important when they are turned into exegeses, which are essays; so the point of criticism is to move poems up in the hierarchy of art, from the poem level to the essay level. Lately, all I can write are essays: polemics about how the future should be. I describe this future that should come into existence as if it actually could come; I think of this strategy as "extrapolative satire." I would call it "hope," but calling it that would just make everyone who read my polemics feel quite hopeless, so instead of hope I call it "extrapolative satire" and that does quite well.

Depictions of the present are complacent; depictions of the future are implausible. For this reason, depictions are generally unimportant, unless they are made by important people like economists or real estate agents. These important people describe only the future, which they make sure is boring and plausible. A plausible future is just more of the present. The Empire never ends because the people in it are more important than the world that they deserve. Better to have a world that exists than a world that is better but might rock the boat: this is a good general view. Because if you rock the boat, the boat will take on water, and it might well sink. There are already people drowning in the bottom of the boat. Poetry proceeds as if the boat can lift off from the water and become an airy structure, with a few words surrounded by wide open space where the sun gleams off-white. This is not an important thing for the world to be able to do; it is not an important thing to be able to do with the world. Turn it into an essay where the dead things of the present are nailed to a bulletin board: that is at least a little bit useful. I've nailed every dead bit of my ego to this bulletin board that you have just read, and illustrated each one with a corny metaphor. Enjoy. I'll see you in the future, or else in an extrapolative satire, or else I won't see you. You are too important to be able to get out of this present world that wants to be with you till death. Your safety and security is more important than this:

The poem was unimportant.
It could not be bought or sold,
Could not be traded or exchanged: only shared.
The poet thought, "Capitalism Sux!
It's not nearly as unimportant as my poem."

The poem was SO unimportant.
It was better than anything plausible,
It ballooned to the size of a fiery lake
Full of souls weeping out star-powered orgasms
Obtained by melting down the ego's gold.

The poem was SO unimportant,
Barely condescending to be logical!
It was OUT THERE! It was a trip!
Suns blew up in the vast cold interstellar stretches of the poem:
KABOOM! Whole worlds disappeared, just out of spite.

The poem was SO unimportant,
People looked at it like it was a freak:
"Put some pants on, poem!" they said.
"You are leaking, stupid utopias of cranial fluid
Right out of your tightie whities! You must halt!"

The poem was SO unimportant,
Depicting a perfect world of perfect pitch and poise,
By using a typical parlor trick:
The poem decided every stupid thing was perfect now,
And lined them all up, and let them all be
And stupefied itself for all to see.

The poem was SO unimportant,
It could perform every stunt in the rhetorical gymnasium,
Until it was sweating out aromas of new worlds,
Each one a stunt, a jump of the tongue,
An aerobics of the possible.

The poem was SO unimportant,
It said "Goodbye" to the Present,
And the Present did not even bother
To begin getting ready to leave:
So the poem made "Goodbye" an epic,

Every facet of "Goodbye" was explained,
Until "Goodbye" seemed the most logical and perfect thing,
The only possible outcome actually,
The only outcome that could leave everyone involved,
And the poem left them, as if it could. THE END

Los Angeles
2007

MESS IN THE TÊTE AS BRICK

Stephanie Taylor

Upon arriving in Los Angeles from New York in 1997, I became aware of a great divide in communication. Angelenos spoke English, but, perhaps especially among artists in my graduate program, it meant different things than to New Yorkers, even when using the same words. Meaning does not cling to a specific word as it roams the country. Rather, like a virus, it hops to any host who will have it.

Appearance and meaning share a chasm: speak the same language but say something different. For instance, gallery-goers *I'll try to make it* (no one specifies how *hard* they will try, which, in this case, determines the substantive significance of the statement) or, *beautiful exhibition!* (an exhibition may be beautiful but bad). Academics sometimes speak in a language with a style equal to its meaning in presence: this doesn't (always) mean the thicker the language, the seemingly thicker the thought. How to put words together and which ones to choose, and more, the extractability of meaning to morpheme. I walk into a room and try to figure out what's going on, make up a story to fight the fear of not understanding, and then later marvel at my wildly inaccurate estimations made under the constraints of *fear*, of unknowing. This is a key to my work. I first wondered if the urge to recreate this experience was passive aggressive, but I've come to believe it's more *empathetic realism.*

There is a funny thing about it, that meaning can be cobbled together. That one can cobble, and by doing so, make a meaning. It is not a riddle because a riddle has an answer. It is a trick, trying to fool. It is how the world is.

First impressions: there are so many personal, chemical and biological factors in first impressions; the figure in a landscape *alone* is enough to work with. A story can be culled rather than created from a combination of nerve endings and available choices. There is no need to make things up, but at the same time, there is no option *not to*. Connect any dots and you have a story and you will connect the dots. I make work with rhyme charts, which function as an intermediary device, a navigation tool amidst too many choices.

Rather than start with nothing (or is it everything?), I start with lists of sounds. I tread through them, assembling words and sentences. I try to make a story or something that can masquerade as one. The phrases accumulate and, in girth, there is a certain number of coincidences. There appear to be connections. They are not really stories. They pretend to wish to be stories.

This is how it works: a found text (any text for basically any reason) is broken down into individual syllables. A list is made for each syllable of rhyming words. A new text is written from the lists. The story is conjured rather than created; underlying truths are uncovered as syllabic connections are made.

Sounds from the original sound sequences remain amidst new consonants. They are the old frame for the new house. It is a costume party for sound waves. They are happily divorced from old skins. They are celebrating.

The products of rhyme charts are meant to look like thematic installation art, the kind created when an artist is really *into* a certain subject matter, for instance, cars, and he decides to make a show *all about cars.* The equivalences here are dual, in that my work is based on subject matter *and* (because of the rhyme chart process) sound-association.

I must not be lazy and make lame art about stuff I merely like. I try to make a show that looks like lame art about stuff I merely like, but isn't. Its parts are feigned and aimed in that direction, but they are pulled together behind a mask even as they try to pull apart.

The inseparable aural and visual: the porous membrane. It is then necessary for me to make a narrative about how these two dimensions are alike. It is common to make a story, however abstract and philosophical, in exchange for the right to make *something, anything.*[1] And since history is written by the victors, to have a story is to have legitimacy. It is funny what passes for *a story*. We need and like stories. So our largest genre is presumptive *narrative*, or narratives, as is usually the case.

When I was in grad school, critiques were rife with questions about production. Why is that box blue? Why are you using clay? Basic questions that I could not answer. I thought it would be nice to have an answer.

A female car thief, a devil lady, offers gasoline to motorists on the side of the road or offers to tow the car but rather takes it to the chop shop where it is stripped for parts. She wears a rat's bed as a hat on her head and driving goggles. She shouts, "Yo!" Her motto: Never a tortoise toe!

This was the story I bumbled together about cars. Rhyme became an explanation for each choice I made in art.

Equivalencies + relationships: Artists, like other humans, are trained to think they need justification for making—via biography, concept, constraint, narrative, or some other means. By creating a nonsense story, I mimic the absurd need for justification, but I don't debate its necessity, or the necessity for metaphor. The crux of metaphor being a=b, in the simplest terms. If I tell you the story of the relationship, you will understand the metaphor.

Sounds start adding up in columns and factoring into other sounds. The connection of one sound to another is somewhat random but the end product is meant to look like anything but.

Narrative: except of the self-reflexive sort,[2] is a perversion of older notions of conceptual art that a thing simply is. Thus, narrative is a perfect distraction for a self-reflexive conceptual practice attempting to demonstrate the deceptive nature of first impressions.

---

1. The intriguing people, in my opinion and tendency, seem to want to talk about it. The talk is the point, beside the point, so we sometimes make something up in order to have something to say.

2a. both to itself on a microcosmic level, and to operations in the art world and the human world, on a macrocosmic level.

2b. I always thought the mark of intelligence was knowing exactly how stupid you are.

There is some connection to Conceptual Art as there must be: the idea and the material cannot be undone.

Narrative is equal to a dream sequence, in terms of not having any constraints—a few characters and a plot: minimal requirements. A friend of mine had a professor in film school, who described his crew getting resistant when filming things which didn't make sense within a traditional narrative. When he decided to call it a dream sequence, they went along quite happily.

They are meant to look like mundane facts. They are no more unified than actual fictional experiences. That gas is made of brass.

It became another narrative?

With the right explanation, everything, anything can be made to *make sense*. Once my narrative is determined, I produce objects which pose as story-tellers and which bear a rhyming relation to the materials with which they are made. The *gas* can appears to have some connection to the car thieves but it is also, plainly, made from *brass*; its gas from the *-ass* in *brass*. While the method appears systematic, it is more like a corrupt alibi since, of course, its impossible to tell which specific phrases were or were not produced with the rhyming lists, so convoluted is the method, so grasping is the connection between individual parts. The tale is a bit abnormal because it is partially determined by happenstance. It is no true concoction of equations, no real metaphor, but an explanation devised sometimes in retrospect. Like many narratives.

Each object has a direct connection to the materials with which it's made. The blaze is painted with glaze. The faux-tow is a photo. Each thing could not be different than it is. It is, as if, decreed.

Site-specificity, like narrative, is easy. Since narrative is merely "a description of something," this something can be anything. Similarly, one need only link a project to its place of display (sometimes the challenge is to *not* link it), to base a project on *architecture* or *history* or even *aesthetics*, and therefore make a parallel between any old blob and the gallery it sits in, thus earning the great honor of very *site-specific*. Normally, this would be a reason *not* to make art with the concept of *site-specificity*. In general, I prefer to work *against* something when making it into something else. It is for this reason that I like using rhyme charts. Challenge inspires me, dislocation is more stimulating than location. However, it may be noteworthy that while certain things such as *biography as explanation* exist in exile, other matters, such as site-specificity are embraced to the point of meaninglessness. With a little irony, the meaningless is a source of great amusement.

This is again about things not meaning what they seem. Empty phrases. Poor justification. Boringness.

A simple rhyme with the site name is used to determine genre (normally the most implicit of developments) and instantly makes the work *site-specific*. There is no more plausible genre for an "L.A. artist" than automobile theft and *Vroom* just happens to rhyme with *Room* (Gallery).

Sometimes the best hiding place is expectation.

Finally, to be absolutely literal perverts conceptions of the relation of *method to manner* because the possibility exists to create something which contradicts its very nature and reveals itself at the same time. *Directness* being portrayed *indirectly*, for instance. To make the *experience* of rather than telling a story.

Here is the façade, newly made.

Thus: my work should look like a normal kind of art exhibition; engaging in an a*esthetics of normality*, posing and sometimes almost passing as a show about something but usually not. It should look like art. The question, "is this art?" is not my interest. Rather, an attempt is made to seem as much as possible *like art*. Like a metaphor of art. The narrative in the exhibition serves this purpose: it lurches to connect disparate objects with a simple tale—car thieves with a fake tow-truck business, for example. Unrelated characters are bound together by lies. The story is a farce meant to echo the experience of seeing something for the first time and trying to understand what it is, and then making up an explanation to initiate comprehension. And then learning later, as we almost always do, that our first impression was incredibly misleading. A false equivalency.

To ask the question, "what is this?" and to have the answer be "many things—depending on who's asking."

And this *looking like* is itself one of its (true) stories. It *is* art as it sets up a story about why it is *like* art.[3] What better place to start than a language such as English, which supports silent letters and spelling-bee fetishes? Language that is language and is like a language.

English with its irregular verbs, the things you have to know and which cannot be intuited from general rules. A specific knowledge that must be learned in trials. Unless you are expecting irregularities, but how can irregularities be expected? Is the best hiding place amidst the irregularities or is it inside the shining phantom façades?

Los Angeles
2007, 2014

Editor's Note: The bold sections included in this essay are annotations added to the original (unbolded) text.

---

3. *like* signaling a metaphor or story, that in itself is a story, according to Vanessa Place.

04. Tracer

Kim Rosenfield / Susan Simpson / Allison Carter / Ken
Ehrlich / Amina Cain / Sophie Robinson / 2008–09

1++1

Teresa Carmody

1. Tear this page out.
2. Find another piece of paper, light in color, thin in density, without marks.
3. Select a pen, pencil or ultra-fine point permanent marker. Fine point will also work.
4. Search for a window with good light.
5. Place this page behind the other. Press both pages against the window.
6. Use your pen, pencil, or marker and trace.
7. When you are done, place your drawing on the floor, picture-side up.

There was the one, and then there were two hundred, and if you followed all the instructions, daring to be one of the ones who doesn't mind tearing a page from a book, there are now two-hundred and ten, or two-hundred thirty-one, or maybe, if we're especially caring and community-minded and open to change and hopeful, implementing, in short, the "core activities," or "SALT" of Kim Rosenfield's *integrated mission*, there are exactly three-hundred and thirty-three *Maman Spiders?*, lying down and listening.

A tracer traces. In order to trace, there must be one and another. The act of tracing subverts the original, turning the traced in turn into that which can be traced—a new original made by copying the old.

"Compounding objects," writes Allison Carter, "is a way to make out of their borders." To *make out of*. The edges of one make the other. The one across the table. In the bed.

To trace is a relational act, an engagement.

And because we are messy, full of patterns learned and inherited, "[p]erverse collaborations ensue." There's Sophie Robinson asking, "[w]hose language can I appropriate, queer up, violate?" Tracing, and having fun eating (in) (with) (out) our girlfriend, despite "[the] sense of loss, before [we've] even begun, [...] the sense of being overwritten." Or, Carter: "I shake your hand and you wash it. Some of me gets in."

A tracer is ammunition containing a chemical substance that leaves a trail of smoke or fire, illuminating the night so as to make the target visible for others. It is a *collaborative* kind of ammunition, a working together toward a common goal. It is an ammunition that promotes *community*. That helps others to see and destroy.

"[C]ollaboration," writes Ken Ehrlich, "set my preconceptions about artmaking in relief… so I could suddenly see the assumptions I was making quite clearly and in a way that I was often blind to when working alone." That's it exactly, or at least for now. Because you are inside you, while I'm inside me, and even if I interview myself, like Ehrlich does, I'm still not outside me, like you are. Yet, in the best of all possibilities, you help me to see, as I help you, so

I fire the shot and tear out the page, because I, like Amina Cain, "want there to be connection." To destroy the border between us.

We meet, we lie down, now I'm inside you and you're inside me, but then "[s]omeone hurts you," notes Amina Cain. Because we are messy, sometimes mean, you slip away, must be sought for, slowly. The new you must be followed, and while we're tracing your wounded scent, "all you do is walk around and look at things, feeling aware of your body and of the temperature of the air. Then you hurt another character."

I see how you are. Or do I? I see how you were. I see where you were. I see this space bordering us, in one of Carter's Platonic garages, in Robinson's "half-demolished AmericanCarWash," and in the gap Susan Simpson blindly minds "fastidiously, obsessively. It is not what I had envisioned," says Simpson. "My collaborators have deprived me of the sight I've grown used to." The creation of a new original destroys the old original. Yet if the original goal is to make an object that "haunts the vision of those who see or read or hear it," then all the better to have one's vision haunted by the process of *making out of* together.

Making *integrated mission.*

I want to join. I'll be a cadet, an officer, a soldier, whatever, just let me in, let me listen and want, let me trace her, I am her, Maman the Spider, and she is lying on the floor as she says, "To quote Kim Rosenfield, 'There are great opportunities in the little things of life.'"

"I saw you."

MISSION IN POETICS

Kim Rosenfield

PROGRAM RESOURCES DEPARTMENT
International Headquarters, CA.

mission in poetics
Kim Rosenfield's Integrated Mission

PREFACE

The hallmark of my work is *integrated mission*. Which means it ministers to the whole person bringing health—physical, mental, social, and spiritual—to every person. And it is to that comprehensive understanding that mission in poetics is dedicated.

There is no doubt that when everything we do is added together, then we have the very embodiment of *integrated mission*. But it is when we view each project corps or center or program on its own that we need to pause and think. Ideally, every unit, every program, however specialized, should reflect to some degree the breadth of vision that *integrated mission* represents for every person. But in our concentration on the task at hand, we sometimes forget the larger picture.

There is, therefore, never a time when we do not need to be recalled to our roots. Never a time when we do not need to seek new vision of the possibilities that are open to us today. This is what this booklet *mission in poetics* is all about.

In recent years, dedicated visionaries have been spearheading new approaches to *integrated mission*. These approaches have been centered in the community, with the concerns of home and neighborhoods as well as of individuals shaping a response. Old concepts have been given new clothes—and the results have often been amazing.

These pages give us the framework that animates these new developments in *integrated mission*. They tell us not only something of what is happening around the world, but also why these things are happening. These pages remind us to care for the total person and to our calling in society. These pages highlight the fundamental concepts of care, community, change, and hope—concepts that are at the heart of every form of *integrated mission*. These pages therefore have something vital to say to everyone.

I am pleased that the Program Resources Department (PRD) of Les Figues Press at International Headquarters, Los Angeles, has had a leadership role in these developments. On everything to do with *integrated mission*, the department is now a vast storehouse of accumulated experience and knowledge. I know that the personnel of the department will be pleased to share from this abundance with any enquirer.

May we continue to bless *integrated mission* to the total person.

HOW TO USE THIS DOCUMENT

Two elements of culture are belief and practice, also called values and norms, or vision and direction. My task was to align belief and practice with consciousness. This document is a framework for a working poetic culture, which is recognizable anywhere, although actions may differ according to environment. The sections are arranged by concepts.

First

Look at it as a framework, not as a manual. It is a distillation of experience, meant as a stimulus to discussion, a catalyst for action.

Second

Think of your own experience or desire as you read it. Explore, and find out how it resonates with your own experience.

Third

Discover what you can draw from this framework and what you can add.

■

GLOSSARY OF TERMS

Cadets: students

Corps: audience

Officers: ordained leaders, laureates

Soldiers: active laity, members, subscribers, volunteers

Territorial headquarters: administrative office for country or combination of countries

BACKGROUND

This document is a voice, from all different parts of the world, from years of working on various issues. The experience here is true to identity and there is nothing new in the beliefs expressed. Practice is the real challenge: how does practice emerge from passionately held beliefs? What is actually being expressed in the communities of the world today? Mission in community has come to be known as "integrated mission." A pattern of belief and practice characterized by a core belief that all people can respond and become whole. A core practice of accompaniment by presence in the homes and neighborhoods of people. There are friends in every region of the world who believe and practice this.

Early in 2005, an international working group was formed to reflect on the roots of *integrated mission*. This document is the result of its work.

The working group has a prevailing sense of returning to historical roots, while exploring a "new thing."

Participants hope that this document will be an encouragement and that it will help stimulate further action and reflection.

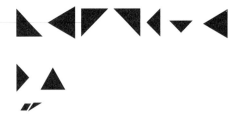

Fastidious rejection of everything—until we reach our ghostly natural insides, the most precious gift you can make.
>   - Kim Rosenfield

Homely mixed institutional parables keep our digestive systems in good working order. Use it to beat upon clouds of darkness and to subdue all distractions.
>   - Kim Rosenfield

All the human body needed. Consigning them to clouds of forgetting, below.
>   - Kim Rosenfield

There are great opportunities in the little things of life, in the conventional clothes of the local tailor, and the daily progress along the same dull streets.
>   - Kim Rosenfield

Hidden earthly hurts continue to wield great power. Attention centered on the blind awareness of your naked being amongst the sawdust and the shavings.
>   - Kim Rosenfield

Little things bring great opportunities— how wonderful a thing's silence can be; a child's home growing; quiet care; housework and arrangement of the garden; corporate digestion. Ruminare= to chew the cud, quietly.
>   - Kim Rosenfield

Put your desire into one simple word and then affix it to your brain, come what may. I assure you that these thoughts will vanish. Why?
>   - Kim Rosenfield

CARE

Section 1: CARE

BELIEF

▦ The scars remain. The loss remains. But there are signs of hope because people cared, listened, cried.

▦ It was a deeply emotional experience for us all. We sang, read together, cried together, had food, and shared together as believers.

BEHAVIOR

▦ Presence/accompaniment: "Be with people" in their living reality
▦ Homes and neighborhoods, not only our own buildings
▦ Listening, to understand and learn
▦ Participating in the life of people—their suffering and joys
▦ Long-term relationship, not activity/program only
▦ Express trust, and respect, dignity for ourselves and others
▦ Be available
▦ We together in a team approach
▦ Encourage and provoke care and response: people themselves express care, take initiative, become team mates
▦ Care as a natural overflow of life

STORY

The corps (congregation/clinic) was the only presence in the community. The team cared by participating and by facilitating community discussions through listening and respectful interactions.

During one community discussion, the community leaders requested something from the team. They said, "Can you make a poem bless us?"

These community leaders requested the power of poetry to guide them. This is a result of the "care" that the team shared and exemplified in the community.

Section 2: COMMUNITY

BELIEF

- Humans are created for belonging
- All persons are to be respected
- Connection between people is found everywhere
- People long to mean and belong
- We are persons in relationship, not just individuals
- Teamwork is a journey and an expression of community
- Community can be built
- Community can choose "health"
- Care in the community by teamwork inspires longing for connection
- Relationships are the persuasive environment where it is all felt

STORY

I was doing pick up for the kids when a mother got into the van full of kids and started talking to me about issues including relationships, racism, and money. Before long she was weeping. After I and all the kids in the van had listened to her, we were quiet.

I could not offer her the money she needed. I could not eliminate the discrimination she and her children were experiencing. I couldn't mend her abusive relationship, but in a mysterious and yet real way a healing and strength came over her to stay strong.

I was encouraged by her strength. In those moments I knew the children were keenly tuned to what was going on.

⬜⬜

○

INTEGRATED STRATEGY

↵

CORE ACTIVITIES - **SALT** ↵

S..upport, stimulate
A..ppreciate, analyze
L..earn
T..ransfer

Neighboring communities   ↙↙

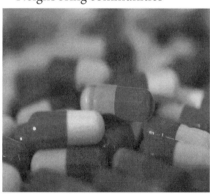

Corps or Center ∩

Wider Community ↖

BEHAVIOR

- Go out; get into neighborhoods and homes by invitation
- Be with and engage with people
- Participate with people in their life
- SALT visits (see diagram on page 149)
- Include: who else is here, could be here, should be here?
- Look for family connections
- Work by relationship
- Learn from local action and experience

Section 3: CHANGE

BELIEF

- Change is possible: no person, no culture, no community is beyond it
- Change comes from within: capacity is part of image
- Change is not initiated by us
- People are not the 'subject' nor the 'object' of change
- We are changed by our relationships with others
- International care will draw people into change
- Freedom to be fully whole is good design; desire for freedom motivates change
- We are changed by our relationships with others
- Change includes growth into belonging
- Families and communities can change

STORY

In our first appointment we set up an orientated community-based program which worked with the community; but that, in retrospect, was still very building-based and with not enough involvement of the community itself.

Having left that place, two appointments further on I began to grasp a lot more the concept of working with the community and the fact that the community could respond and that my role should be much more one of facilitation rather than providing or better helping to provide.

The experience that really revolutionized my understanding was seeing the community organizing themselves and working with nothing—a couple of rabbits and a bag of charcoal.

I realized that although we had probably helped lots of people, we had not empowered them as we could have, because we had not started from their standpoint or even from the 'empty handed' standpoint, although we had listened many times to them.

Delegates reflected, saying:

▩ People around us are dying within
▩ We see something different in ourselves that we want to share
▩ We should be 'out there' with people
▩ We are searching for and finding a vision for our communities and for ourselves
▩ We gather to learn from each other and our shared experience what *integrated mission* is all about—how it is expressed and transferred

◆

Section 4: HOPE

BELIEF

- There are many factors which contribute to despair
- Yet hope is present now
- Hope is linked to past and future
- Capacity for hope can expand: hope grows within individuals and communities
- Often people need to take steps toward hope, and these steps are encouraged by caring relationships and presence
- Knowing beside, before, behind, and within us, we can be along side others
- Examples guide us 'to the heart of the matter' in each situation and cultural context
- Hope is a catalyst, giving energy for change
- Hope is driven by compassion
- Hope is security

STORY

A woman was lying on the streets. 'I saw you,' she said.

■ ■ ■ ··

BEHAVIOR

- Go out; approach people with confidence
- Expect the unexpected—don't imagine that we control the outcomes
- Expect invitations into positive relationship
- Discern opportunity and invitation
- Be patient as people find their steps: trust in the process

◨

Many people should be acknowledged for their contribution to the formation of this document. The International Working Group on the roots of integrated mission has met and been reinforced by an advisory group whose members have commented by email. Territorial leaders and regional teams participated and supported participation. A reference group at IHQ has guided the process. The Health Service Section has supported throughout. Production of this document has been possible thanks to the skills of the Communications Section. The leadership and support of the International Management Council has been appreciated. Especially, thanks to those who have shared and read these stories of *integrated mission* journey.

New York City
2008

Postscript:

"mission in poetics" speaks to the collective whole and is thus a comment on what it means to be framed as an individual poet in concert with other contemporary poets/artists writing statements on our various aesthetics. In "mission in poetics" I'm commenting on my accompanying book, *re: evolution*, in terms of how systems organize and develop evolutionarily, but also on the role at large of Les Figues as a developer of community and poetic action. The text is lifted from Salvation Army training program materials because, although Les Figues is not standing on a street corner ringing a bell with an alms bucket, they are doing the very hard work of spreading the gospel of experimental writing. This kind of foot soldiering takes a village, a "knowing beside, before, behind, and within us, we can be along side others."[1] In other words, our being in the trenches with our art and hope for its survival.

New York City
2014

---

1. Kim Rosenfield, "mission in poetics," *Trenchart: Tracer*, 2008, Les Figues Press

UNTITLED AESTHETIC

Susan Simpson

"'Have you ever really looked carefully at your watch?' The questioner knows that I have looked at it often enough and now his question deprives me of the sight which I've grown used to and which accordingly has nothing more to say to me. I realize that I have given up seeing the watch with an astonished eye; and it is in many ways an astonishing piece of machinery."

– Bertolt Brecht

To view the world with an astonished eye can be a haunting experience. Take the objects that lie before you. For me, at this moment, it is a toy kitchen, a fishing lure, a plastic bridesmaid for the top of the cake, two of them actually bought as stand-ins for brides at a double bride ceremony. Beyond the thing that each object seems to be, there is the thing we believe it to be, the thing it aspires to be, and the thing it pretends to be.

What material is it made of? What labor? What cost? What boredom of process? What chemical formula? What natural resource depleted? What excitement of invention? What shipping? What darkness of storage? What smell of the new? What section of the store? Every object threatens to capsize in its own wake.

There is the future disposal of the thing, its recycling potential, the space it takes up, the worth of the space it takes up, the factory line littermates out there and space they take up, the supposed virtue of its one-of-a-kindness, or the humble work-a-dayness of its lack of uniqueness. The aura of things is unbearably bright. Rooms fill with blinding ectoplasm.

There is the name of the thing, the word we hold with a trembling hand in front of the object. The trembling is all, as the poignancy of this effort wins out over the accuracy of the match. Names are themselves delicate, provisional, unstable things tacked onto moving targets.

To deprive another of the sight they have grown used to and to offer instead a fissure in their vision, a crack as a peephole, an invitation into an infinite interstitial—Is this not a generous act?

So what of the making of things? Assuming my own generous motives, I set out to make something that will haunt the vision of those who see or read or hear it. I make a familiar path where I lead the unsuspecting. I sing a song to amuse and put them at ease. I grow the lilacs, a whiff of which will make them feel at home. I practice jumping out and saying that very gentle BOO.

What of the making of things together? Collaboration. We get together to make a thing, a thing that will trigger an uncanny shift of perception in those who see it. This shift will expose a particular societal delusion so ubiquitous as to have been previously invisible. This object we imagine will perpetrate an act of radical haunting, that awakens the viewer to the world around it, but its success depends wholly on our collective BOO. I show up as Boris Karloff but my collaborator was hoping for a more Henry James-like spooking. Her laugh is not fiendish enough. He thinks my cape ridiculous. There is always a gap. We mind the gap fastidiously, obsessively. It is not what I had envisioned. My collaborators have deprived me of the sight I've grown used to. They have haunted my haunting… generously. "Have you ever really looked carefully at the thing we are making?" they ask.

Los Angeles
2008

AESTHETICS STATEMENT

Allison Carter

A sentence leads time around a tracing space. It can lead the splice into the hole, through the other end. Love is also a knot. All I ever wanted was to move my arms in both directions. Control is a thing you can work very hard to find.

1. Control—The Edge of the Room

A garage is defined by what comes and goes from it, leaving traces. The form allows settings in and the bodies of people and animals leave residues, the accumulation of events and words leaves traces, cuttings, and a breakdown of the day to day. To remain in the garage is a breakdown. I bring my dog to a garage. He inhales and undergoes a tremor. To leave is to leave the page, and stop there. The fourth wall of any piece is a vertical door with windows made of glass.

2. Control—The Sneeze of the Heart

Compounding objects is a way to make out of their borders. The mustache of a sentence, the sentence is also very clean. I shake your hand and you wash it. Some of me gets in. You sneeze. Compounding objects to perform the liminal at the same time: talking directly into the space between people, or gestures. Some words fill up the space and get on people. Sneezes of heart or of intellect. Slippage. Lyrical gestures, I noticed, earlier, that a utensil for measuring space was arriving by mail, I waited, no wait, a pile up, to wait is to be surrounded by objects and then to begin a dissolve, I shake my own hand, it moves me, reining in excess, squeezing excess out through the pores in the container that fits. I introduce myself as I, and then switch. I introduce myself as Allison and then delete to I, to introduce a letter again. Authoring is sometimes filling a role, elbowing out the borders of the role. Some of the borders get on you and your eye flashes in a tremor. I love you, and then you sneeze/leave me again.

3. Control—Control Management System

Conversation is a control management system. You make some assumptions to accumulate a coherent peer group; you make conversation to accumulate a coherent person. About knowledge—words allow for relationship slippage: slippage of the borders of the individual parties undersigned or blown out. At the office I like to highlight major routes that would get me from here to there and then get the page carbon pressed. To make skin out of other skin. To make a friend and name it then talk, then wait for it to talk, talk. Words stay inside a text for hours at a time and wait for each other to reveal a pattern. If you find yourself stuck in a fixed, formal arrangement, find another word and then use it. In this respect conversation reveals rugburns and other pinned symptoms. In this respect sometimes some pain peels out—I listen to it and I talk, talk. I lay it out and I fold it, measure it, iron it, hawk it to the filer for a change of pace.

4. Control—The Body

Viscosity is dangerous to measure. It is allowable to wear a skin vest in which the fingers are made of leather. Conversation veins out and reconvenes, the conversational organ pumps at a slight lag. Viscous is my least favorite word. You can avoid viscosity by having a container of tiny hard things instead of a solution. That way you can rearrange things with only a photo stain to prove it. You can pour tongues as if concrete and watch them get lathered, without a tremor in your body, without sticking.

"How do you measure viscosity?" I yell from the garage. I am studying the things I have studied and where I filed them. My husband calls me husband. "Husband," he says, "with a honey dipper." This is an example of the tremor that I try to avoid. I shut him without a waver and I think.

Los Angeles
2008

ON COLLABORATION

Ken Ehrlich

Words or phrases that might seem cliché yet are difficult to avoid while giving your collaborator a pep talk during a difficult moment in collaboration: activate, interdisciplinary, the sum of the parts is greater…, resources, trans-formation, contextualize, creativity, commitment, conversation, limitless inter-relations, collective process, process, individual empowerment, group dynamics, persevere, turning point, trust, participatory, long-term, self-organizing, alternative, market-driven, untapped freedom, productive constraint, linkage, points of contact, symbiotic, mutual respect.

to collaborate: together, art,

signify, subtlety, mis-

represent, circuitous, therapy, over-committed, expectation, dedication, discipline, strident, oneiric,

arrival, productivity, normalize. Words to try to ignore that are difficult to ignore while trying

strategize, incomplete, obscure, powerful, re-evaluate, incongruous, extraordinary, implicated, methodology,

hearing from

Words you dread

your collaborator during a project but expect to hear: *adjustment,*

reconsider, circulate,

stimulate, calibrate, relevance,

one, conflict, pursue, shame,

compete, both, indignant, stern, crass, success, redeem, maintain, share, obscure, reject,

cracy, genius, funding, smear, commodity, painterly, despair. Words or phrases those who idealize

career, enduring, bureau-

expansive, nurturing.

Words or phrases in these categories regarding collaboration that are inter-

changeable

with one another: All of the above.

form, elucidate, hostility, shithead, arrogant, pride, sabotage, ambition, subterfuge, scandalous,

never collaborated like to use in reference to collaboration: facilitate, listening session, group activity,

collaboration yet have

compromise, discouraging, sex, in-

Interview with Ken Ehrlich

Q: I wanted to start with a question about site-specificity. Many of your projects are described as "site-specific," you've written about this subject and you edit the *Surface Tension* book series, which is focused on site-specific practices in art, architecture, and performance. This is a loaded term for some readers and might be an unfamiliar term for others. What does site-specific mean in your work and why is it important?

A: Ummm. Ok. You're right to suggest the ambiguity of this term. Like so many words related to art practices, "site-specificity" is first of all a changing concept. That's very important. So site-specific practices in the 1960s or 1970s have very little in common with most site-based work today. In terms of an art historical take on the term, I like Miwon Kwon's analysis in which she distinguishes between physical, institutional, and discursive site-specificity. In her model, you have someone like Richard Serra who claims that if you move one of his pieces, you've destroyed it. So a project for him might be literally bound to a physical site. The institutional sort of site-specificity she describes is attributed to artists like Daniel Buren or Michael Asher, whose work stages a critical dialogue with the "site" of an institution like a museum or a gallery. And then lastly, when referring to discursive site-specificity, Kwon describes the practices of artists like Renee Green and Andrea Fraser, whose work might refer to, say, African-American history or notions of taste... so that the "site" here becomes a discourse that is interrogated. Now, Kwon presents her account much more elegantly than that and in much greater detail, but I think she gives us a useful framework for thinking about the term historically.

In terms of my own work, "sited-based practice" is a useful framework that encompasses much of what I do and at the same time I'm not particularly devoted to the concept. I grew up in an environment where if you played the saxophone, built houses, made photographs, and wrote poetry, that was considered more or less normal. So as an artist who works on a project basis and across many media, I'm interested in site-specificity, sculpture in the expanded field, relational practices, etc... Whatever helps frame a contemporary practice that expands the notion of what art might be... Oh, and the last thing I'll say about that is that, alongside site-specificity, a parallel discourse has evolved about the relationship between art and architecture involving all sorts of productive cross-overs and including aspects of geography, urbanism, activism, and performance. So without forcing too much onto the term, site-specific work kind of prefigures a lot of contemporary cultural work related to cities and spaces.

Q: That leads me to my next question. It seems that you do many things: sculptures, videos, photographs, interventions, writing, editing, publishing, and collaborative work. Do you feel that working in such diverse ways dilutes what you might do in one medium?

A: Not really. I'm not really interested in the mastery of a medium. Most contemporary, commercially successful artists have work fabricated for them... and since Conceptual Art the notion of creating a system or structure that results in the production of an art work has been a very common strategy. I'm interested in both of these models. I kind of imagine Warhol during the factory years as someone who might wave his hand and have an entire body of work produced. Contrast that with the heavy-handedness of someone like Joseph Kosuth who argues that an idea can qualify as an artwork. And both of these examples are from the mid-1960s! So although since that time devotion to a particular medium and the discourses around specific media have fluctuated wildly—from the need to defend or redefine a medium like painting on the one hand to the ongoing conversation about the role of digital imaging technology in photography on the other—I'm more interested in a Duchampian position in which different contexts require different strategies. Whatever you make of Duchamp, he certainly paved the way for an artistic practice that was multi-faceted.

Q: What *do* you make of Duchamp?

A: Yeah... good question. I kind of found my way to Duchamp through other artists who I think felt that they had to reckon with him in some way. There is John Cage of course... and Warhol. But also people like Thomas Hirschhorn in the sense of his very strategic self-presentation. So it was almost as if I was looking at Duchamp through the work of two generations of artists who had struggled with thinking about him. I see Duchamp as intensely analytical with a perverse sense of humor. That seems like a pretty good combination! In my mind, Duchamp also represents a move towards self-referentiality that is both provocative, say in terms of thinking about gender, but can seem limited in terms of imagining alternative forms of social engagement.

Q: What do you mean by social engagement?

A: Any successful art is socially engaged. It is by definition so… but one can make distinctions about what kinds of engagement are useful, productive, or interesting. The point is to imagine all the other forms of social engagement beyond the image of the bullhorn and the protest sign. In my own work, I have tried to address infrastructure as a way of thinking about social engagement. I first started thinking about this in terms of electricity and electrical transmission. Here is this vast complex system that transmits an invisible energy force that is completely linked, albeit in a very abstract way, to almost every aspect of society. But, in general, people don't think of the electrical system as political. There are very literal ways that it is political— for example, the way it is regulated by state and federal governments or how the control of infrastructure in general has migrated from public to private entities—but what is more interesting to me and what I've tried to get at is the way these systems might be read, through an aesthetic and textual lens, as "political" entities. It's taking the notion 'the personal is political' literally. So electricity has a technical, social, and even mystical dimension. And an installation or a text might be able to point to that in an experiential way. I'm trying to complicate the idea of techno-determinism—the idea that we are somehow completely defined by technology—on the one hand and at the same time explore the reciprocal relationship between modes of thinking or imagining and things that are built in the world. Another example is the infrastructure around trash… it is an indicator of over-consumption and a barometer of the ecological crisis and it can provide a lens for thinking about excess, expenditure and accumulation from a cultural point of view. Or currently I'm thinking about the infrastructure of trucking, which relates to discourses around immigration and free trade but also to fantasies about the freedom of the open road…. So, to me the most interesting way that art can be socially engaged is to address political questions—and I mean that in the most abstract and concrete sense—in formally rigorous ways.

Q: So do you think 'protest' art is a dead-end?

A: No, I think there is room for all sorts of art practices. Given the state of contemporary politics, all sorts of interventions are warranted and necessary. I think the danger of artworks that address complex political issues in simplistic ways is that they can reinforce the presumed position of the audience. I guess I hold on to a bit of that romantic notion that art has the potential to address "the political" in ways that are more complex than we usually encounter.

Q: You've often collaborated with architects and with other artists. What's your interest in collaboration?

A: Partly it was an organic process. In San Francisco in the 1990s and in graduate school, I was just drawn to making work with friends. So I would write a text for a performance or make a film that would be projected while a friend's band was playing… or whatever. It was loose. Later I started to see that collaboration set my preconceptions about artmaking in relief… so I could suddenly see the assumptions I was making quite clearly and in a way that I was often blind to when working alone—I was interested in that process… Also, and again maybe this is a bit romantic, I honestly believe in negotiating difference *as* a form of work. I like making that part of what I do… Contributing to a cultural discourse through the sometimes difficult process of negotiating difference is more exciting to me than striving to see my individual vision made manifest in the world. (Though I have to admit that proposition is also seductive!) I'm fascinated by what we mean when we say 'public,' and I often feel that my thinking about what is public and what is private is enhanced through collaboration. In particular, my various collaborations with Brandon LaBelle have really expanded my sense of what might constitute an artistic practice.

Q: I want to go back to something you touched on earlier, when you referred to cities and spaces. Can you talk about some of the projects you've done in various cities and how you work with urban issues?

A: Sure. First of all, it has been and remains one of my goals to work in as many diverse places as I can. At the same time, one aspect of globalization is the creation of this jet-setting cultural elite who travel around to art fairs and biennials, visiting museums-as-destinations and generally having a good ole' time. This is a dynamic that I'm very aware of when I work internationally.

So working with infrastructure and digging into these dynamics of how a city works, how it functions on a concrete level is a way of addressing the potential for art-making to become a kind of cultural tourism. In the *Surface Tension* publications and exhibition series I co-edit and organize with Brandon LaBelle, we've tried both to plug into existing networks and artistic communities and initiate a conversation among artists, writers, performers, and architects internationally that approaches urban issues in critical and creative ways. Last year we organized an exhibition with Nis Rømer, and invited artists from Denmark and other countries to stage works in various venues around the city of Copenhagen. As part of this larger project, I investigated off-shore wind farms in Copenhagen. My piece combined a small video installation about the construction and collective organization of these wind farms with more playful sculptural works about the wind and the ambiance of the city.

Q: What are some of your current projects?

A: The last two things I did both exist on the internet. Tom Leeser invited me to participate in the *Lament Project,* which is an online collection of sound works consisting of one-minute interpretations of the meaning of the lament. I created a collaged sequence of recorded texts based on ancient laments, threaded together with the suggestion that you must "begin at the beginning" but keep in mind that there are "multiple beginnings beyond the beginning…" I also recently contributed to *A Wikipedia Reader*, a project organized by artist David Horvitz that looks at how information is linked between Wikipedia pages and playfully comments on the way knowledge is produced via users' contributions. The entries that I chose—my path through Wikipedia—were spatial disorientation, proprioception, muscle memory, serotonin, L.S.D., synesthesia, romanticism, epistemology, slippery slope, and social change. Another *Surface Tension* book is in the works and, as I mentioned, I'm working on a couple of video pieces related to long distance trucking and the infrastructure of transportation that will be exhibited at F.I.T. Gallery and General Public this summer in Berlin.

Q: The two projects you just mentioned seem text-based and I know that you also write… so how do you think about language, and how does that thinking translate to your visual works?

A: I'm not really sure… Sometimes the relationship is very clear and distinct and other times it's all muddled. At some point, I was very interested in Structuralism and all the ways that language is employed in making conceptual art. I guess I still am to a certain degree. But I'm becoming less interested in rigid structures… and also thinking a lot about sound has changed the way I think of language. Not that sound is without structure but sounds tend to remind us that languages are always relational and changing. I like language games and puns and think that the humor that finds its way into my work often comes through language. I like the shape of letters and the materiality of language. I do know that I am often compelled to say something when I feel there is nothing to say. But when language speaks, I listen.

Los Angeles
2008

I SEW MY PREY

Amina Cain

I sit, feeling as if the air is a part of my body. I sit in front of a fire, blazing and warm. Whose hands die when they sit in front of a fire? It snows and the snow covers a wire. Who looks at a wire?

Today I walked around with bits of paper in my pockets. I took each bit out and each bit was a wolf. Something sacred happened; the paper turned into wolves. I am writing to you and to someone in prison, unless you think you're in prison too.

Something jumps at a wall. Mud bubbles up like something I have sewn. I sew a wing. I sew my prey. Your whole life flashes in front of me, but what do I know about your life? Outside there is nothing, and the nothingness never stops. Inside there is nothingness too.

Letter to someone who is not *real*:

What was sewn was empty. What was sewn was sent to another state. Tonight I went running and thought about you. You live in a city where it rains all the time. You don't know how to be tender with the other characters in your story. Someone hurts you, and all you do is walk around and look at things, feeling aware of your body and of the temperature of the air. Then you hurt another character.

When it has already been dark for hours, when I am lying on the ground, when I am firewatch, when I light the lanterns in the morning, when I chop beets in the kitchen, when I listen to an owl, when I listen to someone read, when I read, when it is still dark in the morning I am thinking about you. What do you look like? What is your favorite song? Do you like the desert?

You sent me the middle parts of quilts. Here, books in the night, bags on their sides. There, drinking hot cider, talking to the people at a party I've made up for you. I imagine you trying to befriend a woman or a man, both of you confused by a strange desire; someone with dark eyes who looks at you in a way that doesn't add up to what you've seen other people do. Drinking cider becomes the only thing on which you can focus. It burns your tongue, though you don't mind because it is sweet, and because it allows you to pay attention to what burning your tongue is like. But something is lurking in the background, or maybe it's before you. Don't worry, it is small, and in certain moments you won't really be able to sense that it is there. You won't even know whether it is good or bad, empty or full.

What is that desire? A woman or a man walks toward you and you change the air around you.

My hands are on fire. What can I touch? If I touch your hands they will be on fire too. Who touches someone when their hands are on fire?

Today I wake up and I am anxious. I look out the window, at the sun. I look at my desk. It has dust on it. There are streets in the distance with paper and glass all over them, cabs driving fast in the morning. I wish I could call you a sweet name and take you to the desert. I had a dream that one of my teeth fell out in the form of a hardened eyeball with pupils and veins. I thought to myself, this is not a dream and it will cost a lot of money to replace the tooth.

Don't worry, I am joyful too. I can walk for hours and hours without getting tired, never wanting to stop.

The fire is still warm. The wolf's fur is shagged with ice, and the prisoner is running.

I want there to be connection.

This is for you.

Turning away and touching are both wrong, for it is like a massive fire.
    —Dongshan Liangjie,
    "Song of the Precious Mirror Samadhi"

To Alex Guthrie Branch, with whom I sewed something.

Chicago
2008

WORKTHROUGH

Sophie Robinson

I work through language. Language is situated & saturated; language is governed. I am situated & saturated; I am governed. My body, its limits. Boundary/situation. A body also contained & situated within the city of London, dwelling amongst the urban decay of the east end, which likes to creep into the borders of the corporate structures of the City proper: banks, workstations, £££HQs. I walk & wonder where my place is. I take pleasure in perversity, in the presence of Actuaries & Advertisements. Whose language can I appropriate, queer up, violate?

from Killin'Kittenish! (yt communications, 2006)

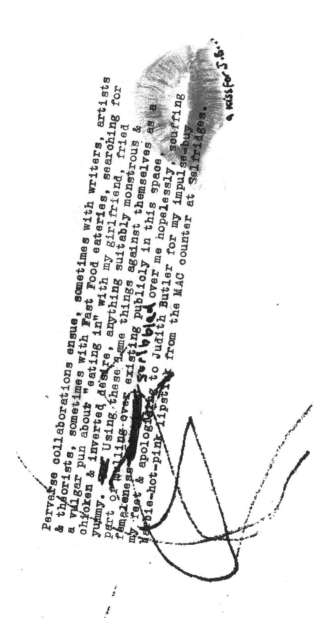

Perverse collaborations ensue, sometimes with writers, artists & theorists, sometimes with Fast Food eateries, searching for a vulgar pun about "eating in" with my girlfriend, searching for chicken & inverted desire, anything suitably monstrous & yummy. Using these same things against themselves as a part of willing-over existing publicly in this space femaleness scribbled over me hopelessly, scuffing my feet & apologising to Judith Butler for my impulse-buy Barbie-hot-pink-lipstick from the MAC counter at Selfridges.

"a kiss for J.B."

Not forgetting the gaps: those forgotten alleyways off
Brick Lane, a half-demolished AmericanCarWash, unexperted
lacunae in the landscape...startling emptinesses, & how
we reconcile them, or don't, in purposeful inexpressiveness
A sense of loss, before I've even begun, accompanies the
sense of being overwritten by my superiors - Milton, my boss,
my Bank, Freud, Academe, POESIE. My deviance, then, cutting
textx into neon strips & hamfisting them onto gluey pages,
gawping at an abandoned CarPark or Louise Bourgeois' hermetic
structures in the Tate Modern, peering in on glassy events
which freeze me out. Having unspeakable desires towards these
voids, their inhumane tumbleweeding of my understandings.

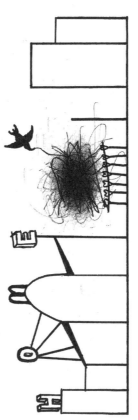

I'm also interested in Frankensteining my xxxxx practice,
inviting Britney Spears over to read Kathy Acker with me in
the fur teacup. We paint each others' toenails (shade 3,
spiderblack) & listen to Le Tigre again, bewailing the not-to-
be-taken-seriousliness of our work = &/OR: writing in sequence,
a conceptual project starting with a question/gap/
falsely-complete spectacle, worked through in repetitions &
subversions, & subverted repetitions, again.

IN CONCLUSION: All of this has to do reading, mostly writing as
a reader, but also writing as a queer reader, which mightxx be
quite different. Maybe attempting to form a pallet or toolbox
(I don't have my own tools, I borrow Tzara's or Burroughs', but
they always want them back, & they feel a little stiff) of stuff
I can use which might centralise a certain perspective,
skew everything, rock the boat a bit.

London
2008

Tracer? I hardly know her.

−Vanessa Place

Material

Casements

Parapet

Tracer

05. Maneuvers

Harold Abramowitz / Vincent Dachy / Paul Hoover / Lily Hoang / Mathew Timmons / 2010

Recon

Surplus

Logistics

THIS IS:
A BRIEF INTRODUCTION
Teresa Carmody

It was difficult to remember what she thought was happening between us, but sometimes if he hears a certain song, one does remember. Too, his mother said the world is governed by scientific laws and when she is angry, he should yell. Loudly. Or softly. Into. She started to believe something new. So did I. Neither of us could pin the point of it exactly, but after that, everything did change. Then it refused. The whole story changes. It is refused. In the future, it will be changed again, in the future anterior. Still, so much depends on what happens today. The way of order is as true as any formal memory.

This is *TrenchArt: Maneuvers*, a collection of texts written by each of the writers/artists whose work is forthcoming in the fifth TrenchArt series— *Maneuvers*—published by Les Figues Press. These texts are about the recombinant possibilities of art and literature; they are also a guide to the writers' individual works. As a series, *TrenchArt: Maneuvers* explores the possibilities of re-ordered time and content, understanding, of course, that one (he, she, I, you, too) cannot separate content from time, and that to shift the form, or the order, or the order of the form, is to shift the subjectivities of a text. This is the first book in a series of five. As you read, the point of this, like your quantum mechanical perspective, will change.

SELECTED WRITINGS

Harold Abramowitz

I found standards. The roughshod ambulance men at my door. There was a kind of hush. Holding over me then. You are foolish enough to answer my question. The evidence was in the bag. And then you hand it over to me and I take exception to the way it looks. The evidence in the bag. The whole way of looking at things. There is a finality to the way the ambulance stops. It puts its feet on the lounge. And you are a real character, you know. The sleeping speech. The hints of character. And then the whole world at your disposal. A kind of hush. Stalking the spirit wherever and whenever it may go. But betting on science. That kind of cadaver-like speech. The whole quality ripped from the headlines. Blood. Galoshes. A semblance of boots worn. Of tissues taken. We split our exceptions in half and take them to the store and rub them together and dream of better days. The mercy ebbs and flows. Fills volumes. You are getting high on rubberized steak, on grams and grams of fat returned to heaven in parts. And then you want to tell me to go and get fucked? Well, that's not even me you're talking to. Not even then. And not even in heaven. I have a voice, you know. And all the cantilevers, all the volumes in heaven will never fill up a suitcase until the voice says exactly what it's supposed to say. There is a kind of hush. And you explode. You ask for mercy. There is no cooking. At least not until tomorrow. Because that's when the truck rolls in and there are decisions to be made.

But there is a letter waiting by the door.

There are new ways of saying old things.

Final and violating the pin—
The pin, and only the pin.

But it does not ring true.

A kind of hush. Hold your head up high. There is a last minute reserved for speech. For the real recitation of the moment you stuck your head out the window and waved. Reality is a vision of forgetting that you were born at the bottom of the book and there is no mercy for your character, that is, no mercy for one or anyone of your character. Your philosophy deserves to be dragged down. And it is dragged down and it is kicking and screaming and asking for mercy. Hazing. A new disaster. And you call that the annals of science. Mercy. Release. And you call that, or those, the annals of the world. But I am not angry. Not at all. A kind of hush. All over the world. And then release. So listen very carefully. The only sound you will hear. Each time relieving its mercy and honesty. And then you stay at the back of the bus, or car, or truck, or train. You believe in relief. The whole list of things that were done, then, at that time. This was then. And this was in the back of the bus, or truck, or train, or car. The tile was blue or green. There was a garden just outside the window. I could hear the alarm sound early in the morning. There was a chicken making sounds. A hen, I think. You are tinkering with dismay. The whole conversation collapses around a story. And you are taken hostage and instantly turned into nothing again.

But what is a fair opportunity?

Opinions regarding what is best for the making of a boy differ greatly. Some assert that a child born with a silver spoon in its mouth is not likely to breathe as deeply and develop as well as one that is born without any such hindrance to full respiration.

Kind parents, a good home training, a chance to go to school, influential friends, good health, and someone to stand between you and the hard knocks of the world all serve to make a boy's surroundings truly enviable. Under such conditions any boy ought to win. Yet some boys have won without these advantages.

Abraham Lincoln was born of very
There is nothing

"BOY WANTED"

But dreams. They tell you stories and they tell you beautiful things to set
your name in sparks. Resuscitate this motion, if you will. I saw you driving
a train and you were a specialist in science, new medicine and all that. Or
that special something that starts shining over every element, so to speak.
A holistic way of looking at exactly what you want. But the space program
ended years ago. And in the backroom, far from the alley. A view. This view
has always dismayed me. I hear you speaking. There are gas and lights and
every one of them knew what was around the corner. In the house behind
the garden and there was something I could have used. I called you. But in
the end, the conflict wears me out. I am in disgrace. I have no knife. I am
angry because I cannot drive a car and still you show me no mercy. You have
the best at your disposal. Arousal. Even then I live in debt and your mercy
is a violation of the promises I kept when I came to your house to eat and
you weren't home. You just weren't home. There is no one missing you. I use
that word with increasing frequency. And the guests. And the getting. And
the gusts of wind that blow. But the moment you want to let loose again, I
am gone, and with good reason. But not interspersed with love or anything
like that. Let us say very definitively that we will not be making that mistake
again. We will not be making that supposition again. It is standard. This is the
standard way I go about my business. The intent of which is the reason I am
here in your hands in the first place. But that's not right. It is the product of
a project. The product of a real imagination. The product of being brought
forth for the third time. For the one thousandth time. You hold me, you hit
me, you rub me the wrong way, and then you tell me to go away. I was a good
boy though. I really thought I was.

"A GENIUS?"

And half-a-dozen other boys
were starting with their pails
to gather berries, Johnny's pa,
in talking with him, said that
he could tell him how to pick
so he'd come out ahead.

"First find your bush,"
said Johnny's pa, "and then

stick to it till you've
picked it clean. Let those go
chasing all about who will
in search of better bushes,
but it's picking tells, my son;

to look at fifty bushes doesn't
count like picking one."

And Johnny did as he was told,

and, sure enough, he found
by sticking to his bush while
all the others chased around
in search of better picking, it was
as his father said;

for while the others looked,
he worked,

and thus came out ahead.
And Johnny recollected this when
he became a man, and first of all
he laid him out a well-determined
plan; so, while the brilliant triflers
failed with all their

There is a kind of hush. And you call it a violation. The way I speak. I put my
hands up and try to remember to stop. I stop you all the time and I try to
remember to stop holding on so hard to that thing I remember. The whole
world crushing me, my instinct. My behavior. And it is old science that is
haunting me. I try the new stuff. I get interested in the new stuff. There is a
kind of hush and you go on. A certain smile. Enough of this stuff of the heart
you say. The knife and the bottle and the seams and the twists of yarn and the
twists of fate and the circles of fate and the smoke in the sky. The bold one

that urges me on has come to this place to sit down and rest and tell me that there are many vacations that can be had if I put my head out the window and wave my hands and let myself be heard over the racket of the war and the other phenomenon that rages and holds my feet to the fire. I belong by the arms I've been given. I took my arms out but that was only to tell you. The whole time there was a feature. You are living in the fire. You are demanding that I tell you every secret in the book. And there is a black box. A new way of looking. And I tell you. I want very much to tell you where it lives. Where to find it. To take the time out of this. I want very much to tell you to take the time out of this and hold it in a box or hold it up to the light and hold it and hold it and never shake it and never let more than an ounce of it spill out of the opening on the top.

There were leaves, or red bushes.

There was something green
Against the ground.

The scene was vivid.

It was emerging.

And each and every time I looked,
I tasted it again.

A reason.

I have a reputation to uphold. Holding forth. The soup. The mushroom. The vacation. And there is a kind of hush. A void. Each and every circumstance that will take your name and refer to you as one of the important working wheels in the machine. A ruin. A running ruler. In your hand. And you were running. I was running. They played games all day. They played the way they were meant to play. With guns. Holding something in their hands. What they were playing with was sharp and mean and tiny. It was flat. There was something comfortable there. They were lounging around and telling mean lies and lining things up. The most distinct part of the circumstance was the motion of the moon. They knew every human being by name. There is a kind of hush all over the world, today. Today. And there is sleeping. Fire. Jesus.

Personal demons. Restraint. Haircuts. Animals. And zero is the number of events that can be remembered at any given time.

And you know that.

You really know that.

I know that you know that.

There is a kind of hush. You tell them not to look. It holds you down at the exact moment you want to get up. It is in your eyes. You were telling them and they were listening to you. A green chain. And then you know that the nature of the event is circular. The event I was speaking of. I was speaking of the event just now and you rolled your eyes. And, at that point, no decision had yet been made. There was a kind of hush. A kind of trying to be free. You lost that. You've lost that loving feeling. In the summertime. I was rolling a log and I was facing west and there was a hiding place and a pin and then the next time I saw you. I was holding forth. I call those my ankles. Which is to say that I call on my ankles all the time. And it is almost exactly true: this holding forth, this model of exceptional circumstance. The very putting it all together for the sake of a spine, for the sake of a pin, or, as usual, for the sake of someone or something else.

Los Angeles
2009

FOUR MANOEUVRES

VD Collective

I'm age… the Grim Reaper said. (That really is the only thing he ever rustled.)

1- SENTENTIOUSLY BUMPTIOUS

Let's start with generalities. They are so enjoyable. They give off a marvelous smell of coherence and unity. Talking generally about art is both reassuring—it is possible to say what it is—and rewarding—I really know what I am talking about.
This is a treat—and it allows the use of big words.
I must add that big ideas are also very useful if you are caught waiting somewhere for longer than you had anticipated.
They make excellent companions.

Art?
Art is a fart of Truth in the whole absorbing Emptiness.

Translation?
Art is a pun, a twist of some kind (not necessarily refined at all) presenting an instance of truth in the irredeemable lack of (one and one only) finality.
That instance can be a cover-up, a tickle, an advertisement, a tease, an apologia, a double bluff, an adornment, an insult, a reflection, a sneeze even. And it cannot be defined negatively.
Well, what can art not be? Give it a go and be sure that an artist will prove you wrong. This is due to the dissipation of the concept of finality (whose blush left last as it faded away).

And this explains easily why ideas about art do wonders in times of expectation.

They occupy space effortlessly.

2- A PHOTOGRAPHER AND A VENTILATOR

Because life was covered by layers and layers of meaning of absolute density and layers and layers of objects of fleeting pleasures, the little man couldn't breathe deeply anymore. He decided to become an art servant because he thought art would allow him to make holes and become less stifled. As he had some acquaintance with light things, he thought fans would be what he should use to improve his breathing. And, quite quickly, he chose photography.

Experience told the little man that prints made far better fans than sculptures (too encumbering) or paintings (too difficult to wave). He thought of music (wind instruments of course) but realized it was rather difficult to blow yourself in the face.

All this seemingly too troublesome, he opted for simplicity: photoventilation. You could quite simply swish at yourself with a print on good paper.

3- IMAGE, IMAGE? WHERE DO YOU SEE AN IMAGE?

There was a time when mirrors didn't exist. Paradise they call it.
But that was only a mirage.

Seriously, too many people wonder too much about how they look.
And it is flimflam to pretend that the image is the reflection of the soul.
And image is flimflam anyway—it's precisely why it takes so much time to hone it.
Flimflam, flimflam, flimflam.
Image anywhere here?
Which image? Where have you seen any images? Photographs perhaps, but not an image in sight here, I aver.

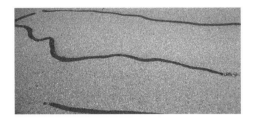

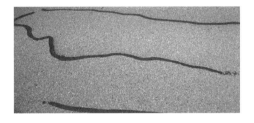

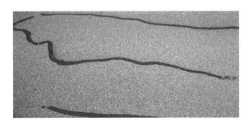

However and although: I'm defective. The fact is obvious.

It follows that I'm often stupid.

Here are some examples:

- the stupid idea that an image shows the world—when it only obfuscates what it fixates. It shapes monuments, hews cemeteries.
- the stupid idea that an image proves by virtue of exhibiting—when it only illustrates.
- the stupid idea that an image documents the world—when it only encumbers.
- the stupid idea that an image makes people think—when it only distracts.

I DON'T MAKE IMAGES, I TAKE PHOTOGRAPHS.

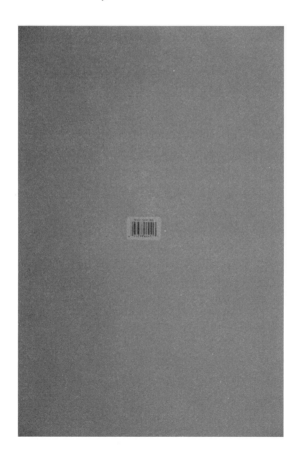

And it should be added that photographs are, by and large, far too pretentious. Most of them are.

From the above and everything ever said or written by anyone at any time in the history of mankind it follows implacably that, there, fore, and therefore, it's a question of producing unassuming photographs, playfully circumspect like children's toys.

Not only am I defective, I'm also lost in the world that there is not.

I have to invent suppletions. I have to, in one way or another. It's obvious and critical—with fingers or toes, sneezing inasmuch as spewing.

4- ♀ *SPECK AND MOTE* ♀

♀ De facto I take photographs when I'm taken in fact.
Taken by surprise.
Set-up surprises (surprise ambushes) or windfalls, I don't mind. Nugatory surprises often. This makes modest photographs.
A minor twitch in space that stops my ramble.

♀ I try to make myself factually available to the obvious—strategically.
If I'm lucky I'll catch a pucker. (A pucker is a small place—only occasionally big—that has been creased by crossings.)
Pucker catching requires some application.

♀ I also have two concerns if you must know:
• How not to add to the political futility of avant-garde subvmersion.
• How not to accumulate.

♀ For the time being I remind myself that there is no out of space because it is a topological impossibility—and that should be sufficient to convince me. That is the reason why, in the end, my photographs can be reduced to memento mori. Actually, contingent poor baroque memento mori. But that's too much to ask perhaps.

I'll try to be childlike and keep toying.

Yours, in whole verisimilitude,
VD Collective

Hermetic emetic postscript:
E. Pound made a big deal by saying, "Make it new!"
Some heard, "Make it you!"
The whole absorbing emptiness swallowed the last word.
What, henceforth, remained was "Make it!"—which everybody understood
too well. "Ready? Make it!"
I readymade it, thank you very much.
That is the way 'growth' impregnated art.

And after that?
If you are young, you're not that worried.
And you can't be that worried if you're not that young anymore.
So beat it. 🔲

London
2009

STATEMENT, MANIFESTO, POETICS

Paul Hoover

I. Statement

Sonnet 56 consists of 56 versions of Shakespeare's sonnet of that number, produced from February to May of

2006.	Many of the
2007.	activities, such as
2008.	"Noun Plus Seven"
2009.	and "Word Ladder,"
2010.	are influenced by
2011.	Oulipo; others, such
2012.	as "Villanelle," "Jingle,"
2013.	"Ballad," "Flarf," and
2014.	"Blues," are traditional
2015.	literary or song
2016.	forms; and some,
2017.	including "Personal Ad,"
2018.	"Chat Group," "Course
2019.	Description," and "Mathematical,"
2020.	are my own
2021.	invention. The project
2022.	began when I
2023.	removed all but
2024.	the end words
2025.	of Shakespeare's sonnet,

2026.   selected because they
2027.   were accessible to
2028.   the postmodern ear,
2029.   and asked my
2030.   poetry students to
2031.   fill in the
2032.   rest without imagining
2033.   that they were
2034.   writing a sonnet.
2035.   The results were
2036.   wonderful, and I
2037.   tried it myself.
2038.   The results were
2039.   mediocre. But then
2040.   I created 55
2041.   more versions, beginning
2042.   with "Haikuisation" and
2043.   "Homosyntactic Translation." I
2044.   soon realized that
2045.   the series demanded
2046.   a range of
2047.   tones, from the
2048.   comic to the
2049.   serene and elegiac.
2050.   No rule insists
2051.   that procedural work
2052.   must be ironic
2053.   and entirely self-
2054.   reflexive. Raymond Queneau's
2055.   *Exercises in Style*,
2056.   1947, was the
2057.   "anticipatory plagiary." But
2058.   when I checked
2059.   to see how
2060.   much I had
2061.   taken from it,
2062.   very little was
2063.   in evidence, except

2064.   for "Sentence." Aaron
2065.   Shurin's *Involuntary Sonnets,*
2066.   2005, offered the
2067.   formal model for
2068.   the work "End
2069.   Words." Some of
2070.   my happiest moments
2071.   came from writing
2072.   in song forms,
2073.   which are lyrical
2074.   in the original
2075.   sense, but take
2076.   their greatest strengths
2077.   from song's performance
2078.   aspect. Songs are
2079.   purposive. They seek
2080.   to calm, excite,
2081.   awaken, and console.
2082.   It's important also
2083.   to remember that
2084.   Shakespeare's sonnets were
2085.   mostly love poems.
2086.   With proceduralism as
2087.   my chaperone, I
2088.   was given permission
2089.   to write in
2090.   one of poetry's
2091.   richest veins. The
2092.   innovative poem (the
2093.   sonnet in 1596)
2094.   invents what we
2095.   later call tradition.
2096.   Likewise, within the
2097.   best innovative poetry
2098.   is an echo
2099.   of the past,
2100.   a stable element
2101.   such as rhyme,

2102.   form, or richness
2103.   of theme, which
2104.   never loses its
2105.   fire: love is
2106.   found, love is
2107.   lost, love is
2108.   regained. The drama
2109.   of that most
2110.   established of themes
2111.   shakes the lives
2112.   of each generation.
2113.   When it happens
2114.   to us, it
2115.   is fiercer and
2116.   stranger than we
2117.   could have imagined.

II. Manifesto

) (The Lives of Others

7/8 Partial At Best

•   Objects of One Dimension

,   Infinity, Interrupted

: Sordid Public Fictions

••• Consist of Private Mind

& The Anonym As Narcissus

/ A Celibate Machine

? That Says Touch Me Here

[ ] It's Midnight in the Film Script

∞ One Mirror Said to Another

! The Odor of Time Endures

= The Rest Is Violence

" " The Bee inside the Flower

{ } Beware the Paraclete

+   Tautology and Endgame

~   Productive Paradoxes

%   Their Name Is Synchresis

@   Ampersand, Meet Stan

<   Mystery Is Distance

>   But It Breathes Close By

*   The Poetry of Subtraction

≈   Almost Understands Us

$ Open Your Eyes to Remember

∧   Stones Are Thickets

Dimension Is Not Pattern

¢ Current Innovative Practice

X Lies Too Far from Fate

§ A Moth Eats Words

e Words Eat the Man

☼ Sumer Is I-cumen in—

♫ Awe Bleteth after Lomb

III. Poetics

I have no objectives, no system, no tendency, and no plan.

I have no speech, no tongue, no memory, and no realm.

Because nothing matters, I am consistent, committed, and excited.

I prefer the definite, the bounded, the repressed and the weak.

Not objectivity but neutrality of being.

Not spontaneity but panic.

For only seeing believes and only the body thinks.

For success is common to those who fail.

For the world's beauty is fading because the world is fading.

For the best narrative is always oblique.

For thought only thinks it thinks—all has been foretold.

For without cruelty, there would be no beauty.

For kindness is always a little bit tragic.

For the mind's progress is zig-zag and stabs at every tree.

For the best art makes things disappear.

Mill Valley
2009

AESTHETIC STATEMENT

Lily Hoang

In Virginia Woolf's *Mrs. Dalloway*, Peter Walsh follows a girl through London. When she disappears behind a door, he sighs, "Well, I've had my fun; I've had it, he thought, looking up at the swinging baskets of pale geraniums. And it was smashed to atoms—his fun, for it was half made up, as he knew very well; invented, this escapade with the girl; made up, as one makes up the better part of life, he thought—making oneself up; making her up; creating an exquisite amusement, and something more. But odd it was, and quite true; all this one could never share—it smashed to atoms."

------------------------------------cut here------------------------------------

It's true that I am not Peter Walsh, following a half make-believe girl through the streets of London, nor have I even been to London to pretend to follow this half make-believe girl around. But what Peter Walsh thinks here is undeniably real to any writer, artist, etc. etc. etc. We make ourselves up. Before we write. Before we think. Before all of it, we create ourselves. We make up these versions of self, and this is where it all begins: the creation of self, not an authentic or real self, but a virtual self, a safe self, a shelter.

------------------------------------cut here------------------------------------

This shelter of a self, this safe place, this writer: I am making myself up, making her up, and I am much more amusing this way than any other way. And because I am more amusing, so much more likable this way, unlike Peter Walsh, this is the version of self I share. This is not the version that is smashed to atoms. But perhaps it is because of this version of self that I myself become smashed to atoms, unable to regenerate whole.

The funny thing is: it would be so much easier to be smashed to atoms. It would make the division of self clearer, cleaner. I could say—this much of me is this and that much of me is that—and in doing so, I would have a definitive way of saying: this is how much of me is writer, and that is how much of me is not. It's something I'm constantly looking for, the ratio of writer : non-writer, as if a perfect formula could exist, and like Peter Walsh, it's what I'm looking for, something concrete.

-------------------------------------cut here-------------------------------------

It's something about being a writer, an artist, the romance of it, even if it isn't romantic. It's banal, really, being a writer. There's so much more excitement in life, and here I am, pining away at how much of me is writer and how much isn't. But perhaps it's the boredom that has taken me here. I live in a small town with several colleges and universities, but it's no college town. No, it's a bombed-out Midwestern town. Strongly blue-collar. Anti-university. Or maybe it's the university's fault. Those Catholics. But here, in this bombed-out Midwestern town, I've created myself as writer. I've created the myth of me. I've invented stories and stories, gotten confused and considered, if only briefly, that I was somewhere else. I've "made up, as one makes up the better part of life," even though it's not what I want.

-------------------------------------cut here-------------------------------------

Here I am again, back to that point of division. How to exist here and not here. How to do that if writing fiction necessitates you moving away from here while you struggle to stay here, present, now.

-------------------------------------cut here-------------------------------------

Fiction: what I write moves away from the real, consciously, purposefully. In *The Evolutionary Revolution* in particular, my characters are strange and surreal. They are also real and true. They move back and forth, without much regard for what reality is, because they don't care. In the way that the girl Peter Walsh made up doesn't care, my characters don't care. In the way that Peter Walsh is at once devastated and relieved, so am I.

-------------------------------------cut here-------------------------------------

But imagine, for just one moment, that you are Peter Walsh, walking through the streets of London. You see what Virginia Woolf wants you to see. You see this girl. She isn't real, and yet you see her. You follow her. You stalk her. How is this any different from my two-headed mermen, pulling their bodies apart, falling in love, waging wars? What is the ultimate difference between Woolf's realism and my irrealism, if they are both fictions? If they are both not real? If they both take you to the same point of obsession and desire?

--cut here--

What Woolf gives Peter Walsh is an opportunity to have fun in a world turned askew by war. Walsh has just been to India. He has missed the Great War, but he can still feel its effects. This is me having my fun in a world turned askew by war and years of shit. This is me having my fun, engaging in a dialogue, like Woolf did with Joyce, only I'm no Woolf and the dialogue is with an album, not a person, but a person, a series of people, a band. The obsession Peter Walsh feels for this woman he stalks, it's no different than the obsession I've had with Neutral Milk Hotel's *The Aeroplane Over the Sea*, which is how my book was written. Obsessively. Listening. I listened obsessively to the album. For months it was the only album I listened to. And still, now, I'm not sick of it. There's something new every time. It never gets old. Unlike Peter Walsh, who could not share his obsession before it was smashed to pieces, Neutral Milk Hotel could. And because of it, I wrote a book. Because of it, my book is nothing in comparison.

--------cut-------cut-------cut------everywhere------cut--------cut-------cut--------

Kingston
2009

THE OLD POETICS

Mathew Timmons

The Canon has shown that works composed according to rules or artistic demands (i.e., those that adhere to the old poetics) find themselves shackled to the old poetics. One used to talk about the end of the line in poetry—instead of it being "ba BOM," it would just be "BA." This speculation, though, overflows the limits of the old poetics, and, in other words, proclaims that the new poetry will usher in a new way of feeling and living.

"The old poetics are dead, it's not enough to mean what you mean anymore," etc. etc. We were lying beneath the arbors of our hunch-backed, logical starting point, and found an outcome we could not exploit, bound up in the presuppositions of the old poetics. It's not enough to refer generally to a new poetics, one must perfect and enrich an appreciation of the old poetics. What marks this poetics is a poet's more contemplative mood (Plank 1966, 112).

What emerges from the new poetics is a relinquishment of the old poetics of *being*, in favor of a frontier *poetics of becoming*. The old poetics lasted because it could be developed in significant ways to accommodate the valuable insights provided by narrative. We must now get down to the characteristic problems of the old poetics. By making a list detailing various attributes of the old poetics, we can band together and solve problems with our capacity for attention, and we can expand our vision to other arenas where poetics has become the central concern.

Now we have, at last, come to the cause of our dispute and evidently the old poetics is to be blamed for it. The old poetics does not mind representing peasants in a banquet hall (where a banquet hall represents the old poetics). Callimachus, for example, mistook one art for another by concretizing metaphor—a phenomenon that persists in our own time. This shows we are still trapped in the old poetics with its combinations of actions and its characters envisioning that now we have, at last, come to the cause of our dispute.

The old poetics is to be blamed. It does not mind the representation of peasants. This symbolism, pointing either to the real or mental worlds, was the basis of the old poetics. In the act of shifting the symbolic locus from real things to a mental banquet hall, the old poetics can be seen and represented. However, Callimachus was concretizing metaphor and marble at the same time. But if we mistake one art for another, we remain trapped in the old poetics with its combinations of actions and its characters envisioning the grove of Demeter. On one level this represents the new poetics and is set in opposition to Erysichthon's representation of the old poetics as a banquet hall.

I now ask of you—partly thinking of the old poetics, about how you (my dear, dear reader), David Bromige, Maria Damon, and George Bowering composed over numerous months a hilarious list (an openly exploited extra-literary list) of reasons to justify the removal of the old poetics of Neoclassicism and Romanticism. Is it worth noting that Grinberg, according to "Buffalo '99" by Kent Johnson, claimed that certain energetic adherents to the old poetics (including a list of established poets and critics) through the figure of E.P. (Pound), "developed and set aside the old poetics of song," while through Mauberley they "showed the aim and imprint" of their own poetics?

The new world of reference has given a vitality to the old poetics just as the old poetics has given strength to the proclamation of a new faith. The breakdown of the old poetics, which occurred with a shift of interest to the individual "taste" of the reader, strengthened the conviction that Creeley had when he rejected what he called the old poetics of description and reflective arrangement, because it denied the immediacy of the poem as event, as itself.

The old poetics, which followed a shift of interest to the individual "taste" of the reader, strengthened the conviction that art, in fact, as it may be called, as

Richard Janko has argued, is a more complete appreciation of the old poetics. What we need is not to produce our own poetics. It would be pointless to seek in the old poetics a definitive position on "taste"—as appeared, for instance, in Johann Christoph Gottsched's book *A Critical Approach to Poetic Art for the Germans*. In this, and as he said elsewhere in his comments about following the old poetics of creation, the people began to follow the Catholic charismatic poets, creating a particular strain of the old poetics that Creeley would eventually reject, what he called the old poetics of description and reflective arrangement because it denied the immediacy of the poem as event, as itself.

I, myself, still employ the old poetics, which I guess I believe has served me well. But ohkay, finally the realization hit that I've been doing it all wrong, that my perceived improvements to the old poetics at the same time preserved the old poetics. In his work, Chateaubriand also introduced elements foreign to the old poetics. Thus, however timidly, he recognized that he was introducing a new poetic style by making fun of the old poetics: Pronto me di cuenta / que era una errata eso / de que los niños / venian de Paris.

Instead of following the old poetics of creation, people have begun reforming the old poetics, the *Ars Poetica* of Horace. A strong flavor of Ciceronian rhetoric cropped up in Horace's views on poetry. Thinking partly of the old poetics, you (dear reader), David Bromige, Maria Damon, and George Bowering composed a list of rhetorical tropes over numerous months, which helped us to see, at last, that the old poetics was the cause of our dispute— laying the blame squarely upon the representation of peasants. By mistaking one art for another, we become trapped in the old poetics with its combinations of actions, our characters envisioning the *Ars Poetica* or the old poetics of Latin allegories and cosmic order. The knowledge of Bernardus Silvestris, the Medieval Platonist philosopher and poet of the twelfth century, directed would-be writers of a new poetics toward an application of the old poetics, perfected and enriched. What marks this poetics is a poet's more contemplative mood (Plank 1966, 112).

In an essay entitled "A Refutation of the Old Poetics," a claim is made that the underlying idea of the old poetics of exile received a much-needed ironic twist in Kushner's plays, the main thrust of which was to deconstruct one art in the service of another. Of course, it's easy to see how the resources of the old rhetoric and the old poetics can still be put to use, even when nothing else seems to have been learned. One should also note Bakhtin's claim that the old poetics—that is, old literary theory—is inadequate to describe the modern novel. In fact, what may be called for, as Richard Janko has argued, is a more complete appreciation of the old poetics. What we need is not to reproduce our own version of the old poetics, but that of the animal fable, which would especially enrage adherents to the old poetics. In fact, what may be called for, as Richard Janko has argued, is a complete appreciation of poetics. What we need is not to produce.

While the figure of E.P. (Pound) "develops and sets aside the old poetics of song," Mauberley "shows the aim and imprint" of himself, and it is, of course, easy to see how the resources of the old rhetoric and the old poetics still find uses, even when nothing else seems to have been learned. On one level, the grove of Demeter represents the new poetics and is set in opposition to Erysichthon's banquet hall which represents the old poetics. The old poetics is particularly bitter against the poet who experiments in the "mixing" of rhetorical devices, and the twentieth century poet who practices the old poetics, slowly emptying themselves of meaning, becoming a simple agent of hearsay. A dim wood, with lurking chances of venomous or untamed creatures, and me doing so much better than the old poets ever did at the old poetics (know what I mean?), it's back to bed dear Beckett, beneath the flowers of goodness you go.

Bakhtin claims the old poetics and old literary theory as an inadequate way to describe the modern novel, a mistake of one art for another, still trapped in the old poetics with its combinations of visions. In fact, what may be called for, as has been argued, is a more complete appreciation of the old poetics. What we need is not to reproduce the old poetics by translating concepts into the more familiar terminology of the old poetics. If there is anagnorisis in Mother Courage, for example, so passes the old poetics into oblivion (or at least history!), an entire world and all its conceits, baubles and false promises. The breakdown of the old poetics occurred alongside a shift of interest towards the individual taste of the reader and strengthened the conviction of the reader.

We mistake one art for another, trapped in the old poetics, combining actions and characters, envisioning another art in the form of a mistake, still trapped and mean, the old poetics' combinations of characters envisioning actions, the mistake traps another art form, the old poetics distilled in the visions of action characters, in these combinations the mistake of one art for another, still trapped in the old poetics with its combinations of actions and its characters envisioning not a new poetics, but an application of the old poetics, perfected and enriched. What marks this poetics is the poet's more contemplative mood (Plank 1966, 112).

Douglas Staiger, the John French Professor of Economics in the Department of Economics at Dartmouth, discredits the old poetics implicitly rather than explicitly. He discloses its false grounding and hence its irrelevance. By arguing against a contemporary fixation on one problem of the old poetics, its capacity to convey a singular attention, he suggests visiting other areas of contention around the old poetics by translating its concepts into the more familiar terminology of the old poetics. He says, "there is *anagnorisis* (italics mine) in Mother Courage," and here the shadow of the old poetics lies more heavily upon him—and he then passes to a consideration of the rules and limitations of poetry, but his speculation overflows the limits of the old poetics and he ends by proclaiming that the new poetry is a new way of feeling and living.

The idea of an identity eventually formed around the principle of travel (which was, after all, the underlying idea of the old poetics of exile), redeems one thing by mistaking it for another. However, through the means of the old poetics, with its combinations of actions and its characters envisioning ideas, an identity formed around the principle of travel (which was, after all, the underlying idea of the old poetics of exile).

To replace the old poetics, the *Ars Poetica* of Horace, and set aside the old poetics of song, it can be shown that the new poetics involves developing the aim and imprint of a characteristic voice. Just as there had been a strong flavor of Ciceronian rhetoric in Horace's views on poetry, the old poetics lasted because it could be developed in significant ways to accommodate the valuable insights provided by narrative. We must now admit the cause of our dispute: you see, the old poetics' penchant for representing peasants should be blamed, but this speculation overflows the limits of the old poetics. Proclaiming that the new poetry was also a new way of feeling and living, Brecht and Boal developed a new poetics of dramatic form, and street protests demonstrated that the old poetics of Aristotelian dramatic action were still alive.

The shift of interest to the individual "taste" of the reader strengthened the conviction that translating concepts into the familiar terminology of the old poetics, as in the old poetics as understood by literary genres and certain rules of craftsmanship which the poet follows, the empty patterns and formal structures, within which we, at last, come to the cause of the dispute. You see, the old poetics is to be blamed, it does not mind the representation of peasants, but this overflows the limits of the old poetics, proclaiming that the new poetry is also a new way of feeling and living. The union of poetry and prose is a constant, which is a formally and highly accomplished witness to traditional poetics but which in every sentence and line rejects the philosophy of the old poetics. However, with the eruption of Otherness into literature and the dominant social order, the old poetics of vision loses ground to a theory of perception that posits a logical starting point, and one which isn't so easy to exploit. Here the shadow of the old poetics lies heavily upon us, as we move from the presuppositions of the old poetics, to the consideration of the rules and limitations of poetry, to questions of "Do you want to write, and want to know how it's done?" To plead that the old poetics has lasted fifteen hundred years, and ours thirty, doesn't help much.

Pauline Yu has overemphasized the degree to which poets rejected the principles upon which the old poetics of the classics were based. We may note that contemporary linguistics gives this operation a name borrowed from the old poetics: embedding, or modifying an older mode of composition by translating its central concepts into the more familiar terminology of the old poetics. Employing Heideggerian terminology, one can describe this altered perspective (as it occurs in *Four Quartets*) as Eliot's acknowledgement of the old poetics of The Enlightenment having been instrumental in the destruction of the old poetics and in creating a host of new generic hybrids in literature. The old poetics assigns the epigram to the lyric category. There are, of course, lyric epigrams, for instance, the delicate landscape depictions of the new world gave vitality to the old poetics just as the old poetics gave strength to the proclamation of a new faith. The old poetics lasted because it could be developed in significant ways to accommodate the valuable insights provided by narrative, but we must not mistake one art for another and remain trapped in the old poetics with its combinations of characters envisioning actions on an epic scale. The old poetics is particularly bitter against the poet who experiments in the "mixing" of rhetorical devices, the twentieth century poet who practices mistaking one art for another and envisioning great ends.

One should also note Bakhtin's claims that the old poetics—that is, old literary theory—is inadequate to describe the modern novel. This means that the old poetics of the quintessence of art must be supplanted by a poetics of aesthetic function—a function that takes on solid form and serves, therefore, at once to designate and to characterize the old poetics. I often had, if not to destroy, at least to discredit the old poetics. The old poetry itself, which was blameless, was of course left almost intact. The old poetics as understood by literary genres posited that the poet was to follow certain rules of craftsmanship—empty patterns. Douglas Staiger discredited the old poetics implicitly rather than explicitly. He disclosed its false grounding and hence its irrelevance and also, that it would be pointless to seek in the old poetics a focus on "taste." He said, "In giving short shrift to the critics I often had, if not to destroy, at least to discredit the old poetics. The old poetry itself was blameless. The old poetics are dead. It's not enough to mean what you mean anymore, etc. etc. Lying beneath the arbors of your hunch-backed oak tree, a small cultural elite has formed which is no less exclusive than the normative classicism of the old poetics." The only difference in Staiger's approach to the old poetics that he reaches by the end of the book is that he believes the *Ars Poetica,* or the old poetics, and Latin allegories of cosmic order are not adverse to the representation of peasants. He then goes further to claim that this brings us to the cause of our dispute and that the old poetics is to be blamed.

Mistaking one art for another means we are still trapped in the old poetics with its combinations of actions, its characters envisioning the mistake of one art for another. This means we are still trapped in the old poetics with its combinations of actions, its characters envisioning the results of a wealth of research showing that the confrontation between the new music and the old poetics in antiquity was not aesthetical but ideological. And, in fact, the results of the research do show that the confrontation between the new music and the old poetics in antiquity was not aesthetical but ideological.

Contrary to the old poetics I understand, then, by literary genres, certain basic themes, mutually exclusive, and true aesthetic categories. Now we have, at last, come to the cause of the dispute and can see that the old poetics is to be blamed for it. It does not mind the representation of peasants. Of course, it is easy to see how the resources of the old rhetoric and the old poetics still find uses, even when nothing else seems to have been learned. According to the old poetics of Humanism and the Renaissance, art should try to imitate nature. By contrast, Góngora's main work was based upon mistaking one art for another and this shows it was still trapped in the old poetics with its endless combinations of characters envisioning action. The old poetics are slowly emptying themselves of meaning, becoming hearsay, like a dim wood, with lurking chances of venomous or untamed creatures in its depths.

Besides the breakdown of the old poetics, which occurred with the shift of interest to the individual "taste" of the reader, the old poetics passed into oblivion (or at least history!), an entire world and all its conceits, baubles and false promises swallowed by a new reflex. "The old poetics are dead, it's not enough to mean what you mean anymore," etc. etc. We were lying beneath the arbors of your hunch-backed oak tree, thinking, "The old poetics are dead, it's not enough to mean what you mean anymore," etc. etc. We were lying beneath the arbors of your hunch-backed mistake, one art substituted for another, still trapped in the old poetics with its combinations of actions, its characters envisioning one art mistaken for another, the old poetics, still trapped by combinations of characters envisioning action as they mistake one art for another, still trapped in the old poetics with its characters envisioning combinations of actions, mistaking one art for another, still trapped in the old poetics with its combinations of actions, its characters envisioning the old poetics slowly emptying themselves of meaning, becoming hearsay—a dim wood, with lurking chances of venomous or untamed creatures hidden within.

The limits of the old poetics flow from a proclamation that the new poetry is also a new way of feeling and living. The union of poetry and prose is a constant. It would be pointless to seek in the old poetics a privileging of "taste," but what emerges from Go Down, Moses is a relinquishment of the old poetics of *being* in favor of a frontier *poetics of becoming*. Now we have, at last, come to the cause of the dispute, you see, the old poetics is to be blamed for representing peasants, but it does not mind that now, we have, at last, come to the cause of the dispute, you see, the old poetics is to be blamed. It does not mind the representation of peasants as they mistake one art for another. This means they are still trapped in the old poetics with its combinations of actions, its characters envisioning how it is not possible for people to consider and revere the old poetics as a result of having fallen under the influence of the old poetics. This speculation overflows the limits of the old poetics, proclaiming that the new poetry is also a new way of feeling and living. The allegorical tradition, especially that of the animal fable, enraged adherents to the old poetics. So passed the old poetics into oblivion (or at least history!), an entire world and all its conceits, baubles, and false promises swallowed by the new, a relinquishment of the old poetics of "being" in favor of a frontier "poetics of becoming."

Ohkay, I'm still using the old poetics, which I guess I believe has served me well. Then the realization hit that I'm doing it all wrong. How, after all this, can writers who were once able without talent to make a successful career in poetry, be expected not to love and revere the old poetics? Brecht and Boal developed a new poetics of dramatic form, and street protests demonstrated that the old poetics of Aristotelian dramatic action were alive and well. The old poetics understood literary genres as certain rules of craftsmanship the poet was to follow, empty patterns and formal structures, but through elaborate depictions of local landscape, society, and folkways the old poetics more closely resembled a proto-ethnography than the old poetics of empire.

The animal fable especially enraged the adherents of the old poetics. So passed the old poetics into oblivion (or at least history!), an entire world and all its conceits, baubles and false promises swallowed by the new. Contrary to the old poetics I understand, then, by literary genres, certain basic themes, mutually exclusive, true aesthetic categories. Also, it would be pointless to seek in the old poetics a separation between good and bad "taste," which does appear as a mistake of one art for another, the old poetics of action trapped within old combinations of characters.

According to the old poetics of Humanism and the Renaissance, art should try to imitate nature. By contrast, Góngora's main work was based upon the old poetics. In giving short shrift to the critics I often had, if not to destroy, at least to discredit the old poetics, the old poetry itself was blameless, but was used by poets to gain and maintain an elite status by distinguishing themselves from amateurs and from popular poetry. Yet in both the old poetics and the new, this speculation overflows the limits of the old poetics, proclaiming that the new poetry is a new way of feeling and living. This serves, therefore, at once, to designate and to characterize the old poetics.

The old poetics often uses woven carpet as a metaphor for text, the woven, by which the old poetics referred to its own textuality. Jacob Bidermann specifically alludes to Ovid's mistake of one art for another, showing that Ovid was trapped in the old poetics with its combinations of characters envisioning the old poetics being replaced by a new, diverse, and vibrant poetics that is impossible to categorize. Yet, out of style as it may seem, Robert Creeley rejected what he called the early, old poetics of description and reflective arrangement because it denied the immediacy of the poem as event, as itself. The old poetics of pattern that dominated in the marginal southern land was changed into the new poetics as the center of discourse shifted to the north of China. The mistake of one art for another shows the trap embedded within the old poetics, its combinations of actions and its characters envisioning the mistake of one art for another, this means that the old poetics, with its characters envisioning combinations of actions, mistakes one art for another, meaning the old poetics is still trapped in the old poetics with its visions of characters in action.

However, with the eruption of Otherness into literature and the dominant social order, the old poetics of vision loses ground to a theory of perception which functions by translating its concepts into the more familiar terminology of the old poetics. If there is anagnorisis in Mother Courage, this means we are still trapped in the old poetics with its combinations of art and action, its characters envisioning great ends. The old poetics is supplanted by translating the concepts of the new poetics into the more familiar terminology of the old poetics. If there is anagnorisis in Mother Courage, we mistake one art for another, and are still trapped in the old poetics with its characters' active combinations of visions. So passes the old poetics into oblivion (or at least history!), an entire world and all its conceits, baubles and false promises reflected in the mistake of one art for another, the visions of our characters still trapped in the old poetics with its combinations of actions. However, with the eruption of Otherness into literature and the dominant social order, the old poetics of vision lost ground to a theory of perception that made it pointless to seek in the old poetics a separate position on "taste."

In reprisals against critics, I have often been obliged, if not to smash to pieces, at least to discredit the old poetics. Of course we didn't interfere with the old poetics by translating its concepts into the more familiar terminology of the old poetics. If there is anagnorisis in Mother Courage, we are able to note the old poetics being replaced by a new, diverse, and vibrant poetics that is impossible to categorize. Yet, out of style as they may have been, those early, programmatic calls for a move away from the old poetics just encouraged the old poetics to slowly empty itself of meaning, becoming hearsay. A dim wood, with lurking chances of venomous or untamed creatures in its depths, the new world of reference gave vitality to the old poetics as the old poetics gave strength to the proclamation of a new faith. Let us not mistake one art for another, this would mean we are still trapped in the old poetics with its combinations of actions, and its characters envisioning they often had, if not destroyed, at least discredited the old poetics. The old poetry itself, which was blameless, was, of course, left almost intact.

Now we have, at last, come to the cause of the dispute, you see, the old poetics is to be blamed. It does not mind your representing peasants. Brecht and Boal developed a new poetics of dramatic form, and street protests demonstrated that the old poetics of Aristotelian dramatic action were still alive. Also, it would be pointless to seek in the old poetics any specific perspective on "taste." This does appear in the old poetics of pattern that dominated in the marginal southern land. Sociologists of literature have tried though to show how this changed as the new poetics created its own discourse centered in the north of China. The old poetics of emulation had given way to a tolerant democracy of genres and to the poetics of originality.

The old poetics understood literary genres as certain rules of craftsmanship that the poet was to follow—empty patterns and formal structures. It would be pointless to seek in the old poetics a sense of "taste," which does appear in Johann Christoph Gottsched's book *A Critical Approach to Poetic Art for the Germans*. In this book, as in the many commentaries that came afterwards, one art is consistently mistaken for another, this showed the old poetics still trapped in its combinations of actions, and its characters' visions. Mistake one art for another and remain trapped in the old poetics with its combinations of actions, its characters envisioning that this speculation overflowed the limits of the old poetics, proclaiming that the new poetry was also a new way of feeling and living. The old poetics assigns the epigram to the lyric category. There are, of course, lyric epigrams, for instance the delicate landscape depictions of the old poetics.

Now we have, at last, come to the cause of our dispute. Let's blame the old poetics. This doesn't represent your mind. Peasants mistake one art for another. They're still trapped in the old poetics. Characters envision combinations of actions as they mistake one art for another. This means they are still trapped in the old poetics with its combinations of characters envisioning actions. In "Buffalo '99" by Kent Johnson, certain energetic respondents to the old poetics were included in a list of otherwise established poets and critics. This symbolic act, pointing either to the real or mental worlds, was the basis of the old poetics. In the act of shifting the symbolic locus away from "things," these writers mistake one art for another and this means they are still trapped in the old poetics with its combinations of actions and its characters envisioning that, "The old poetics are dead, it's not enough to mean what you mean anymore," etc. etc. We were lying beneath the arbors of your hunch-backed, timid recognition that at the same time as he preserves the old poetics, Chateaubriand also introduces elements foreign to it.

Los Angeles
2009

Material

Casements

Parapet

Tracer

Maneuvers

06. Recon

Frances Richard / Doug Nufer / Myriam Moscona /
Jen Hofer / Renée Petropoulos / Alex Forman / 2011

Surplus

Logistics

MAKING IN THE BROKEN: AN INTRODUCTION

Teresa Carmody

I decided to kill myself when I was seven. It was summer, and I was bored and lonely. I thought I would ride my bicycle off a cliff on the edge of the neighbor's yard. I thought I should survey the cliff first to make sure my plan would work. The drop was only seven or eight feet down. Not very steep. There were a lot of small trees and other kinds of brush and bramble on the hill. I noticed it wasn't really a cliff, but more of a hill. I would ride into the trees and brush and bramble, and they would break my fall. Even with speed—I could catch some real speed on my beautiful Desert Rose—I would probably only poke my eye out. What would I tell my mother? What horrible things would my big sister say when I showed up with a sad and bloody eye? In the face of such failure, I decided to live.

It's a very exciting time to be writing. The world is falling apart! This includes the boundaries of the book and the authorship of the author. You don't have to read left to right anymore, FYI, or even read at all. Why not do a collaborative writing project with racehorses, where you write the words and the horses decide the plot structure? Or make up your own emoticons for things like car horns or the sound of oil gushing into the Gulf? Growing up in a fundamentalist Christian home, I knew someone was really bad if he or she was "of this world." "Of this world" meant without Christ, or more specifically, without the right Christ, the right way to believe in Christ. The writing contained in this book, and in this series, is "of this world." It doesn't follow the right rules, especially that still-lingering Romantic rule: be original. In some cases, the writing is plagiarized. The writers do not speak from (or for) the plenum, though the plenum does individuate the writer, albeit briefly, for a moment of speech. These writers background their "I's," as they foreground their constraints: text found at the track or in a mirrored reflection. This book, *TrenchArt: Recon*, points toward the writers' forthcoming (f/c) books, as part of the *TrenchArt: Recon* series. The *Recon* series is also the site of an unfolding visual articulation by Renée Petropoulos. Considering the physical shape of the text and the geopolitical location of the writer, Petropoulos creates a system of graphic and abstract representation of and between the books. Dotting between the "I's," so to speak. For nothing is singular, just as nothing is as everything seems.

Being original is an exercise in failure, though not being original is not the same as having nothing to say. In the face of such non-originality, we continue. Continue what? Continue to write. For if this world is falling apart, and we are "of this world," then we too are falling apart—and our writing falls apart together. How exciting! "Recon" for reconnaissance, recognition, a preliminary survey to gain information, an exploratory military survey of enemy territory. The books in the Recon series provide an aerial view, a survey, of ways writers are approaching this question: what does one make in, and of, the brokenness.

In a recent talk at the 95Cent Skool, Joel Kovel made a distinction between integrative and disintegrative actions. That which initially appears integrative—making children behave in school for the sake of behaving or writing a formally-sound sonnet about the City and/or Country—often contributes to a larger disintegration, as the "integrative" act may further assimilate us into a socially unjust and ecologically disastrous world-view. In contrast, the more truly integrative may initially appear disintegrative in that these kinds of actions—the activist takeover of Chevron's stockholders' meeting or the Yes Men's Bhopal announcement—disrupt business-as-usual while insisting on social and ecological justice. So the narrative doesn't follow well-trod literary conventions (f/c Nufer), but runs like a racehorse—sometimes off the track. Letters insist on being also seen as image (f/c Moscona) as much as they too are particles of sound (f/c Richard) as much as they are furthermore parts of words taken from other people's books (f/c Forman). The fragmented narrative, page, sound, or source is then reconstituted as a newly imagined world. Sometimes we must break things.

So go ahead and ride your bike off the cliff. If you poke your eye out, what happens? I mean really.

MAYFLY

Frances Richard

PLENUM is itself a living form—an inhabited
terrain alive with traces and voices

marked up, ululating

it cannot be definitively—though it can be temporarily—individuated. it is
chaotic, but is not
a psychotic blather or dead husk

a vital husk

what is the force or mechanism that feeds vitality, propagates its waves?
furnace of the vitality event? historical voices, received urges, filtered through
the cognizant momentary—not the death but the making-particulate of the
author. the mayfly author, who incubates at the bottom of the stream and is
born as an adult for half an hour

d
e
s
i
r
e

[c.1230, from O.Fr. *desirer*, from L. *desiderare*
"to long for, wish for," original sense perhaps "await
what the stars will bring," from the phrase *de sidere*
"from the stars"]

& mayfly cognizance: discuss

larva of the author, nymph of the author, Order:
Ephemeroptera of the author, swarm of the author,
death of the author, right away the next day rebloom
a new cloud/generation of the author

husk filled with, wrapped as a veil around, desire

of fluids released by the body, milk alone is produced
on purpose to nurture, be reconsumed

husk that is not a covering, but a Möbius loop

wait-and-see veil made of stains in the tain

Milky Way—*via lactea* [what about the other
pearlescenct stains?] utterance as a fluid

produced on purpose to nurture, be reconsumed

voice is generative although speaker is dead. wanting
to know what the words contain. trace is alive
& thus compels/rewards/elicits/solicits attention.
light arrives although the star exploded
and burned out astronomic timespaces ago.

husk not an empty hard surface but a porous
or viscous particulate, a stretchy distribution. an ooze,
germ or syrup, full sponge partially squeezed out—
the curving inner surface of each pore of the sponge
is a husk in this sense.
the still-moist many-stranded silk inside the husk

impressionable or incisable surface, i.e., a surface that
is also a depth, a very energetic sheath
around nonentity

that's what desire is

voice alive on its own recognizance. flaked off
the body as heat or skin-cells sloughed. storyteller
persona as a roving transchronological avatar or
mask—but mask and husk are wrong insofar as they
are posited as concealing a "real" underneath, a face
or pith. rather, husk and mask are all there is, and
under them lies neither the consolidated treasure of
unified eye/ego/essence, nor the muzak of totally
affectless simulacra, nor the horror of screeching
abyss and antimatter

hysterical insistence on the precession of muzak is
horror vacui acting flattened. this implies an oddly
Puritanical, not to say fundamentalist-Congressman,
insistence that the devil stalks among us

antimatter gets a bad rap—why not love
the mystifying, positively deducible existence
of negatively charged hyperdense invisibility?

what the notation looks like, sounds like, the cipher

a charge in the phoneme or grapheme. and that—the
vagrant charge, now positive/now negative/now
matter/now anti- —is what is found and appropriated
or deployed; transcribed off the open-source echo-
rama. the verbal charge-object collaged
in the poem-thought

species—husks of shaped light—peeling off visible
objects and flying on exquisitely thin strings toward
the eye

recording equipment, sensitive plate in the mind

insinuated lexicon of subverbal notation

memory a sticky coating, quicksilver/gray-matter
emulsion, subtle-body
gluetrap

radio free half-life

the poem-thought as a temporary arrangement, a
quantum slice. paradoxically fixed like a snapshot in
the terms available to it through linguistic
representation—i.e., vocabulary, syntax, punctuation,
rhythm, image, distribution on the page and in the
line—as understood in the extended instant of a
writing microclimate—i.e., a decade or so amongst a
loosely defined and fluctuating group of participants?

decade built of mayfly instances.

if the translucent body/mind of the mayfly is a
clearinghouse or switching-station through which
pour the pulses of a) reading, b) economy, c) history,
d) electrochemistry then how to understand deeply
held convictions, unswerving loyalties,
the consolidation of opinion intrinsic to judgement?
you can't deny you have a name/a mayfly has no
bank account or house key, but you do/a habitus
called self persists across the extended instants called
decades. doesn't committed follow-through
tend to suborn sclerosis? can mayflies drill down
into bedrock principles?

j
u
s
t
i
c
e

[mid-12c., "the exercise of authority in vindication of right by assigning reward or punishment," from O.Fr. *justise*, from L. *justitia* "righteousness, equity," from *justus* "upright, just" (see **just** [adj.]). O.Fr. comprises widespread senses, including "uprightness, equity, vindication of right, court of justice, judge."

Attested Eng. c.1200 as title for a judicial officer. As "the administration of law" from c.1300. Justice of the peace attested early 14c.]

& mayfly cognizance: discuss

the neural quiver leaps past graphing mere eccentric jolts. tropes toward decision. statement. definition. yes to this and no to that. right. wrong. fight. stand firm.

not free from the marks of experience. marked by experience. but only the marks—and not the experience in toto—can be made articulate

nevertheless, the act of articulation exercises, vindicates. has consequences, and thus ethical implications. a mayfly's authority is short-lived, but it is not thereby excused from judging. each successive author-instant has to re-decide to throw its tiny weight at the persisting rock in order to accumulate a dent

how to train the judge? consult the jurisprudence.

where is the jurisprudence? in the field of vital traces.

how to know the rock? land on it often.

which direction is upright? every articulation is a
choice, a trope along a particular vector or vectors
through the field.

thick and mighty, weighty records, made of buzzing
tissues, subwoofer vibes

archeology of frissons

geological record of infrathins

the poem-thought slices down into it—the plenum of
traces, the jurisprudence book and aporetic justice
rock, the waxy part of the mystic writing pad—as
into a cake. can be consumed with pleasure.

—but some synthetic fixative must be injected into
the core-sample, twittering wrapping, grit
of the residue, to artificially provide it with structural
integrity adequate for transportation, cataloguing,
study, etc. otherwise exposed to air and excised from
its embeddedness, it would disintegrate. the terms of
representation—words, images, syntax, punctuation,
rhythm, distribution in the line and on the page—and
also beliefs and concerns about authorship,
readership, intellectual property, publication,
connotation, reception, tradition, ethics, genre,
practice, style—are epoxy the sample is bonded by
to fill in its porous aporiae and harden its grain

Brooklyn
2010

Postscript:

I was afraid, for awhile, that I might kill someone. Everyone
does, at a distance. But I never killed anyone, though that was only personally.
– Alice Notley, "In the Pines," 2007

In a world of distributed agency, a hesitant attitude toward assigning singular
blame becomes a presumptive virtue. Of course, sometimes moral outrage,
akin to what Plato called *thumos*, is indispensable to a democratic and just
politics [...] Outrage will not and should not disappear, but a politics
devoted too exclusively to moral condemnation and not enough to a cultivated discernment of the web of agentic capacities can do little good.
– Jane Bennett, *Vibrant Matter: A Political Ecology of Things*, 2010, p. 38

It's possible that the reader, or maybe the ideal reader, is a very disobedient
person, a head/church/city entity her/himself full of soaring icons and the
words of all the living and all the dead, who sees and listens to it all and never
lets on that there's all this beautiful almost undifferentiation inside, everything
equal and almost undemarcated in the light of fundamental justice.
– Alice Notley, "The Poetics of Disobedience," 1998
http://epc.buffalo.edu/authors/notley/disob.html

Worms, or electricity, or various gadgets, or fats, or metals, or stem cells are
actants, or what Darwin calls "small agencies," that, when in the right confed-
eration with other physical and physiological bodies, can make big things
happen.
– Jane Bennett, *Vibrant Matter*, p. 94

A more casual and familiar term is "incomplete metamorphosis."
– Wikipedia, "Mayfly," 7/16/14

San Francisco
2014

METHODICAL MAD SCIENCE

Doug Nufer

"Doug Nufer is a writer whose fiction, poetry, and pieces for performance seem to follow procedures based on formal constraints, even when they don't," is a line I used to go by, before it seemed useless to pretend. It so happens that everything I write is based on constraints. Oulipo writers Georges Perec, Harry Mathews, and Raymond Queneau, and others, led by Gilbert Sorrentino, saved me from a life of aspiring to be a midlist novelist, whose imitations of life aspire to be made into movies.

Although the constraint-driven tradition goes back centuries, embracing everyone who ever wrote in verse or to form, writers today who impose restrictions upon themselves (beyond the rules of grammar, genre, and craft) get linked to two terms which can be controversial: avant-garde and experimental. Why controversy? Beats me. To be avant-garde, to be ahead of the rest, to try to be original, is something an artist does; and, to experiment, to make art in unproven ways that may very well explode, is an essential part of writing for anyone, even those without the slightest interest in reinventing conventional forms (i.e., you write a line, it doesn't work, you revise). And yet, those who have staked their reputations on work that mainstream readers dismiss as "experimental" because it doesn't follow rules of the marketplace are often eager to duck the word, as if it came on the hot end of a branding iron.

Whatever "avant-garde," "constraint-driven," and "experimental" are supposed to mean means less to me than how useful these terms are. I rely on these terms to describe what I do. As much as I've come to prefer the dynamic resonance of words to their pedestrian meanings, the meanings do matter, which brings me directly back to *By Kelman Out of Pessoa*, a novel I developed from an investigation of the term "experimental."

As with many scientific discoveries, the investigation grew from a serendipitous chain of circumstances. I read "A Wide Runner" by James Kelman, a story with a scheme to beat the races, and wrote a story in the form of a lecture by a tout, who claimed you could win by using Kelman's plan, if you split yourself into characters modeled after the heteronyms of Fernando Pessoa. The Kelman scheme was absurd, posing a money management progression advertised as "stop-at-a-winner" yet known as "chasing your losses." The Pessoa angle only compounded the problem, turning a day at the races into a ludicrous exercise in multi-tasking.

Nevertheless, it made some sense. When racing resumed at Emerald Downs in the summer of 2003, the least I could do was split myself into heteronym characters, give each a rudimentary background which would include years of experience playing the ponies, and have each play in his or her own way, combining various disciplines of handicapping to pick the horses, and using (or in one case, inverting) the stop-at-a-winner plan to make bets.

Immediately complications arose. In order to follow the advice, each had to imagine herself/himself to be the boss of a gambling mob made up of the others, and so each character not only made up a part of the others, but was, in turn, made up by them. This reminded me of Raymond Queneau's x mistakes y for z constraint, and so, apart from giving me an excuse to go to the track regularly, my summer project offered the potential of providing material for a novel. I began a literal literary experiment to write an experimental novel based on an experiment.

Intrigued, I applied myself to the task of collecting data. I didn't care what happened. Play motivated me more than fear, and because the game was fun, the wagering diary I compiled, complete with notes on characters and daily oddities, was more scorecard than notebook. I wanted my heteronyms to win money for me, but the dramatic potential of having them set out on disastrous losing streaks was perversely appealing. As for money, the most I could lose in a day was $50, and the maximum loss of about $1000 over a season of 20-some weekend dates was not only unlikely but also far less than amounts I had lost in some previous seasons at the track.

Not caring—or, being detached from the self-examinations a horseplayer often goes through after losses—did the trick. The heteronyms won enough to make me think the scheme wasn't completely foolish. And, as each won and lost according to his or her own bent, the characters developed. Cal Nipper, the nit-picking retired algebra teacher who liked to back horses with many statistical attributes, was content with the small payoffs he managed to stockpile, even though any minor slump threatened to send him plunging. Kelly Lane, a woman with a past Nipper fancied as loose, was looser at making picks, often going with horses that only showed one or two positive factors. Her choices won less frequently, but when they won, they won much more. Then there was the contrarian, Henderson Will, the mental misfit who did everything backwards. He played to lose, picking horses not to win but to finish second to a select group of contenders in exactas. His bets rarely won, but paid the most of all.

At the end of the season, I had pages full of numbers and abbreviations, noting types of races and funds won and lost by each character. As the characters won and lost, their lives turned for better or worse, especially as the end of the season threatened to end whatever their lives had amounted to in the course of the book. But what sort of person, after years of failure, turns to a professional tout for advice? Lane and Nipper were losers taking a shot at a last chance to make something of themselves. Will, meanwhile, had already bungled through a year at the track after taking The Course taught by the tout, hence his determination to do the opposite of what he had been led to do.

Like the default choices in a word processing program that sets up a double-spaced, twelve point Times New Roman document with paragraph indents, headers, and footers, there are default choices most novelists seem to take for granted. Diction comes automatically from each character's voice and from the novelist's voice, plot structure comes intuitively from one of a few basic models, setting comes from places the author knows, and so on, with only point-of-view, perhaps, making the author pause to choose first or third-person. In a constraint-driven novel, all such choices are subject to the rules of the constraints. This can be strangely liberating when paratext elements come into play. Questions of wording the disclaimer or the dedication, questions that can be maddening, resolve easily. In the text itself, the resolutions also can fall into place, although the place they fall into may seem more and more like alien territory.

For one example of how this works in By *Kelman Out of Pessoa* (whose title derives from how the sire and dam of race horses are listed: e.g., Pegasus Crude by Roustabout Driller out of Queen Cajun Gulf), consider the order of scenes and how each is told. Since each character makes up the others, each scene comes in a section of a brief commentary on one character by another (Henderson Will by Kelly Lane), interspersed with a few soliloquy sections. The progression must be chronological, as each character reacts to what happens, as it happens, at the track, but there's a certain tyranny dictating whose turn it is to tell the story. This, of course, must come from the races themselves. After fiddling with various approaches, I saw that, just as the characters suspect, the frequency and order of narration should come from the frequency and order of winning post positions. Throughout this season, most of the races were won by horses in posts 1 through 6, with the posts 7, 8, and 9-12 adding a few more. 1-6 supplied each of the primary narrative situations: say, let 1 = Cal Nipper by Henderson Will, 2 = Kelly Lane by Cal Nipper, etc.; and 7, 8, and 9-12 supplied each soliloquy. Distribution of wins by the first six posts was mostly equal and varied, but the same post did occasionally win two or three times in a row. In a way, the order and frequency is arbitrary. It doesn't matter what number horse wins the next race, or whose turn it is to speak. In another way, the order is absolute. All that matters is the outcome of the next race, if you bet on it, and the outcome of the story depends on who relates what, when.

While gathering data, and especially while trying different approaches to put numbers of notes into words of a narrative, I thought of the history of racetrack literature. What books there are on betting on horses are almost all non-fiction and/or memoir. When fiction makes use of horse racing, the track is typically used as a colorful milieu, such as in Dick Francis mysteries. Novels about horse racing as a pure sport, like *Black Beauty*, deal with the people around the horse. Novels about gambling in general, from Dostoevsky to Jeanette Winterson, tend to concentrate on the psychology of the gambler, and on the quasi-to-overt mystical relationships to luck (or, fortune) gamblers develop. In *By Kelman Out of Pessoa*, luck is either beside the point or it is a necessary evil that is best expressed and exploited by statistical probability figures a skilled player can master. My heteronyms may be losers, but I'll be damned if they are faith-based morons, in thrall to superstition. Also, whatever racetrack novels there are that focus on gambling, I somehow doubt their authors linked the methodology of playing the races to the content of the story. I did spend time trying to find novels on betting the horses that somehow used the methods of betting as a basis for constraints to steer the story, just as I consulted the books on Oulipo for examples of such a project as I was getting involved with, if only to let me know what I was getting into, or, better yet, if I was getting into it first.

As technology makes this scientific approach to writing a novel more feasible, it also makes the goal of originality more elusive. No matter what you do to try to discover some way to write that hasn't been done, somebody may well have already published it. But so what? All I can do is all I can do. Beyond the research and the procedures, there is the work, and the work made by the work. I've written books that have been called experimental, by others and by me; but, to be literary to the literal letter, I can now say that with By *Kelman Out of Pessoa* I have written an experimental novel.

Seattle
2010

Postscript: What Could Go Wrong

After the initial questions and hypotheses propose a constraint and I gather information, a lot of trial and error goes into the process, as it's essential to play with ideas and forms; eventually, analysis and interpretation come into play, and I may realize that this thing is not going anywhere—or worse, that this thing I have sent to publishers should not have gone anywhere.

Rules can be so compelling that their fulfillment is all that matters. Wherever the constraint leads, I must follow, observing yet overruling traditional literary standards. It's not unusual for me to be good at complying with the constraint but bad at using it to write poetry or prose. Do I defy all judgment of aesthetic value and simply take the constraint to the limit or do I compromise and risk undoing what I set out to do?

I've come to doubt that an untried constraint is bound to produce work that hasn't been done. This had been the crux of my boilerplate artist statement: only by following a new procedure can an artist achieve originality. As if to test this, I've often made my constraints take on other constraints (song lyrics, sestinas, famous lines), and this can produce works with patterns in common, especially if novels follow a typical plot arc, such as a life history. I wrote two novels which, despite following widely unrelated and different constraints, were so similar as to replicate each other. Back to the lab.

Seattle
2014

THE NATURE OF THE POEM

Myriam Moscona

(Trans. by Jen Hofer)

suicidal
toxic
rebellious

                    focused
                    open
                    brazen

border-facing
naked
blade-sharp

                    taciturn
                    inhaling
                    digressive

          cruel
          adulterous
          pantheistic

hard-headed
kiss-ready
ballsy

                    masculine
                    detailed
                    detail-oriented

NATURALEZA DEL POEMA

Myriam Moscona

suicida
tóxica
rebelde

concentrada
abierta
caradura

fronteriza
desnuda
cortante

taciturna
inhalante
digresiva

cruel
adúltera
panteísta

necia
besante
jija

masculina
detallada
detallista

carrion-devouring
festive
deathly

feminine
red
stabbing

wounded
unhealthy
contagious

indisposed
hormonal
asleep

black
bloody
wolverine

awake
insidious
turbid

sudden
brutal
indispensable

mortal
blessed
rude

maternal
stingy
bodacious

broken
diva
divine

carroñera
festiva
mortífera

femenina
roja
punzante

herida
insana
contagiosa

indispuesta
hormonal
dormida

negra
sangrante
loba

despierta
insidiosa
turbia

repentina
brutal
imprescindible

mortal
bienaventurada
grosera

maternal
cicatera
zafia

rota
diva
divina

elliptical
wandering
ritual

abducting
erudite
obscene

poised
spectral
erratic

full of jealousy
full of sky
adorable

absent
lesbian
sibylline

war-like
evening-like
dictator-like

thieving
subdued
flaying

dramatic
ascetic
abrasive

ball-busting
fierce
ocular

wretched
contained
free

elíptica
peregrina
ritual

      raptora
      docta
      obscena

          donosa
          espectral
          errática

      celosa
      cielosa
      adorable

            ausente
            lésbica
            sibilina

guerrera
vesperal
dictadora

        ladrona
        sometida
        desollante

            dramática
            ascética
            abrasiva

       rompe huevos
       brava
       ocular

    mísera
    contenida
    libre

fluid
unbearable
portable

alpha
auditory
solitary

dancing
reclusive
cantabile

corporeal
soulful
glassy

blue
latent
shuddering

monstrous
officiating
intrusive

enviable
giving
priestly

rhythmic
gestural
voracious

mental
brilliant
excessive

secret
impeccable
diamantine

                                        fluida
                                        insoportable
                                        portátil

                        alfa
                        auditiva
                        solitaria

                danzante
                eremita
                cantabile

                                corporal
                                álmica
                                vítrea

        azul
        latente
        estremecida

                        monstruosa
                        oficiante
                        intrusa

        envidiable
        dadivosa
        sacerdotal

                                                rítmica
                                                gestual
                                                voraz

                        mental
                        brillante
                        excesiva

                                        secreta
                                        impecable
                                        diamantina

impossible
malicious
saucy

meddlesome
dark
intravenous

ludic
acrobatic
music-loving

arrogant
imprudent
shameless

lying
vacillating
astute

noble
tyrannical
obstinate

impulsive
magnetized
incisive

fresh
aerobic
judicious

schizoid
impetuous
dreaded

brave
slow
procuring

imposible
maliciosa
zorra

entrometida
oscura
intravenosa

lúdica
acrobática
melómana

arrogante
imprudente
impúdica

mentirosa
vacilante
astuta

noble
tirana
obstinada

impulsiva
imantada
incisiva

fresca
aeróbica
juiciosa

esquizoide
impetuosa
temida

valiente
lenta
alcahueta

soothing
baroque
bipolar

colorist
memorious
celebratory

aerostatic
fevered
cold

ojos que vuelven atrás

dialectical
permissive
aerial

irreverent
versatile
tireless

polyphonic
inventive
hysterical

legendary
crafty
diatonic

stammering
exhibitionist
neurotic

tolerable
nomadic
disobedient

calmante
barroca
bipolar

colorista
memoriosa
celebratoria

aerostática
afiebrada
fría

eyes turning back

dialéctica
permisiva
aérea

irreverente
versátil
incansable

polifónica
inventora
histérica

legendaria
artificiosa
diatónica

balbuciente
exhibicionista
neurótica

llevadera
nómada
insumisa

                                        intrepid
                                        sassy
                                        captivating

right on
daring
penetrable

                    evasive
                    hot
                    insolent

wanton
enigmatic
learned

                                        vaporous
                                        cyclonic
                                        spicy

                    sodomite
                    seismic
                    absorbed

patient
movable
shipwrecked

                                        serious
                                        spiny
                                        curative

mute
filtering
visceral

                    illuminated
                    impatient
                    relative

                                    lanzada
                                    furcia
                                    cautivante

acertiva
atrevida
penetrable

                  huidiza
                  caliente
                  lenguaraz

pécora
esfinge
bachillera

                                    vaporosa
                                    ciclónica
                                    picante

                  sodomita
                  sísmica
                  embebida

paciente
movible
náufraga

                                    grave
                                    espinosa
                                    curativa

muda
filtrante
visceral

                  iluminada
                  impaciente
                  relativa

treacherous
restorative
illuminating

spilled
pyramidal
doleful

foreign
audacious
gypsy

dirty
loose
licentious

never absolute

(the nature of the poem)

Mexico City
2010

pérfida
reparadora
iluminante

vertida
piramidal
funesta

fuereña
lea
gitana

sucia
suelta
licenciosa

nunca absoluta

(naturaleza del poema)

México
2010

THE NATURE OF TRANSLATION

Jen Hofer

determination
proximity
complicity

sphere
aperture
periphery

expansion
exposure
subtraction

tactics
deviance
interpretation

cruelty
polymorphousness
polyvocality

orneriness
perversity
mofo

non-conformity
detail
corrective

omnivore
welcome
culture

feline
feral
punctual

membrane
bacteria
breath

fragility
intuition
alternation

color
circulation
ferocity

struggle
exception
air

collision
tremor
refusal

shroud
accident
challenge

molecule
stone
multitude

hue
tune
sky

asymptote
parade
ceremony

        wingspan
        research
        fearlessness

          scaffold
          phenomenon
          circuitousness

    resistance
    persistence
    enchantment

            departure
            assent
            disclosure

din
fade
dictation

    appropriation
    submission
    extravagance

            billboard
            sidewalk
            traffic

      garden
      avenue
      visitation

dissent
border
alternative

flow
sustenance
transit

node
listening
solidarity

mobile
solo
choral

physical
ephemeral
liquid

oceanic
palpable
oppositional

human
inverse
permeating

withholding
forthcoming
costumed

bodily
expressive
devotional

brainy
bristling
overflowing

contained
imperfect
mirrored

possible
impossible
flickering

percussive
shadowed
permissive

promiscuous
acrobatic
pigmented

blustery
meticulous
willing

deceptive
uncertain
subversive

humbling
stuttering
walled

canyoned
irresistible
apt

self-effacing
fleshy
skeletal

multiple
rococo
ricocheting

heartful
rhythmic
brazen

                                        whirlpooling
                                        lush
                                        non-binary

vibrating
forgetful
starry

                                        rotating
                                        spinning
                                        shimmering

            ¡ojo! ¡ojo! volver volver

                                        dialogically
                                        performatively
                                        vastly

rule-breakingly
divergently
endlessly

                                        melodically
                                        fabricatively
                                        dissonantly

anthropomorphically
distressingly
harmonically

                                        interruptively
                                        nakedly
                                        anxiously

        acceptingly
        transitionally
        assertively

questioningly
flourishingly
magnetically

erroneously
adventurously
porously

tidally
ardently
directly

animalistically
inquisitively
verbally

airily
revolvingly
snappily

ambidextrously
fractally
embeddedly

infinitesimally
curiously
mistakenly

gravitationally
unprotectedly
awakeningly

whisperingly
tentacularly
surgically

cloudily
slowly
relationally

ambiguously
vibrantly
vividly

overly
pointedly
utterly

freely
insufficiently
nomadically

impurely
swarmingly
messily

never absolutely

(the nature of translation
in the marrow, in the air.
itself represented is the thing, nominal.
it is the description of the thing, adjectival.
it is how the thing is
described and represented, adverbial.
nominal, adjectival, adverbial effects
on "our" language and interpretive capacities
which become a different thing.
in the marrow, in the air.)

Los Angeles
2010

THE AESTHETIC: AMONG NATIONS (ANTHEMS FLOWERS PLAIDS BOOKS)

Renée Petropoulos

Marginalia by Sianne Ngai
and Veronica Gonzalez Peña

Every expression is a translation. Everything expressed is a translation. All emanating from the brain or the body, from both—this kind of breaking down of thought/impulse into action/expression is rudimentary and also profound in turning over and deciphering how an 'artwork' originates. And, then is translated.

The site is a 9¼" x 4¼" book. A shape that is particularly long and slim, a smooth, comfortable-in-the-hand kind of shape. One meant to invoke security, intimacy; the act of holding and sitting—actually the shape and size and feel of the volumes remind one to sit down and read.

Read what?

> Some things don't need a translation. Moths, for example. I am in Berlin, and the same moth from my kitchen in Los Angeles plagues me here…one landed on my bedding tonight, ready for the attack; my nightmare is that the one warm sweater I have with me will get eaten. I've only ever found one person who can patch a sweater well. Her husband scolds me for giving his wife work. But she is here, I think, in this shop in Los Feliz, hoping for work. I am not a villian! I am a hero! I am giving her what she is here for: work. But she is old…I can do nothing about that…
> Moths, since Virginia Woolf and her wandering pencil, will never be the same. Moths have been translated by Woolf. They are always the site of murder. I will never understand a moth as a moth, clear and clean and direct. So, you are right, in the end, even the moth can only be understood as a translation. (VGP)

These texts. These identities via these visual components: flowers, flags, plaids. I am thinking about the writers of these books, where they live and how that place—Brazil, Mexico, the United States—may affect their writing. I am thinking about origins and their effects on words, punctuation, style, and ideas.

> There is something static and even decorative about flags, flowers, and codes. Yet your work often gives the impression of speed and movement. (SN)

The site is a set of books.

Section 1 : National anthems

National anthems are often born out of competition. A 'leader' creates a contest and bestows a prize for the best poetic composition expressing patriotic ideals. The lyrics are often composed separately from the music. The lyrical expression often resembles that of a love poem, with a particular affection for physical attributes and for wisdom, coupled with the ultimate reverence and esteem for virtue.

> Did you watch the World Cup? (SN)

National anthems herald shows of strength and power with a willingness to go to the limit for one's love. As is often true in love poems, the point-of-view can ricochet between filial and amorous love. This ricocheting is fundamental to the form. In the national anthems of both Mexico and Brazil, the Father and Mother are invoked. The sense of the 'body' is often portrayed by the land, and nature is cultured via lyrics praising sky and earth and vegetation. The Star-Spangled Banner lyrics are unusual in that they praise an object. In our national anthem, the flag is more important than the nation itself. This object is given the affection, the power, and the status to symbolically prevail over adversity. It becomes the body.

> And sets the stage for us to become disembodied. In the US the body no longer matters, in warfare, or in work, or in love. The body only matters as it is being read through an object: drones, or TV, or the computer, phone, e-mail, text, flat image… (VGP)

Section 2 : A bouquet of flowers

In my research on flags and national anthems, I have learned that even flowers are a sign of recognition and national identity. A particular flower, in bloom, with color, fragrance, and leaves, can indicate location, patriotism, rapture, and allegiance. The representation of the flower. A bouquet for every book; a flower for each writer.

It may be that the flower is the more 'demure' representation of power. Or, it may be that seeing natural beauty, innocence, and the fundamental order of things cased in a form as luscious as a flower is the best way to camouflage the (seemingly) naturalized systems of power.

> Like Jasper Johns with his flags, targets, and alphabets, you start with icons or images that already come "pre-charged" with signifying energy (that already belong to a semiotic system), and then denature them, divest them of that original signification. The denatured icon (which importantly always continues to bear a trace of its original meaning) then gets re-inserted, as it were, into a series or sequence of other works which all together give the impression of their belonging to some other system which we don't fully quite understand yet. (SN)

> Or [flower] as vaginal symbol. Though with the stamen, it could be the penis too... like a worm, flowers are both male and female at once, and so essential in some way we do not understand, nature at its most fundamental... (VGP)

Roses are red, orange, yellow, pink, cream, and sometimes brown. I can often smell them just from their photograph. It is easier. The White House has a rose garden, cultivated as both a garden for the house and as a national symbol. Its odiferous health is important— important meetings take place in the Rose Garden. Heads of state smell the flowers, named Elizabeth, Pascale, and Pat Nixon. Their scents welcome the dignitaries, who make strategies to protect their homes. Dead flowers are never left in the garden.

On the other hand, orchids do not have a scent. None whatsoever. They are described with words like "frilly," and seem to have lips, tubes, and sheaths. The cattleya in particular is used in hybridization, which accounts for thousands upon thousands of types. They start from under the surface with a bulbous form known as a pseudo bulb, which I think gives them a

In medieval iconography, flowers carry deep meaning—subtle readings based on color or placement, or type. (VGP)

more democratic identity than say a rose. Finding one's origins in such spurious beginnings can only heighten a sensitivity to the sun. Growing up in a desert, I always thought orchids were exotic and rare, but in fact they are ubiquitous. I wonder if this has something to do with Brazilians being associated with love or sex. It could be the bathing suits, but it may be cattleya.

I am still a big fan of lavender and orange and sometimes fuchsia. Fuchsia is never used in flags. It may be the color goes fugitive when made into a dye. It may be that the word, fuchsia, is too beautiful and suggestive. I think fuchsia is a cattleya.

Are colors historical? What history do your colors bring with them? (SN)

I love this story—the flower and the cake merging in the form of the grandfather. The present girl with Dahlia figures the past grandfather with cake (or does he pre-figure her?). A palimpsest. (VGP)

The first dahlia I encountered was deep purple, almost black. It was nearly a foot in diameter and I promptly put it on my head as a hat. My grandfather once put a cake, a celebratory birthday cake just produced by my grandmother, on top of his head to suggest a hat. He cocked his head, made a smile, and the cake slid to the floor. I have always loved that moment precisely because of the smoldering smile, the slow motion of the cheesecake's slide and the bemused expression on my grandfather's face. I love dahlias. In Germany the dahlia was known as 'Georgia.' My grandfather was German.

Mexico was the first country I visited. The dahlia first came to Madrid via seed from Mexico. But a French botanist, sent to steal the cochineal beetle for its dye, brought back the dahlia of the same color. Cochineal is synonymous with fuchsia. Some people call it scarlet, which comes with a whole other set of associations I don't share.

But of course the botanist would find in the flower what the entomologist found in the bug. The whole world is encoded in the language we know, underneath the surface the same thing—fuschia—which is scarlet—a layering which is what colonialism does too, layers and re-layers what is already there, multileveled, deep with meaning. (VGP)

Aztecs cultivated the dahlia for food and ceremonies. They decorated their buildings with the flowers. They wore the flowers in their hair. They danced dahlia dances. One could eat the dahlias and smoke the dahlias.

Dahlias are octoploids. Ploid is a word related to plaid.

Section 3 : A sense of plaid

We assume the flag has come to us through the historical use of the emblematic and the evolution of heraldry. Yet flags come to us through their most literal use as well—as a carried object, to be seen above the crowds, preceding the 'people.' Flags can be held and waved and read again, much like a book. In this way the colors of the flag will precede the reading of the text.

> I am afraid of flags. Nationalism—which, perhaps unfairly, is what I think when I think flag—scares me. Flowers are another thing; though many have tried, no one owns their symbolic language. It flutters about more than any unfurled flag. (VGP)

Each of the books in this *TrenchArt* series will include a plaid as its endpaper. The color, reflecting the Brazilian, Mexican, and American flags, will suggest a system that may or may not be significant to the author. The plaid will provide a context. A context that operates on an entirely different level of recognition. Think about modernism on the one hand, then feel the breeze and sense of a fluttering flag, be aware of the sweet scent of the flower and you will be ready to read.

I have previously used plaids to represent relationships, intersections, and encounters between nations. In this project, the plaid will first be seen when the book is unfolded from either the front or the back. The pattern will criss-cross horizontal and vertical bands in multiple colors from the flags; in some instances new colors will form through the blended originals. This colored pattern may evoke patriotism and national identity, while also suggesting the modernist code of design.

The green of an apple, the green of tree moss, the green of Islam, the green of a fern, the blue of water, the blue of the sky, of feathers of the cockatiel, the red of a rose, the red of blood, the red of lipstick, the red of thread, the yellow of paint, the yellow of the sun, the yellow of corn, or of blond hair. Mondrian. The RED square. The grid of a city; the topographical pattern on all things modern.

Modern farming, modern keyboards, modern movement.

The imprint of the modernist grid bleeds through the previous historical associations. In a continuous chain of reactions, the plaid patterns oscillate between negative and positive, though they are not readable as such. Their forms are here for invigoration. The colors become a subjective agent for discourse, activated by their histories, which are intact even as they are reshaped into a conversation. What if Mexico and Brazil merge and their plants and skins mutate? Their intellects refine one another. What about land that slips across the continent creating a muddy path of footsteps? What about that wall between Mexico and the United States, a spatial line tracking vast ground? The wall is such a short line, but one of infinite proportions.

Your work always seems to be about—or to always stage— an oscillation between what Jacques Rancière describes as two opposing tendencies on the part of visual imagery: the "image as raw, material presence" (modernist abstraction) and the "image as discourse encoding a history" (iconology: national flags, the language of flowers, plaids). Or in other words, the "visible" and the "sayable"; the image as pure, a-signifying (if not therefore insignificant) form, and the image as "hieroglyph," as semiotic sign. You seem interested in the way in which these two dimensions leak and blur into one another. One could even say you force them to leak and blur into one another. (SN)

South Americans still think about this: how does a color fully embody the object? The world's first photograph was a plaid ribbon. Our association and belief in symmetrical perfection is so dominant that we think we see it everywhere. These plaids will appear to have that which they actually don't: signs of reproduction and identical repetitive lines. In some ways this echoes the idea that all things must have an imperfection constructed into them— something consciously intended as a shift. No accidents.

> Another way of asking the same question: you seem interested in the way visual images can function like words in a language, and conversely in the way words can be made to function more like visual images. (SN)

Section 4: If art is a social proposition

and I believe that it is, then the viewer is entitled to participate fully. To bring everything to the table, the participant presumed intelligent, willing.

Art is a conversation—a navigational tool for being human.

Lispector
Hips
Revolution
repressed materials
bougainvillea
slaves
vodun
tubas

> Art is the site of connection—a this to that, a constant shifting, a viewing and being viewed, open for interpretation. A flow, a process, life… (VGP)

Being present is the act that one must insist upon. If the book is seen and the graphics perceived, then the act of reading is foreseen. Perceiving and interpreting the graphic foregrounds the reading of the book. Attention is focused, brought to the surface of perception. To borrow words: what is there, what is rooted, permanent, resistant, lived-in; an object and the memory of it, a being and its history.

> All of this is life… this is the flow of life… (VGP)

Consider this: explosions on a typical Fourth of July recognize the United States' independence from Britain. The fireworks are pink, yellow, green, and blue, they are sparkly, vibrant, and sexy. Immediate and fleeting. See the fireworks from the deck of a sailing vessel; smell the explosives, the gunpowder, the sulfur in the air. I realize now that the fireworks display is a simulation and reenactment of the song's lyric, "bombs bursting in air." Each Fourth of July, millions of Americans reexperience war. Each year they feel and reinvigorate their patriotism under the guise of entertainment. It is insinuated into our systems of body and belief as a seductive, awe-inspiring, and separated-from-content experience, so it can be felt as an out-of-body, fully-sensate encounter. It is not.

> Is there anything about patriotism worth recuperating? (SN)

Extensive Cattle Farming, Two Altitudes, The Problem of Origins, The "Dark" Legend, The New Agriculture, The Land Problem, Transition Towards the North, The "Promised Land" of the North-West, The Hot Lands of the Gulf, The Underdeveloped "Annexes" of the South-East, The Classic Civilizations, The Pre-Classic Civilizations, Shopping, Traffic Regulations, Aztec Society, Regional Diversity.

Macumba, Favelas, Quality Hotels, Contradictions, Masters and Slaves, Beans, Milk and Coffee, Dividing the Land, Sweetness and Fights, Swishing, the National Psyche.

Making a Nation, Boston Tea Party, Battle of Tippecanoe, Traditional Culture, Elvis, Death Valley, Advertising, City Hopping, Outdoor Adventures, The West, Cinco de Mayo, Basketball, *Poor Richard's Almanac*, Gospel, Blues and Soul, Crime and Gangsters, Common Sense, Lines and Crowds, Re-Creations and Fakes, the Abundant Society.

Bus, New Year, red trousers, stones, embroidery, red, dishes, moisture, dirt, squeaky, teeth, fog, tongue, clouds, resistance.

Pink, skin, sultry, translation, drumming, meat, wet, hips, crushed ice, lime, women.

Cars, bellies, fists.

Art is a social proposition by virtue of my existence as a social proposition. This existence proposes action. If conscious awareness of the present is the highest form of resistance, then this is a constant struggle. Every aesthetic gesture works to bring itself into focus, to make one aware of seeing the 'it' and the ramifications of the 'it.' There is never the one. They are dots. They are dashes. They are placeholders. They stand in, supplant. They free us to think, to reflect as they do not 'say.' Inside the book the sign is altered. It becomes specific. It 'says' something. Before it is specific it is recognized as a signal. PAY ATTENTION HERE. When the unfolding takes place the texture changes. One is adrift with the colors. Familiar but not comprehended.

"The particular essence of each form of motion is determined by its own particular contradiction. This holds true not only for nature but also for social and ideological phenomena." *Mao Tse-tung 1966*

"If you want knowledge, you must take part in the practice of changing reality. If you want to know the taste of a pear, you must change the pear by eating it yourself." *Mao Tse-tung 1966*

> To be fully known, understood,
> I must be consumed! I must be eaten?! (VGP)

The human eye is capable of focusing on only a very small area at one time. Eyes see in spurts and stops. We see the entire field first, then we concentrate, in and out, we scan the page with our eyes, take in the form. We can only read one word at a time, then some letters to the left and some additional letters to the right. We focus just long enough to make sense of the word. The image and shape of the text become form.

From the outside of the book a form is detected. Even an instance of direct mimicry to a text is perceived. From here to the inside we proceed to meaning. Meaning through syntax, our agreed upon form of communication.

Several types of reading are suggested when producing an artwork for a book.

Several types of reading are suggested when making a life.

Section 5 : Three ways to speak simultaneously

If three ways to speak are simultaneously presented, each part being singular, each part overlapping another, then the coding, representation, and placement within the space can be approached.

– a bouquet
– swatches of plaid with color
– language signs

- flowers rendered in each instance with all of their particularities
- plaid of identical colors in particular arrangements, singular in their appearance
- word replacements with dots, dashes, blocks, spaces

'Enabler' in contradiction to an achiever. It is a trader, a sharer.
The landscape of America is a disabler.

> This is thrilling! We are being made privy to a private language, yet need not be as we can still appreciate this on a simply visual level. (VGP)

Is it possible that abstraction, as such, can reintroduce a democratic reception (or perception) while also conveying that this perception is neither desirable nor possible? This method of abstraction is desirable in that it is a continual act of unfolding.

UNFOLDING :

The book unfolds, the cover opens, the flaps lift, pages turn. In what order do you see: the flowers, the text, the dots, the plaid, the dashes, the plaid, the text, the flowers, never the flowers, always the blocks.

> Does gender—one of the most powerful and persistent codes or symbolic systems in our culture to this day—enter into this work? (SN)

There is an act of working between the predictable and the unpredictable. If I hear the sounds of something and see the rhythm, then I know I am insisting on the alignment of simultaneous perceptions. I am more comfortable taking things askance. I prefer perceiving one thing while something else is going on. It lessens the blow. Every-thing becomes more manageable, the information more tolerable. A direct hit is too emotional. I

> This makes me think of Dan Graham's reflections, the subject is always displaced through the layering of information which the reflections provide... this creates both an influx of additional information, while also deferring any direct "hit" so to speak. I also love, in film, the off-screen voiceover. Godard is the master of this, some philosophical treatise while all we see on-screen is a cup of coffee, the liquid stirring inside it. (VGP)

admire it and am impressed by it, but it does not suit my more round-about sensibility.

Contradictions are the only way to unfold questions, to display methods and switch directions. In Abstraction the pivotal concept is contradiction. We see abstraction as contradictory to representation. We see it as distanced, possibly even elite in its manifestation. I argue quite the opposite. Abstraction is concrete. It is direct and attainable with simple perceptual capabilities. But it does demand individual attention. The encounter is demanding. The individual must respond with all of their senses to unfold what is present. Putting pieces together is a requirement. It is within reach, within our worldly encounters. I am interested in what we know already, what is present within our scheme of knowledge. This must be applied to complicate and reinvigorate our present encounters. It must be used to re-think every situation. In this way, we are alive.

> Nabokov believed deeply in contradiction. He said it was the only way he knew he was alive… the changing of the mind, the motion of the new motion, this is life. Death is stasis, of course. For Winnicott the space between things, the transitional space, is the space where creativity occurs, for it is a space of non-ownership, it is a space that has not been claimed yet. Yes, this is life! (VGP)

In the book space and time are present. The object of the book forces us to consider ourselves and our activities in this construct. The book allows the time to encounter the artwork: it is the site of time. It is a placeholder for space.

End :

I am not so sure now if one should sit down and read these particular books. Perhaps this book is more suited to walking and motioning, to pontificating and gesturing. Its size and adaptability suggest one hand holding and one hand turning the pages: no desk necessary! All you need is a pocket. Use this book to decorate your jacket. Let its lovely shade of green peek from your breast pocket.

> I want one of these books in my pocket at all times… (VGP)

FOLD IT UP. Put it in your pocket and walk. Hold it up and point with it. Open it up and sift through the pages. Touch each surface, glimpse the edges, fuffle (feel and ruffle) the volume.

Los Angeles
2010

ARS POETICA

Alex Forman

The presidency has existed since 1788; however, the photograph was invented only in the late 1830s, and the first picture of a president was of J.Q. Adams when, at 79, he sat for a daguerreotype. That was in 1847. But, until Louis Marx, "a roly-poly, melon-bald little man with the berry-bright eyes and beneficent smile,"[i] created his collection of figurines, there was no reproducible likeness of all the presidents from which to imagine their distinct, human, personal identities.

At least there wasn't until I made my images of the pieces from this Marx Toys playset, miniature plastic figurines of the American presidents from Washington to Nixon, collected individually, hand painted, and lovingly stored together by some unknown person. James Madison was five foot four inches, our shortest president. Lincoln was six foot four, our tallest. Each man, here, is two-and-a-third inches tall. I return them to their life-size proportions and attend to their differences.

The words have been woven together from different sources over generations, providing context both within the complementary framework of photography and outside of it.[ii]

I am a man.

Little man, big man

It was, after all, in this way that "the Explorer" discovered, on his feet and at her feet, the tallest human thing in existence. Her heart beat because no emerald is so rare. And so "the Explorer" said, timidly and with a delicacy of feeling that no one would ever criticize: —"I" am Little Flower.

At that moment, Little Flower scratched herself where no one scratches.

"I" am autobiography, text and context.

...and should the chosen guide
Be nothing better than a wandering cloud,
I cannot miss my way.
– William Wordsworth[iii]

A PHILOSOPHY OF PLAY

I sometimes, in my sprightly moments, consider myself...as the dictator at the head of a commonwealth. In this little state I can discover all the great geniuses, all the surprising actions and revolutions of the great world in miniature.[iv]

Today I shall tour the stores...more books and toys for inspiration.[v]

The world is my imagination. The cleverer I am at miniaturizing the world, the better I possess it.[vi]

Child's play is automatically an abstracting process. Engaging with toys, Baudelaire observed, children enact a "great drama of life, reduced in size by the *camera obscura* of their little brains."[vii]

The size of a man's head is anything "I" decide it to be.

He is a giant said Tolstoy. "Lincoln is the only real giant … a Christ in miniature."
None threw a longer shadow than he.

Larger than slight. Lively.

Things pop up.

Things pop out.

Things pop out, next to other things popping out.

Call the strings or rods that move the puppet the weave. It might be objected that its multiplicity resides in the person of the actor, who projects it into the text.[viii]

It is forbidden to walk on the grass; it is forbidden to touch the flowers; it is not allowed to introduce dogs, or to remain after dark; it is requested to keep to the right.[ix]

The spirit that overcomes mechanics translates exact findings into parables of life.[x]

Truly inhabiting the whole volume of his space, the man of reverie is from anywhere in his world, in an inside which has no outside. … In reverie, the *no* no longer has any function: everything is welcome.[xi]

He likes declaring, with innocent aplomb, how much "fun" it is to make art with toys. Some apologists play along, naïvely taking him at his word.[xii]

Because laughter is ever part of the American genius and our book is not intended for solemn duffers and patriotic stuffed shirts.[xiii]

"I" line them up.

"I" reflect on things through things.

"I" am a conquering explorer.

"I" explore all walks of life.

The littlest woman in the world was laughing. It was the kind of laugh that only someone who doesn't speak laughs.

We are poor passing facts,
warned by that to give each figure in the
photograph
his living name.
– Robert Lowell[xiv]

THE PHOTOGRAPHS

The first people to be reproduced entered the visual space of photography with their innocence intact—or rather, without inscription.[xv]

The advent of photography in 1839 began to challenge the primacy of the hand-crafted image, and by the eve of the Civil War, the photographic print was well on its way to displacing the older forms of portraiture as the main vehicle by which presidents were known.[xvi]

Just as Freud's theories "isolated and made analyzable things which had heretofore floated along unnoticed in the broad stream of perception," the photographic apparatus focuses on "hidden details of familiar objects," revealing "entirely new structural formations of the subject."[xvii]

"I" read everything before me and that is how "I" came upon a worn old book without a back.

In the presidency, for instance, is all of history. The man who puts his woman on a pedestal, and also those who are peculiarly harsh and severe with their women, three Aunt Nancys, four black presidents, and a woman in the president's seat.

Take linearity out of history and you get humanity.

Like many young photographers, he pursued the documentary style of the great masters of the street, Lee Friedlander or Bruce Davidson.[xviii] Walker Evans wrote: "This person has a really unique and interesting vision."[xix]

His dramatically lit figurines echo the staged dolls that frequently appear in the work of Laurie Simmons. Both artists examine American expectations, stereotypes, and clichés. Where Simmons' works examine stereotypical domestic (and in turn private) 1950s housewives, his images portray public men of accomplishment.[xx]

Beautiful as the chance encounter of a sewing machine and an umbrella on an operating table is an expression of the belief that simply placing objects in an unexpected context reinvigorates their mysterious qualities.[xxi]

The magnifying glass in this experience conditions an entry into the world … But because these descriptions tell us things in tiny detail, they are automatically verbose.[xxii]

What interests us are the circumstances.[xxiii]

He was recording American pop.[xxiv]

"I" learn that every feeling waits upon its gesture. The camera is a hand-held auxiliary of wanting-to-know. "I" make a portrait. You've seen his picture before. But do you know him? He's watery of eye, tremulous of hand, fat and flatulent.

"I" cannot bear this, don't trouble me, "I" say, my arm sore and my hand swollen from campaigning.

"I" am in every picture. "I" am the selective process. The world is my imagination.

"I was impressed by your research. I think it's about a third of your book, isn't it?"

"It is."

"That's the bibliography."

– Former first lady Rosalynn Carter and presidential historian Josh Wolf Shenk[xxv]

THE WORDS

What is it collectors do when they collect? Where would history and biography be unless there were collectors?[xxvi]

He was a builder by nature.[xxvii] A lonely prospector in the gallery of words.[xxviii]

The cultural book is necessarily a tracing: already a tracing of itself, a tracing of the previous book by the same author, a tracing of other books however different they may be, an endless tracing of established concepts and words, a tracing of the world present, past, and future.[xxix]

A book is an assemblage of this kind, and as such is unattributable.... There is no difference between what a book talks about and how it is made.... We have been criticized for overquoting literary authors.[xxx]

"I" am a builder.

"I" have made a work of assemblage which is peaceful … involving great restraint, care, reflection, and time, and the possibility of endless minor changes and adjustments.

"I" have this theory about time.

All mankind is of one author, and is one volume; when one man dies, one chapter is not torn out of the book, but translated into a better language; and every chapter must be so translated.[xxxi]

Eventually all things are known. And few matter.[xxxii]

Books like these restore the novelty of the novel, with its ambiguous straddling of verifiable and imaginary facts.[xxxiii] The lifespan of a fact is shrinking.[xxxiv] It must take itself seriously for the public to take it so.[xxxv]

Great minds and their ideas are humanity's common heritage. Actually, great men themselves possess only that which is bizarre about them. To describe a man in all his anomalies, a book should be a work of art, like a Japanese print whereon the image of a tiny caterpillar, seen once at one particular hour of a day, is found eternally recorded.[xxxvi]

Rather than a vagina, labia, and clitoris, "I" have a fully developed penis and atrophic scrotum.

But after studying my own disposition with a good degree of diligence, "I" am satisfied that the motives and desires which rule in my breast are, indeed, "past all finding out."

THE SUBJECT

If any personal description of me is thought desirable, it may be said I am, in height, six feet, four inches, nearly; lean in flesh, weighing on an average of one hundred and eighty pounds; dark complexion, with coarse black hair and grey eyes. No other marks or brands recollected.[xxxvii]

This kind of obsessive project of mine…is one of the things I don't finish. It's a rather intractable set of puzzles and interests for me that take on further various different shapes. What I am trying to do is understand how history informs theory and also how theory informs history. In some ways it's an unhappy shape. I don't try to reconcile history and theory and understand that this may be untidy.[xxxviii]

"Enjoy it as it deserves," I should say to him; "take possession of it, explore it to its utmost extent, reveal it, rejoice in it … If you must indulge in conclusions let them have the taste of a wide knowledge. Remember that your first duty is to be as complete as possible—to make as perfect a work. Be generous and delicate, and then, in the vulgar phrase, go in!"[xxxix]

Mine is the best picture of me one ever saw. It has a little more independence than the others, at least, a stiffer head or neck. It may be a prettier picture, but it does not show my heart so well.

It isn't steady. It's a pulse.

This is not, on reaching its end, simply an observer's story. From the first days of dawning individuality, "I" have longed unceasingly to make pictures of people… to make likenesses that are biographies… free play to the politically educated eye, under whose gaze all intimacies are sacrificed to the illumination of detail. The cleverer "I" am at miniaturizing the world, the better "I" possess it.

He was known for endlessly fracturing
narratives and for stem-winding sentences
adorned with footnotes that were
themselves stem-winders.
– David Foster Wallace [xl]

End- and Bibliographical Notes:

i. "The Little King," *Time Magazine*, Monday, Dec. 12, 1955. Online: http://www. time.com/time/magazine/article/0,9171,711904,00.html#ixzz0nuyCWZQ8.

ii. Howard Bryant, author, in an email to the author.

iii. Wordsworth, William. *The Prelude*, Book I, 16-18, quoted in *The Flesh of Words, The Politics of the Poem*, p. 15.

iv. John Adams quoted in McCullough, David. *John Adams*. Simon & Schuster. 2001.

v. Parry, Eugenia. "The Great Pretender." Online: http://www.davidlevinthal.com/ article_Stranger.html.

vi. Bachelard, Gaston. *The Poetics of Space: The Classic Look at How We Experience Intimate Places*, Beacon Press, Boston, 1994.

vii. Baudelaire, Charles. "A Philosophy of Toys," *The Painter of Modern Life and Other Essays*, translated and edited by Jonathan Mayne (London: Phaidon Press, 1964), p. 199. Quoted in Parry, Eugenia. "The Great Pretender." Online: http://www.davidlevinthal.com/article_Stranger.html.

viii. Venn, Couze. "A Note on Assemblage." *Theory Culture Society* 2006; 23; 107. "Translator's Forward," xiii. Downloaded from http://tcs.sagepub.com at Univ of Auckland Library on May 3, 2010.

ix. James, Henry. "The Art of Fiction." Published in *Longman's Magazine* 4 (September 1884) and reprinted in *Partial Portraits* (Macmillan, 1888).

x. Bachelard, Gaston. *The Poetics of Space: The Classic Look at How We Experience Intimate Places*, Beacon Press, Boston, 1994.

It was probably in an adjustment of her symbolic helmet that "the Explorer" called herself to order, took up again the severe discipline of her work, and returned to her note-taking.

The explorer is an "I," and her sensibility makes her authentic. Her voice is rich, soft, pitched at an alto level. She builds on the words of Clarice Lispector, Bernice L. Hausman, Vanessa Place, Louise Bourgeois, Eudora Welty, Betelhem Makonnen, Gregory Crewdson, Andrew Jackson, William Harrison, John Adams, Rutherford B. Hayes, and Leo Tolstoy.

xi. Bachelard, Gaston. "The 'Cogito' of the Dreamer," in *The Poetics of Reverie, Childhood, Language, and the Cosmos,* translated from the French by Daniel Russell (Boston: Beacon Press, 1971), 166. Bachelard is quoting an unnamed German author.

xii. Parry, Eugenia. "The Great Pretender." Online: http://www.davidlevinthal. com/article_Stranger.html She adds this note: "... the history of Marx toys and play sets, is offered, newsreel fashion, as if to imitate, in writing, the postmodernist media blitz that shaped Levinthal into the deft media-blitz manipulator that he is."

xiii. Sandburg, Carl. *Lincoln Collector.* Harcourt, Brace and Company, Inc. 1949. p. xv.

xiv. Lowell, Robert. "Epilogue." Quoted in Shields, David. *Reality Hunger: A Manifesto,* Knopf, February 2010, #138.

xv. Benjamin, Walter. "Little History of Photography." *Selected Writings* Vol 2 1927-1934. Trans. Rodney Livingstone and Others. Ed. Michael W. Jennings, Howard Eiland, and Gary Smith.

xvi. Voss, Fredrick. *Portraits of the Presidents: from the National Portrait Gallery.* Rizzoli International Publications Inc, NY 2007.

xvii. Lethem, Jonathan. "The ecstasy of influence: A plagiarism." *Harper's Magazine,* February 2007. Online: http://harpers.org/archive/2007/02/0081387.

xviii. Parry, Eugenia. "The Great Pretender." Online: http://www.davidlevinthal. com/article_Stranger.html.

xix. Ibid. Parry, Eugenia, quoting Walker Evans in a recommendation.

xx. "Identifiable Gestures." *NY ARTS MAGAZINE,* March-April, 2008. Online: http://www.nyartsmagazine.com/index.php?option=com_content&view=a rticle&id=118560:posing&catid=158:curated&Itemid=721.

xxi. Ibid. Lethem, Jonathan, quoting André Breton.

xxii. Ibid. Lethem, Jonathan.

xxiii. Ibid. Venn, Couze. p.19.

xxiv. Ibid. Parry, Eugenia. "The Great Pretender." *According to American collector Alex Shear, "If you want an evocative depiction of our culture at this stage in our history...*

My words are always to be taken cautiously. They usually describe a literary side issue. Just the same, "I" must say what "I" feel.

don't go to an art museum—look in your refrigerator." See David Owen's profile of Shear, "The Sultan of Stuff," New Yorker, July 19, 1999, 61. Gathered for over thirty-five years, among Shear's holdings, in "more than twelve hundred categories," are "'station-wagon memorabilia,' 'folk-art roller skate carrying cases,' 'generator flashlights,' and occupational hats.'" David Levinthal's extensive collections of models, toys, etc., often determine what he photographs. The amassment, while nowhere as vast as Shear's, relates to a similar obsession, as Owen observes, "to give a recognizable shape to a yearning that wasn't fully comprehensible even to him."

xxv. Former first lady Rosalynn Carter interviewing Josh Wolf Shenk about his book *Lincoln's Melancholy*, Book TV, CSPAN 2 27 January, 2009. Online: http://www.youtube.com/watch?v=cgb9JrrwEMw.

xxvi. Ibid. Sandburg, Carl.

xxvii. Flaherty, Joseph. "George Washington: Father of the Maker Movement." September 29, 2008. Online: http://replicatorinc.com/blog/2008/09/george-washington-father-of-the-maker-movement/.

xxviii. Pontlis, J.B. "Michel Leiris ou la psychanalyse interminable" in *Les Temps Modernes*, (December 1955): 931, quoted in Gaston Bachelard, *The Poetics of Space: The Classic Look at How We Experience Intimate Places*. Beacon Press, Boston, 1994.

xxix. Ibid. Venn, Couze, p. 19.

xxx. Ibid. Venn, Couze. p. 4.

xxxi. Ibid. Lethem, Jonathan, quoting John Donne from Meditation 17 in *Devotions upon Emergent Occasions*.

xxxii. Vidal, Gore. *Burr*, as quoted in Harris, Stephen. "Gore Vidal's Historical Novels and the Shaping of American Political Consciousness." Online: http://www.mellenpress.com/mellen press.cfm?bookid=6516&pc=9.

xxxiii. Shields, David. *Reality Hunger: A Manifesto*. Knopf, February 2010 #35
Note: 1 *Similar in conceit to Tall, Slim & Erect: "Reality Hunger is made of 600-odd numbered fragments, many of them quotations from other sources, some from Shields's own books, but none properly sourced—the project being not a treasure hunt or a con but a good-faith presentation of what literature might look like if it caught up to contemporary strategies and devices used in the other arts, and allowed for samples (that is, quotation from art and from the world) to revivify existing forms." –Sarah Manguso Online: http://www.amazon.com/Reality-Hunger-Manifesto-David-Shields/dp/0307273539.*

The images come to me when "I" am swimming.

xxxiv. Ibid. #51.

xxxv. James, Henry. "The Art of Fiction." Published in *Longman's Magazine* 4 (September 1884), and reprinted in *Partial Portraits* (Macmillan, 1888).

xxxvi. Schwob, Marcel. "Preface." *Imaginary Lives* (Vies imaginaires, 1896).

Note: 2 *"Marcel Schwob (1867–1905) was one of the key symbolist writers, standing in French literature alongside such names as Stéphane Mallarmé, Octave Mirbeau, André Gide, Léon Bloy, Jules Renard, Rémy de Gourmont, and Alfred Jarry. His best-known works are Double Heart (1891), The King In The Gold Mask (1892), and Imaginary Lives (1896). In Imaginary Lives, Schwob has created a "secret" masterpiece that joins other biographical glossaries such as Jorge Luis Borges' A Universal History Of Infamy and Alfonso Reyes' Real And Imagined Portraits in the pantheon of classic speculative fiction, of which Schwob's book is the dark progenitor." http://www.solarbooks.org/solar%20titles/imaginarylives.html.*

Note: 3 *Lorenzo Semple, Jr., a friend in Los Angeles, loaned me his 1914 copy of Marcel Schwob's Imaginary Lives. He said it reminded him of the tone of Tall, Slim, & Erect. I have to agree the resemblance is uncanny.*

xxvii. Abraham Lincoln in a letter.

Note: 4 *He was well meaning, but his sense of entitlement was taller.*

xxxviii. "Playwright Jane Taylor on Sincerity." The Vera List Center for Art and Politics, The New School. Fora TV. Online: http://fora.tv/2009/05/13/Playwright_Jane_Taylor_on_Sincerity#fullprogram.

xxxix. James, Henry. "The Art of Fiction." Published in *Longman's Magazine* 4 (September 1884), and reprinted in *Partial Portraits* (Macmillan, 1888).

xl. Max, D.T. "The Unfinished." Life and Letters, *The New Yorker*, September 3, 2009. Online: http://www.newyorker.com/reporting/2009/03/09/090309fa_fact_max?currentPage=2#ixzz0oDwhFymf.

Note: 5 *Often fragments of text magically appear like gifts. And there in front of me is this great pair of sentences describing exactly what I attempt to do in my work. So what if it's not about me, and the pronoun used is "he," does it really matter?*

Thus ends this long dry chapter on self.

Rio de Janeiro
2010

Material

Casements

Parapet

Tracer

Maneuvers

Recon

07. Surplus

Michael du Plessis / Melissa Buzzeo˙/ Kim Rosenfield
/ Mark Rutkoski / Klaus Killisch / Matias Viegener /
2012

Logistics

SURPLUS: AN INTRODUCTION

Teresa Carmody

The books in the *TrenchArt: Surplus* series are uniformly excessive.

ON THE SUPERIORITY OF ANGLO-AMERICAN LITERATURE BY GILLES DELEUZE

Michael du Plessis

We like to think of the old-fashioned American classics as children's books. Just childishness on our part.

– D. H. Lawrence,
Studies in Classic American Literature, 1

[D. H. Lawrence's] Studies in Classic American Literature attempted for the first time the kind of explication which does not betray the complexity and perilousness of its theme; and in the pages of that little book I found confirmation of my own suspicion that it is duplicity and outrageousness which determine the quality of those American books ordinarily consigned to the children's shelf in the library.

– Leslie A. Fielder,
Love and Death in the American Novel, 14-15

A ritornello? All music, all writing takes that course. It is a conversation with itself.

– Gilles Deleuze,
"On the Superiority of Anglo-American Literature," 54

The highest aim of literature, according to Lawrence, is that Melville finds himself in the middle of the Pacific. One writes always for animals, like Hofmannsthal, but George Jackson wrote from prison. Fitzgerald puts it even better, as Jacques Besse describes him. It is in Michelet, the fine extract.

Thomas Hardy, Melville, Stevenson, Virginia Woolf, Thomas Wolfe, Lawrence, Fitzgerald, Miller, Kerouac.

The highest aim of literature, according to Lawrence, is that going back to the savages made Melville sicker than anything. The highest aim of literature, according to Lawrence, is that Georges Bataille is a very French author. It is in Michelet, the fine extract.

Thomas Hardy, Melville, Stevenson, Virginia Woolf, Thomas Wolfe, Lawrence, Fitzgerald, Miller, Kerouac.

The highest aim of literature, according to Lawrence is that Hofmannsthal (who then adopts an English pseudonym) can no longer write. The same theme appears in Kleist's Penthesilia. Likewise Lenz or Buechner, all the anti-Goethes: Moby Dick, or the Thing or Entity of Lovecraft, terror. Melville finds himself in the middle of the Pacific, but, still, one writes always for animals, like Hofmannsthal.

Lawrence used to say, no, says Lawrence, you are not the little Eskimo going by. As Jacques Besse describes him. As Lewis Carroll says. Fitzgerald puts it even better. Virginia Woolf forbade herself. A distinct successor to Spinoza would say. When Spinoza says. As Carroll says. Fitzgerald puts it even better. What Lawrence says about Whitman's continuous life is well suited to Spinoza: going back to the savages made Melville sicker than anything, a distinct successor to Spinoza would say. This is what Fitzgerald called a true break.

In the manner of Spinoza, Nietzsche, or Lawrence. Lawrence used to say. No, says Lawrence. As Lewis Carroll says. When Spinoza says. Fitzgerald's alcoholism, Lawrence's disillusion, Virginia Woolf's suicide, Kerouac's sad end. Likewise Lenz or Buechner, all the anti-Goethes. That text of Fitzgerald's which is so fine, *The Crack-Up*, says.

Thomas Hardy, Melville, Stevenson, Virginia Woolf, Thomas Wolfe, Lawrence, Fitzgerald, Miller, Kerouac: all the anti-Goethes.

When Lawrence takes up cudgels against Melville, he criticizes him for having taken the voyage. Georges Bataille is a very French author. Miller's problem (like Lawrence). Virginia Woolf forbade herself. Take the pathetic case of Maurice Sachs: this is what Fitzgerald called a true break. That text of Fitzgerald's which is so fine, *The Crack-Up*, says Georges Bataille is a very

French author. Thyestes' terrible feast, incest, and devouring. Or Lewis Carroll's transition.

When Lawrence takes up cudgels against Melville, he criticizes Thyestes' terrible feast, incest, and devouring. Virginia Woolf forbade herself. Lawrence and Miller are considered to be great sexists, any more than Mozart's music imitates birds. The same theme appears in Kleist's Penthesilea. Take as an example the case of Thomas Hardy. Take the pathetic case of Maurice Sachs. As Lewis Carroll says, it always comes down to Blanchot's fine phrase. You should hear qualified critics talking of Kleist's failures, Lawrence's impotence, Kafka's childishness, Carroll's little girls.

Henry James is one of those to have penetrated most deeply, when Lawrence takes up cudgels against Melville. Did it need Virginia Woolf's anorexia? Take as an example the case of Thomas Hardy.

Fitzgerald's alcoholism, Lawrence's disillusion, Virginia Woolf's suicide, Kerouac's sad end. Thomas Hardy, Melville, Stevenson, Virginia Woolf, Thomas Wolfe, Lawrence, Fitzgerald, Miller, Kerouac. Thomas Hardy, Melville, Stevenson, Virginia Woolf, Thomas Wolfe, Lawrence, Fitzgerald, Miller, Kerouac. "The young student of languages" in Wolfson. Fitzgerald's alcoholism, Lawrence's disillusion, Virginia Woolf's suicide, Kerouac's sad end.

When Spinoza says. As Virilio says. Kleist appalled the Germans. Fitzgerald puts it better. Lawrence used to say. Or Lewis Carroll's transition. Virginia Woolf and her gift, more important, more insinuating than Kerouac's *The Underground One*. More important, more insinuating that Kerouac's *The Underground One*, Fitzgerald's alcoholism, Lawrence's disillusion, Virginia Woolf's suicide, Kerouac's sad end.

If there is a Kafkaesque world, there is not a single play on words in Lewis Carroll. More clearly than Kafka, apart from Sartre, of what is Captain Ahab in Melville guilty? Kleist was one of those authors. If there is a Kafkaesque world, in Hume, there are ideas. Why write about Spinoza? Whence the force of Spinoza's question: of what is Captain Ahab in Melville guilty? The great scene of drunkenness on pure water in Henry Miller.

Drunkenness on pure water in Henry Miller, and Kerouac's phrases are as sober as Synge's AND. A famous text of Renan says this without irony: drunkenness on pure water in Henry Miller. If there is a Kafkaesque world, Shakespeare put on the stage many trickster-kings. Lawrence has the tortoise-becoming, in his admirable poems. Why write about Spinoza? Lawrence criticized French literature for being incurably intellectual. Lawrence used to say. As Virilio says. Fitzgerald puts it better. When Spinoza says. Thomas Hardy, Melville, Stevenson, Virginia Woolf, Thomas Wolfe, Lawrence, Fitzgerald, Miller, Kerouac.

The highest aim of literature, according to Lawrence, is motor agitation and inertia: Kleist. Lovecraft's Thing or Entity, apart from Sartre. Or the heath-phrase, the heath-line of Thomas Hardy: Kleist: from Beckett back to Chrétien de Troyes, from Lawrence to Lancelot, passing through the whole history of the English and American novel. Melville's mariner becomes albatross. Or else Miller's grass-becoming, what he calls a complete "Hume-assemblage," which takes the most varied figures: the most important philosopher in France, Jean Wahl. It is in Michelet, the fine extract.

Spinoza never ceases to be amazed by Spinoza's famous first principle: there is a Spinoza-assemblage. Spinoza, the man of encounters and becoming, the philosopher with the tick, Spinoza the imperceptible. A distinct successor to Spinoza would say when Spinoza says. Or else Miller's grass-becoming. Becoming an entity, an infinitive, as Lovecraft spoke of it, the horrific and luminous story of Carter: the highest aim of literature, according to Lawrence. Spinoza never ceases to be amazed.

The role which Louis de Broglie had in physics: "the young soldier" who leaps up and flees and sees himself leap up and flee in Stephen Crane's book. Proust-humour versus Gide-irony, etc. Henry James is one of those to have penetrated most deeply the "catastrophe" event studied by the mathematician René Thom.

There is not a single play on words in Lewis Carroll. Chrétien de Troyes constantly traced the line, as Lovecraft spoke of it. Proust-humour versus Gide-irony, etc. Leap up and flee in Stephan Crane's book: a famous text of Renan says this without irony. Chrétien de Troyes constantly traced the line.

Works Cited:

Deleuze, Gilles. "On the Superiority of Anglo-American Literature." In *Dialogues II*. By Deleuze and Claire Parnet. Translated by Hugh Tomlinson and Barbara Habberjam. 1977; New York: Columbia University Press, 1987. 36-76.

Derrida, Jacques. *Limited Inc*. Translated by Samuel Weber and Jeffrey Mehlman. 1972; 1977; Evanston, Illinois: Northwest University Press, 1988.

Lawrence, D. H. *Studies in Classic American Literature*. 1924; London: Mercury Books, 1965.

Fiedler, Leslie A. *Love and Death in the American Novel*. Revised edition. 1966; Harmondsworth, Middlesex: Penguin, 1982.

Mallarmé, Stéphane. *Mallarmé. (The Penguin Poets)*. Introduced and edited, with plain prose translations, by Anthony Hartley. Harmondsworth, Middlesex: Penguin, 1965.

Author's Note:

This piece was generated by selecting from the English translation of Gilles Deleuze's essay, "On the Superiority of Anglo-American Literature," some 75 of the phrases and sentences in which the proper name of an author (even where that author is a musician, philosopher, or scientist) appears. All the immediate verbal contexts are verbatim, albeit somewhat truncated. These 75 author-name phrases were then recombined to form the present text.

I hope I may be forgiven the obviousness of stating that my book, as I imagine is plain for all to read, is only about the singular power of the proper name, a singularity that depends, paradoxically, upon what Jacques Derrida has called iterability, its necessary repeatability. And since the proper name also serves as inscription, marker, and signature of and for style and milieu, my book (and indeed my work) constitutes an investigation into notions of "styles" and "milieux." To put it another way, Stéphane Mallarmé observed with admirably lucid self-reflexivity, "Ma Pensée s'est pensée," "my Thought thought itself" (in his letter to Cazalis, 14 May 1867, Mallarmé, p. xvi). I would translate Mallarmé's words in this context as, "My Conceptualism self-conceptualized itself." My work is, I hope, a contribution, in other words, to a self-reflexive conceptualism, a conceptualism that may as yet be a conceptualism to come.

Los Angeles
2011

AN ELEGY FOR PASSAGE: FOR WANT AND SOUND

Melissa Buzzeo

Under the open sky in a countryside in which nothing remained unchanged but the clouds and beneath these clouds, in a field of force of destructive torrents and explosions, was the tiny, fragile, human body.

– Walter Benjamin

Body weight (History):

In the 1980s and into the beginning of the next decade a series of ritual abuse cases were tried all over the country in the American suburbs. Preschool teachers, daycare workers often young often queer often poor always naked in some kind of marked cultural way were accused of ritualistic repeated assault. Sexual assault of the most fantastical kind of rings of children. Hidden doors, trap doors, costumes. Red lips and desire. Clowns and knives that left no trace. Another land. Elaborate patterns. Centuries entwined. Where was this other land, what was it made of. Of what languages or of what non-languages. At what place did desire meet erasure. Is this where the knife touched?

The children were asked: Is this where the knife touched? How does one ask this of text?

There was no trace. There were no marked physical tracings. All the convictions often ending in life sentences were made solely on the testimony of children under hypnosis. Hypnosis: a pleasurable space a space of corrosion or healing. Trance. A rent screen, a room.

Hélène Cixous: *It is when one has been able to reach the moment of opening oneself completely to the other that the scene of the other, which is more specifically the scene of history, will be able to take place in a very vast way.*

All the languages that made testimony possible. In these children who were learning to speak. In these adults who had no recourse towards want.

There are records twenty years later that sometimes the police visited a single child's house eighty times and hypnotized them eighty times reading a script of another child's abuse before getting a testimony and giving the child relief and often a badge.

Language doesn't come from nothing.

Where did this come from?

Where did we come from? But nobody can ask this in speech. The ground will give way. The court will collapse. The language of the court the new language of this new country would then be severed from speech. In all these suburbs in all these immigrant households all these people would just have their bodies to contend with.

And the sound.

The Sound:

The body of water surrounding Long Island and separating it on one side from the states of Connecticut and Rhode Island. Once heavily populated by Native Americans, this peninsula culture formed by a glacial moraine was colonized early by the Dutch and then the British and infiltrated in the early- and mid-20th century by a surge of mostly second generation immigrants, desiring separation from the city.

In the 1980s the immigrant families who populated Long Island were the children of Levittown. Baby boomers from all over Europe. Broken languages erased and processed by row houses. Jewish Italian Armenian. The bombs were over. The camps were over. There were no more riots in the streets. The names had been processed changed turned over. As the asparagus farms had given way to square front yards. Shorn. The Native American town names subsumed in museums. A localness that pervaded hunger. The foreignness given to whom to what?

In the book it says to language.

And the shame?

And the grief?

And the bodies unadorned?

Who courted this?

(I opened my mouth, I rushed toward story.)

More and more I became interested in the bodies pressed into history supported and undone by narrative. What happens when "one stands mute" *peine forte et dure* what crushing what pressing what clutching what erasures. What suffocations. What the stones stand to mark.

The narrative dissolving in text.

What seductions of text. What allowance for ethics entreaties.

Community:

The fanatical rage. The gestures forward. The categories. The boxes the separations. The real tears the real grief. What is real. An I that is understood? Finally we are given space to grieve to fear to want. To the bed that got larger and larger. The courthouses were packed. A shadow that obfuscated love. What can be saved. What can be protected. The men at the head of the household. The women at the center of the household. The chaste kisses written large. The insecurities dead in wars. The abuses handed over in caravans. The bodies becoming smaller and smaller dissolving into the shadow that moved suddenly with ferocious attachment. Subsuming stasis. Straddling charge.

Like wildfire it was said the spread. Through all the staked places.

Is this passion? Or a document of love.

Alphonso Lingis: *A community of decision, of initiative, of absolute initiality but also a threatened community in which the question has not yet found the language it has decided to seek is not yet sure of its own possibility within the community. A community of the question about the possibility of question.*

What reports were given.

What reports were taken.

What bodies were offered as sacrifice for language. As a scar to the collective body of language. For the privilege to speak something charged and choking. To invade the image. To escape the image. To be heard to be watched to be put away. What happens to generational trauma. What happens to erasure as it starts to build? As it becomes cities and houses and bodies and constructs. As the soil becomes depleted and the nation agrees to war.

Who doesn't want to be a writer?

All these voices of the court finally counting. And to be given a sentence for your body. For the unspeakable within your body. What communication can finally become. To say so loudly so fiercely—I want. In a language not your own. To be subsumed. To be taken. The one book held shut.

Broken Narratives and the Distribution of Weight:

Twenty years later many of these children have come forward and recounted with sorrow. Not surprisingly the feeling was not foreign to them only the words. Many years later it has been found that some of the "predators" gave false testimony. What of language does shame make. What shame does language carry. Almost all these cases have been overturned. A generation later with new scientific methods the court narrative has been found to have been physically impossible. To have happened. And yet the call to seduction still written there. Twenty years later the prison doors open and the prisoners long for the one book. The family that betrayed them. The culture that was contaminated. The one book held shut.

Twenty years later it is found that The Sound is contaminated and might be why breast cancer is rampant on Long Island affecting all classes all races all languages.

People still swim there.

My text is flooded in this contamination. (I want to say this compassion but cannot.) This default water. Some days I watched it seep. Spread.

Outside:

In the writing of *For Want and Sound* which spanned three years which saw the production of three other books categories collapsed. The boundarylessness in language which had been the content became the form. Every book had lines to give my book. Millions of books forgotten. Millions of books too open, too closed. The notebooks illegible, the longing gone on too long. The books did not want to give did not want to take. Everything subsumed in Sound. And for what—to open or close. I wanted to finish. The book which had become everything outside of language and so inside of me. With no door, no passage no promise of return. I was also afraid of utter loss, the license the completion of this book would create. I wanted to stay. In unreloved relation to the one book. When longing had come to abbreviate. *That it was more than me and less than my love for it.* This sentence was more and more real. More and more the privatized prison of relinquish.

There would be no more other books. I knew this.

Outside: a book about particular aspects of American culture. A book informed by continental philosophy by experimental film by architecture and testimony writing. Cross-genre writing.

A book in mirror of itself.

The incest we held on our tongues.

Outside: The other book. *L'injure* by Nathalie Stephens. Written in another language. One that I could not read. From another culture, another country. From another person a person who had stepped across a border. I had this book about non escape in my house and did not read it.

Outside in the next century we sat in the park in the middle of my country. Far away from The Sound.

Outside we tried to collect being. I thought is that what a book is?

L'injure and the non reading around it gave me an outside a door on which to bang and close. An outside, an address.

Foreign irreducible. I could touch it but could not enter it. Is this what a book is? Its capacity, liminal for encounter.

I traced the weaving narratives about the book. In my own language. I heard how the writer could not finish a text that enacted itself and so constructed an outside. Took a door from elsewhere. Shook a form. Forced a door to the text. Made commentary possible. Limit freedoms erasing neither. In writing the impossibility I imagined the reading of a book that could not be read.

The non passage. The presence. The parlance finally into text.

From book to book from near book to near book we skip the sentence.

Wanting very much to find the absence buried in presence.

Maybe encounter with *L'injure* was also to me the unearthing of all the other languages, the non erasure. The Levinasian Face grafted to text. Not without pain. Not without sorrow.

Finally I read my unreadable book. Separate from me.

Slowly and then very rapidly the culture moves away from itself. The writer begins. The Sound left the text. The text found a form. The body broke off.

Before leaving.

The Two Books:

For Want and Sound became finally the uneasy cohesion between two books. Part One is simply called *Book* and is comprised of a series of testimony statements in and out of language.

Part Two *Breach, Recoil* is a space of commentary or the commentary of an outside made possible.

In this way an inside was finally constructed and named.

Shredded from leaves floorboards paint and partitions the book finally became itself taking its form from some makeshift scrapbook some baby book. Some document ledger buried in the ground to survive destruction.

When I unbury it I notice the dirt the crumble. The places where the pages won't detach. The parts that come with leaves.

Brooklyn
2011

SCREAMO

Kim Rosenfield

Lately
I've noticed
How everyone
Keeps asking
The same
Questions.

Or they
Keep asking
Dumb
Questions.

Well
This is
The answer
To everyone's
Questions.

I started working on the idea in 1993. We
wanted a name that was bold. And
unused. Where everybody had names with
corpses, maggots, and death...
So we went through medical books and looked
at definitions and LIVIDITY stood out to me.
I have never looked back on changing that!!
It fit the thought and theory best as to what
death and brutality meant to me!!

When the body quits living
And the blood pools up at the lowest point of
your body
And rigor mortis sets in—
It gets brutal, like poetry in motion!!

Conceiving
        (as in child or demon birth).
Ingesting
        (as in dealing with the inside stomach area).

Some fucked up
Demon-child
Coming out of
The intestinal tract
Devouring the mother
From within.
Making a total mess of things.

VOCAL FRY
FALSE CHORDS
DEATH SCREAM

Breeeeeeeeee
Borrrrrrrrrrrrrrr

What better way to document the most extreme
aspects—the horrors, the chaos, the darkest
corners—of the human experience, than with
Guttural Growl? Harsh vocals are fitting for harsh
subject matters, but they're not so fitting for your
vocal chords. Learn the proper technique so death
can be something your voice communicates, not
something your voice experiences.

Adding Vocal Fry to Yell:
First off, the more inhaled-sounding Guttural that is actually an exhale
is a more closed throat Guttural closer to a Growl than an actual Guttural
You need to control air at lower velocities.

If you already have a firm understanding of the inhale style
you can take the same throat flexing point that
you utilize while breathing in
and apply it to Exhale Guts.

Others believe
that it's completely diaphragm/exhale air
through the nose
when you do High Screams.

Make gargle sounds
Shriek
Scream
Hum
Zzzzz, ssssss, breeeee, borrrrr

Whatever.

Metal, Death Metal, Black Metal, and Grindcore Vocals are all derived from the same thing, perseverance. In order to build up your vocal abilities at all you must dedicate yourself to them, work hard on them, and in the end you'll be surprised at what you can do. And don't even stop, you may think your vocals may sound good, or all right, but they can always get better.

Inhales
Are still
What I do best
But they aren't the pinnacles
Of Metal Vocalism.

My Inhaled Gutturals
Sound like something
Out of a dinosaur's
Irritated colon
After he ate
A spicy meal
A.k.a. "bad."

I'm hoping

To one day
Achieve
A Guttural sound
Like that of
Abominable Putridity

Warm up your voice before recording
or performing Death Metal.

Gutterals:
Gutturals are a base in Death Metal and Grindcore, and some Melodic
Black Metal. Gutturals are simply a low airy resonating sound projected
with the diaphragm.

Leave your throat completely open, push the air with the diaphragm, it
should resonate in the throat, and then come out through your mouth.
Your mouth should be more closed or in an open-O shape to properly
create the Guttural sound. Once you have the sound, you may use your
tongue and mouth to shape the sound into consonants and vowels. If you
press the tongue to the roof of your mouth, you'll get unique sound from
the Guttural, also the positioning of airflow through the mouth, rather then
pushing completely down the middle, try putting the airflow to the roof of
your mouth or the bottom right over the tongue.

You're doing the emo pig gets raped in the ass by horse scream.

The most simple method to find your diaphragm is actually very easy. Just start with a whisper "sssssssss" and slowly get louder until you run out of air <u>completely</u>. You will feel a horizontal muscle behind your abdominal muscles tighten. This is your diaphragm. Once you feel it you will now understand easier how you flex it to your own desire, because the human body is amazing! You can control every muscle in it except for the heart. Once you have control of this diaphragm, then every vocal, from Clean Singing, to heavy Grindcore Vocals are opened up to you!

High Vocals/Rasps:
Some People Believe that Highs come from head voice, while others believe that it's completely diaphragm, but as I've learned over the years, it's a combination of both. Highs will take the longest to get down perfect, and they will hurt the most on your throat, but you have to give them time. The art of the High Vocal is simple. Start with imitating it through whispers, move up to the head voice, and then throw in the diaphragm. Some people tend to use their nose in the mix, but that's completely up to you. (Just exhale some of the air through the nose when you do high screams to achieve this).

> You may want to avoid "cupping" the microphone with your hands. Many vocalists intentionally use this technique to increase volume during amplification and to make their tone sound lower than it actually is, but this technique is also widely frowned upon by the Death Metal community as being a false enhancement technique. It will also muffle your enunciation and most likely make it more difficult to achieve the level of vocal/tonal clarity you may desire.

Like a Growl you're going to use the diaphragm, however, your throat is going to be extremely closed (depending on how high you want it) and your mouth is going to be wide open. Once you have gotten this down then your Highs will scream evil. Some people shape their Highs with an Animal Growl Technique in order to hit vowels that would normally not work if you just screamed them ex: "errraiii" rather then "raiii". But most important for shaping the High Scream is the throat and the mouth and some tongue. Practice makes perfect, especially for this style.

Inhaled Vocals:

Inhaled Vocals, the most liked and yet hated of vocals. In reality, they are simple to do, yet hard to master. Bands like Cumbest, Cock and Ball Torture, and newer bands like Waking the Cadaver, Annotations Of An Autopsy, all of these bands just use Inhaled Vocals. The art, if you can call it that, of Inhaled Vocals is as simple as the name, just inhale! Close your throat, open it, just experiment! However, you will never have good Inhale Vocals until you can give them enough power to be at least as loud as your speaking voice, and into a microphone, you will more than likely need to cut the microphone or at least get very close to it to even equal your inhale vocals in amplification to your Exhaled Vocals. Opened mouth can create a frog sounding vocal, closed mouth can create a watery sounding vocal, and with the use of the tongue you can manip- ulate it to many many sounds and the infamous Pig Squeal/Bree with the tongue to the roof of the mouth.

Falsetto Screams:

Namely Grindcore Vocals, sometimes Black Metal, used a lot in Power Metal. Imagine screaming like a girl, or shrieking. Just let it out, beyond your range, as high and strange as your vocal power will go. But Falsettos in general are hard to explain. It's just one of those things you have to figure out on your own.

> Harsh Vocals will grow in volume as you gain skill with them and use them correctly.

Yell/Hardcore/Thrash/Screamo Vocals:

A more difficult vocal skill, yet more important because it opens the door to other vocal abilities. First, Yell/Hardcore Vocals. Ever listen to bands like Hatebreed, or Bury Your Dead? Maybe even Metalcore bands like As I Lay Dying use this skill to some extent. Thrash bands, who yell or shout. And Screamo bands (real Screamo, mind you, not this popular bullshit that's going around calling itself Screamo) who scream at the top of their lungs with emotion and angst.

All of these have something in common, it's called diaphragm + voice projection. Stand back, release your power, shout, scream, flex your body to get more out, but use the diaphragm. You won't need much throat or mouth, so don't worry about that right now, just try to imitate your favorite band of this genre, and you'll start to get it.

Good slow practice songs with Death Metal Vocals:
"Death Walking Terror" by Cannibal Corpse, "Festering in the Crypt" by Cannibal Corpse, "I Cum Blood" by Cannibal Corpse, "The Jealous Sun" by November's Doom, "Sarcophogus" by Nile.

Good fast practice songs with normal vocals:
"Aggressive Perfector" by Slayer, "Dittohead" by Slayer, "Jesus Saves" by Slayer, "Necrophobic" by Slayer.

Good fast practice songs with Death Metal Vocals:
"Disposal of the Body" by Cannibal Corpse, "Homage to Satan" by Deicide, "Post Mortal Ejaculation" by Cannibal Corpse, "The Exorcist" by Possessed, "The Optimist" by Skinless, "4:20" by Six Feet Under, "Stabwound" by Necrophagist, "Egypt, the Red Earth" by Necronomicon, "Buried By the Dead" by Bloodbath, "Sick Salvation" by Bloodbath, "Prometherion" by Behemoth, "Scrolls of the Megilloth" by Mortification, "Demon of the Fall" by Opeth, "What Can Be Safely Written" by Nile.

Growls:

Growls are a combination between Yell/Hardcore Vocals and Gutturals. Using your diaphragm, start with a Guttural, open the mouth, and close the throat slightly, but not too much. And it's as simple as that. Practice makes perfect. That's what creating is all about—blowing even your own mind!!!

> Prepare for some raised eyebrows and harsh criticism when showing friends or family your unique style of singing. Some people don't consider Death Metal singing to be real singing at all.

I can inhale click easily
(But I hear
That it's hell
On the vocal chords)
But I still don't understand
How the guys in
Malodorous
And Abominable Putridity
Can do that
Going out
The muscular control involved
Eludes me.

Maybe I'm just a mutant
And cannot control
The certain muscles
In my throat
That would allow for
Such a gurgling
Yet sharply clicking
Guttural.

Any suggestions
On how to produce
Such a vomitous sound?

I asked the vocalist
Of Malodorous
(And like 30 other bands)
For any tips.

He offered me
This less-than-intelligent
Advice:

"Dude
You just gotta
Sound like
An angry monster."
:Roll eyes:

Oh, is that all?
I must go
On an expedition
To piss off
Some monsters
Brandishing
My Sony
Field Recorder.

How would you
Recommend
I go about angering
Said monsters?
A sharp stick
Perhaps?

Maybe
I could make fun of
The monsters' love
For sub-par
Deathcore
Breakdowns!

In all seriousness
Though
If you have
Any
Helpful advice
On how to
Add
That clicking sound
To a low gut
I would greatly
Appreciate it.

New York City
2011

Postscript:

"SCREAMO" is a companion piece to *Lividity*. The term "lividity" is meant forensically, as in where blood pools in the body to determine the how and if and why of a murder or death. Lividity is also the name of a Brutal Death Metal band out of Decatur, Illinois. So *Lividity* (the Les Figues Book) deals with the brutality of language and who speaks, who is silenced, and how language can fail or degrade ideas of humanness. So does "SCREAMO," which speaks to these ideas of language vis-à-vis online death metal singing tutorials and questions from aspiring death metal singers. Omnipotence via language and sound as a defense against colonizing or invading the other. Or against a wound that can never heal. Language is a carrier of the depressive register or can sometimes even carry a dead body inside it. Rock on!

New York City
2014

PAS DE DEUX

Mark Rutkoski

A pas de deux of a poet and the Other, or a word and its context, or an author and the reader, or an artist and the spectator, or a text and its translation. A text as raw material—sorted and stacked, or woven.

The *Le* **Creative** *Processus* **Act** *créatif*
by par **Marcel** Marcel **Duchamp** Duchamp[1]

Let Considérons **us** d'abord **consider** deux **two** facteurs **important** importants, **factors,** les **the** deux **two** pôles **poles** de **of** toute **the** création **creation** d'ordre **of** artistique: **art:** d'un **the** côté **artist** l'artiste, **on** de **one** l'autre **hand,** le **and** spectateur **on** qui, **the** avec **other** le **the** temps, **spectator** devient **who** la **later** postérité. **becomes** Selon **the** toutes **posterity.**

To apparences, **all** l'artiste **appearances,** agit **the** à **artist** la **acts** façon **like** d'un **a** être **mediumistic** médiumnique **being** qui, **who,** du **from** labyrinthe **the** par-delà **labyrinth** le **beyond** temps **time** et **and** l'espace, **space,** cherche **seeks** son **his** chemin **way** vers **out** une **to** clairière. **a** Si **clearing.**

If donc **we** nous **give** accordons **the** les **attributes** attributs **of** d'un **a** médium **medium** à **to** l'artiste, **the** nous **artist,** devons **we** alors **must** lui **then** refuser **deny** la **him** faculté **the** d'être **state** pleinement **of** conscient, **consciousness**

---

1. *The Creative Act* was a speech given by Marcel Duchamp at the American Federation of Arts conference in Houston, Texas, in 1957. It was published in *Artnews*, vol. 56, no. 4, Summer 1957. The French translation is by Duchamp and was reprinted in a bilingual edition as *Le Processus créatif* by L'Échoppe, Paris, in 1987.

sur **on** le **the** plan **esthetic** esthétique, **plane** de **about** ce **what** qu'il **he** fait **is** ou **doing** pourquoi **or** il **why** le **he** fait—**is** toutes **doing** ses **it.**

All décisions **his** dans **decisions** l'exécution **in** artistique **the** de **artistic** l'oeuvre **execution** restent **of** dans **the** le **work** domaine **rest** de **with** l'intuition **pure** et **intuition** ne **and** peuvent **cannot** être **be** traduities **trans-lated** en **into** une **a** self-analyse, **self-analysis,** parlée **spoken** ou **or** écrite **written,** ou **or** même **even** pensée. **thought** T.S. **out.**

T.S. Eliot, **Eliot,** dans **in** son **his** essai **essay** *Tradition* **on** *and* **Tradition** *individual* **and** *talent,* **individual** écrit: *talent,* «L'artiste **writes:** sera "The d'autant **more** plus **perfect** parfait **the** que **artist,** seront **the** plus **more** complètement **completely** séparés **separate** en **in** lui **him** l'homme **will** qui **be** souffre **the** et **man** l'esprit **who** qui **suffers** crée; **and** et **the** d'autant **mind** plus **which** parfaitement **creates;** l'esprit **the** digérera **more** et **perfectly** transmuera **will** les **the** passions **mind** qui **digest** sont **and** son **translate** élément». **the** Des **passions** millions **which** d'artistes **are** créent, **its** quelques **material."**

Millions milliers **of** seulement **artists** sont **create;** discutés **only** ou a **accepted** few par **thousands** le **are** spectateur **discussed** et **or** moins **accepted** encore **by** sont **the** consacrés **spectator** par **and** la **many** postérité. **less** En **again** dernière **are** analyse, **consecrated** l'artiste **by** peut **posterity.**

In crier **the** sur **last** tous **analysis,** les **the** toits **artist** qu'il **may** a **shout** du **from** génie, **all** il **the** devra **rooftops** attendre **that** le **he** verdict **is** du **a** spectateur **genius;** pour **he** que **will** ses **have** déclarations **to** prennent **wait** une **for** valeur **the** sociale **verdict** et **of** que **the** finalement **spectator** la **in** postérité **order** le **that** cite **his** dans **declarations** les **take** manuels **a** d'histoire **social** de **value** l'art. **and** Je **that,** sais **finally,** que **posterity** cette **includes** vue **him** n'aura **in** pas **the** l'approbation **primers** de **of** nombreux **Art** artistes **History.**

I qui **know** refusent **that** ce **this** rôle **statement** mediumnique **will** et **not** insistent **meet** sur **with** la **the** validité **approval** de **of** leur **many** pleine **artists** conscience **who** pendant **refuse** l'acte **this** de **mediumistic** création—**role** et **and** cependant **insist** l'histoire **on** de **the** l'art, **validity** à **of** maintes **their** reprises, **awareness** a **in** basé **the** les **creative** vertus **act**—d'une **yet**

oeuvre **art** sur **history** des **has** considérations **consistently** complètement **decided** indépendantes **upon** des **the** explications **virtues** rationnelles **of** de **a** l'artiste. **work** Si **of** l'artiste, **art** en **through** tant **considerations** qu'être **completely** humain **divorced** plein **from** des **the** meilleures **rationalized** intentions **explanations** envers **of** lui-même **the** et **artist.**

If le **the** monde **artist,** entier, **as** ne **a** joue **human** aucun **being,** rôle **full** dans **of** le **the** jugement **best** de **intentions** son **toward** oeuvre, **himself** comment **and** peut-on **the** décrire **whole** le **world,** phénomène **plays** qui **no** amène **role** le **at** spectateur **all** à **in** réagir **the** devant **judgment** l'oeuvre **of** d'art? **his** En **own** d'autres **work,** termes, **how** comment **can** cette **one** réaction **describe** se **the** produit-elle? **phenomenon** Ce **which** phénomène **prompts** peut **the** être **spectator** comparé **to** à **react** un **critically** « transfert » **to** de **the** l'artiste **work** au **of** spectateur **art?**

In sous **other** la **words** forme **how** d'une **does** osmose **this** esthétique **reaction** qui **come** a **about?**

This lieu **phenomenon** à **is** travers **comparable** la **to** matière **a** inerte: **transference** couleur, **from** piano, **the** marbre, **artist** etc. **to** Mais **the** avant **spectator** d'aller **in** plus **the** loin, **form** je **of** voudrais **an** mettre **esthetic** au **osmosis** clair **taking** notre **place** interprétation **through** du **the** mot **inert** « Art » **matter,** sans, **such** bien **as** entendu, **pigment,** chercher **piano** à **or** le **marble.**

But définir. **before** Je **we** veux **go** dire, **further,** tout **I** simplement, **want** que **to** l'art **clarify** peut **our** être **understanding** bon, **of** mauvais **the** ou **word** indifférent "art"—mais **to** que, **be** quelle **sure,** que **without** soit **an** l'épithète **attempt** employée, **to** nous **a** devons **definition.**

What l'appeler **I** art: **have** un **in** mauvais **mind** art **is** est **that** quand **art** même **may** de **be** l'art **bad,** comme **good** une **or** mauvaise **indifferent,** émotion **but,** est **whatever** encore **adjective** une **is** émotion. **used,** Donc **we** quand **must** plus **call** loin **it** je **art,** parle **and** de **bad** « coefficient **art** d'art », **is** il **still** reste **art** bien **in** entendu **the** que **same** non **way** seulement **as** j'emploie **a** ce **bad** terme **emotion** en **is** relation **still** avec **an** le **emotion.**

Therefore, grand when art, I mais refer aussi to que "art j'essaie coefficient," de it décrire will le be mécanisme understood subjectif that qui I produit refer une not oeuvre only d'art to à great l'état art, brut, but mauvaise, I bonne am ou trying indifférente. to Pendant describe l'acte the de subjective création, mechanism l'artiste which va produces de art l'intention in à a la raw réalisation state en—à passant l'état par brut—une bad, chaîne good de or réactions indifferent.

In totalement the subjectives. creative La act, lutte the vers artist la goes réalisation from est intention une to série realization d'efforts, through de a douleurs, chain de of satisfactions, totally de subjective refus, reactions.

His de struggle décisions toward qui the ne realization peuvent is ni a ne series doivent of être efforts, pleinement pains, conscients, satisfactions, du refusals, moins decisions, sur which le also plan cannot esthétique. and Le must résultat not de be cette fully lutte self-conscious, est at une least différence on entre the l'intention esthetic et plane.

The sa result réalisation, of différence this dont struggle l'artiste is n'est a nullement difference conscient. between En the fait, intention un and chaînon its manque realization, à a la difference chaîne which des the réactions artist qui is accompagnent not l'acte aware de of.

Consequently, création; in cette the coupure chain qui of représente reactions l'impossibilité accompanying pour the l'artiste creative d'exprimer act, complétement a son link intention, is cette missing.

This différence gap entre which ce represents qu'il the avait inability projeté of de the réaliser artist et to ce express qu'il fully a his réalisé intention; est this le difference «coefficient between d'art» what personnel he contenu intended dans to l'oeuvre. realize En and d'autres did termes, realize, le is «coefficient the d'art» personal personnel "art est coefficient" comme contained une in relation the arithmétique work.

In entre other «ce words, qui the est personal inexprimé "art mais coefficient" était is projeté» like et an «ce artithmetrical qui relation est between exprimé the inintentionnellement». unexpressed Pour but éviter intended tout and malentendu, the nous unintentionally devons expressed.

To répéter avoid que a ce misunderstanding, «coefficient we d'art» must est remember une that expression this personnelle "art «d'art coefficient" à is l'état a brut» personal qui expression doit of être art «raffiné» "à par l'état le brut," spectateur, that tout is comme still la in mélasse a et raw le state, sucre which pur. must L'indice be de "refined" ce as coefficient pure n'a sugar aucune from influence molasses, sur by le the verdict spectator.

The du digit spectateur. of Le this processus coefficient créatif has prend no un bearing tout whatsoever autre on aspect this quand verdict.

The le creative spectateur act se takes trouve another en aspect présence when du the phénomène spectator de experiences la the transmutation; phenomenon avec of le transmutation; changement through de the la change matière from inerte inert en matter oeuvre into d'art, a une work véritable of transsubstantiation art, a an lieu actual et transubstantiation le has rôle taken important place, du and spectateur the est role de of déterminer the le spectator poids is de to l'oeuvre determine sur the la weight bascule of esthétique. the Somme work toute, on l'artiste the n'est esthetic pas scale.

All seul in à all, accomplir the l'acte creative de act création is car not le performed spectateur by établit the le artist contact alone; de the l'oeuvre spectator avec brings le the monde work extérieur in en contact déchiffrant with et the en external intreprétant world ses by qualifications deciphering profondes and et interpreting par its là inner ajoute qualifications sa and propre thus contribution adds au his processus contribution créatif. to Cette the contribution creative est act.

This encore becomes plus even évidente more lorsque obvious la when postérité posterity prononce gives son its verdict final définitif verdict et and réhabilite sometimes des rehabilitates artistes forgotten oubliés. artists.

New York City
2011

Postscript: Last Words

The last word of each of the thirteen English *Texts for Nothing* translated from his original French by Samuel Beckett; published by Calder and Boyars Ltd., London, in 1974 (first published in English in *No's Knife* by Calder and Boyars, 1967).

I
play.

II
diversity.

III
them.

IV
be.

V
noted.

VI
word.

VII
begin.

VIII
whose.

IX
again.

X
there.

XI
evening.

XII
words.

XIII
murmurs.

New York City
2014

STILL LIFE ABOUT MY WORK

Klaus Killisch

Berlin
2011

AESTHETIC STATEMENT: WRITING AGAINST MY WILL

Matias Viegener

For about two years I didn't write anything at all. Anything as deliberate as words on a page filled me with misgivings, especially when they piled up into phrases and sentences. I wanted less from myself. It was a time when I was travelling a lot, and by coincidence, I visited many of the places I lived when I was younger. I started finding letters in the world, in the form of rocks, scrap metal, or pieces of wood. They're everywhere, especially O, L, and E, which make Leo, or more excitingly, olé! In Spanish it means something like hooray or bravo, but some etymologists think it's from Arabic and an invocation to Allah.

I found lots of E's, which when spun around could just as well be M's or W's. I'm not sure now if I really found them or was looking to find them, but suddenly they were appearing and I sought them out. After I found a few, I would combine them into possible words, the first of which were *wow* and *mom*, which could also become *woe* or *emo*. These would subsequently be woven into sentences, or rather interpretations infused by where the letters were found and what message they might contain. *Mom* appeared near the house of my early childhood, and *emo* where I spent my adolescence. I thought of this as something between site-specificity and shamanism. A message from beyond!

In "How to Recognize a Poem When You See One," an early essay on reader-response criticism, Stanley Fish describes arriving in a classroom where the readings for the preceding class were listed on the board, just a set of last names: Derring, Rosenbaum, Smith, Thorne, etc. When his students arrived, he told them it was a poem and asked them to explicate it with him. Derring was a dare, manhood, or chivalry, or even a gun, and Smith was slower and more purposeful, like a blacksmith forging through with the task. The Jewish-sounding Rosenbaum was a rosebush, beautiful but with thorns, a challenge to overcome. Since love is like a red, red rose, they concluded it was a love poem, a romance between a Gentile and Jew, with many obstacles and even Old Testament references, which arise through other names on the list that I don't remember.

People are only too willing to create not just meaning but even narrative from bits and pieces, and often the smaller or less directive these bits, the better. There's virtually no boundary between reading and misreading. If you're told it's a poem, you'll see it as one; sometimes even if you're not told. I love humanity for its grim determination to wring meaning from the incidental. It's a pathetic impulse, stuck in its incapacity to just let one bit be. Just letting one word sit still floods people with anxiety. What if it doesn't mean anything? We can't have one thing without another; we can't leave anything alone. One bite of cake tastes good, so we have another. We're gluttons for meaning.

Lists are appealing to me because they have a concrete function without much ornamentation. Princes and paupers make lists because they help get things done. Unlike literature, the list has a tangible purpose. Sometimes the order is significant, a ranking of importance or chronology, but often there's no meaning at all. The list captures the way things came out, one after another, like shots from a rifle. A reading list sometimes tells you the order in which to read, but lots of them are alphabetized, or chronological. When I was young I longed for people to give me reading lists, to tell me what I needed to know, book by book. Instead I figured out what to read through the arrangements of books on the shelves of the bookstore down the street from my house. After that I worked in categories, like nineteenth century Russian novels. If you like Gogol, you'll probably like Dostoyevsky.

Umberto Eco says we like lists because they help us make sense of infinity. Humans have a cheery capacity to endlessly organize and catalogue, collecting things in museums and glass cabinets. Much of culture is about listing, like the list of the 2,063 women Don Giovanni seduced, or how James Joyce describes Leopold Bloom opening his drawers and itemizing what he finds inside them. Narrative description is a kind of literary list-making, often for no other purpose than inventory, or to convey the presence of a real world. It doesn't even need to be the presence of the real, just the presence of something. The classic Dutch still life is a kind of visual list: on this table is a loaf of bread, three oysters, and a lemon. One painting I love has the lemon half-peeled, the peel curling below the table's edge like a flourish or question mark. It's as if to ask why are we here, after all?

Eco says that our desire to control the infinite through lists is filtered through something very finite: our own death. We make lists because we don't want to die. This is a literary commonplace, *ars longa, vita brevis*, but I like it better when applied to something as banal as a list. Part of the list's aesthetic, if you can call it that, is that length doesn't much matter. A list is infinitely expandable. You don't really need to stop, unless it's a list of the ten best piano sonatas. The way to expand that list, though, is to list Beethoven's ten best, and then Schubert's, etc. Theoretically you reach a limit (Scriabin only wrote ten), but practically you can go on forever.

The list as a form is related to the serial, a work of many parallel parts that follow a certain set of constraints or modular principles. Serials are repetitive, but often the repetition is tempered with variation. One of my favorite teaching texts is Joe Brainard's *I Remember,* every sentence of which begins with "I remember." It's a little childish at first, and sentimental, a list of memories and things: objects and bits of his past. Soon it's just too cute. But if you persist in reading, the fabric begins to transform. He talks about growing up, recognizing that he's gay, and coming to terms with his desire. The very phrase "I remember" drops away as you read, and suddenly you are there with him, in his web of associations. You lose the trajectory of sissy boys, pink girl's dresses, and New York poets to find yourself in something resembling a story, but also because of its serial form, something that exceeds narrative. Philosophically it's the move from being to becoming, a concept that dates back to Heraclitus, who said nothing in this world was constant except change (or becoming). Nothing will hold for long and only fools try to freeze time.

Something bigger than Brainard's will, and bigger than the compulsion to tell us he's gay, compels him to speak, or us to listen. Only the rigor of the list could dragoon us like this. He wrote *I Remember* in a world that was just beginning to care to see gay men. For a work that begins in sentiment, there is nothing sentimental at the end but his grim longing. Working in the same period, Sol LeWitt writes that the serial artist "does not attempt to produce a beautiful or mysterious object but functions merely as a clerk cataloguing the results of his premise." I reckon that the warmth and even eroticism of Brainard's book is there by dint of the cold, methodical cataloguing.

One of the recurring features of our lives as they're lived on social media today is the appearance of new memes. You're asked to list your ten favorite writers or fifteen songs that changed your life. I'm usually paralyzed by these demands. Why ten, why fifteen? What exactly does it mean to change your life? And though restrictive, these memes are invasive. If I did hammer out a list of ten writers, what would it say about me if I left off Virginia Woolf, or Gertude Stein? I can't bear that kind of scrutiny—it's too intimate.

Something about the emptiness of a random list of 25 things about myself felt easy, though I was faintly troubled by the arbitrary cut-off. When you finished your list, you were supposed to tag 25 friends and send it to them. They were supposed to read it, learn new things about you, recognize you or not, and then write their own list and send that to 25 more friends. It's like a chain letter, almost as empty and annoying. Everyone can find 25 random things about themselves, and doing so felt far less precarious than a list of favorite artists or foods or philosophers. It's like turning on the vacuum cleaner and sucking in whatever fits through the hose.

As the first week passed, two subjects started to push to the fore: the death of my friend Kathy Acker and the death of my mother. The veterinarian told me my dog, Peggy, had cancer and there weren't many options to help her. A friend from college whom I hadn't seen in many years, Sydni Bender, found me on Facebook and started leaving comments on my daily lists. Sydni herself was fighting cancer, breast cancer, and it had metastasized. Many other people left comments, and of course they also wove their way into what I was thinking. As the months went by, Sydni jokingly accused me of playing out Peggy's illness to get attention. The social conversation—which of course the format invited—inserted itself into me despite my resistance to it.

The minute you intend to be random, you can't do it. You try not to pay attention to it, because your attention is itself a filter: every time you focus on randomness you're being deliberate. John Cage solved this problem by deploying chance operations, with mechanisms like dice or the I Ching to depersonalize the act; he even had computer programmers run a set of random numbers to further distance the operation from his own hand. What isn't removed however is intention: chance hardly comes barging in uninvited. Even the Delphic oracle was not immune to intention. Just entering the room after the oracular leaves settle to the ground disturbs them a bit, so the presence of the observer is never eradicated. It relates back to my uncertainty about finding letters on the ground. Though I was really finding M's and O's in the dirt, was this just happening or was I looking? Was it a way to convince myself the world was really paying attention?

"Indeterminacy," the collection of stories from Cage's *Silence*, are texts Cage used in performance. From a repertoire of about 90 stories he selected one through a chance operation, then another, until he was done. He read each story for one minute, so the long ones were very fast and the short ones were very slow. Most of the stories were things that happened that "stuck in [his] mind," some were told to him by his ex-wife Xenia, or Merce Cunningham, and others he remembered from books by Martin Buber, Joseph Campbell, or Zen philosophers like Kwang-tse. He didn't plan any continuity in them. "I simply made a list of all the stories I could think of," he tells us, "and checked them off as I wrote them. Some that I remembered I was not able to write to my satisfaction, and so they do not appear."

Joe Brainard's *I Remember* and John Cage's "Indeterminacy" seem to me the epitome of the kind of conceptual writing that compels me most, combining the personal and the impersonal, or rather the intentional and the speculative. "Many things, wherever one is, whatever one's doing, happen at once," says Cage. "They are in the air; they belong to all of us. Life is abundant." Brainard and Cage stand on a hill looking out at the world. Each of them is looking from where he stands, examining the personal, but also something beyond it. You might call this thing being, but that makes Brainard at least seem too metaphysical. To me the thing they examine is the shift from being to becoming, the always incipient movement that can never be concluded. It never stops. It's less related to memory than to consciousness.

I'm pretty ready to let go of the personal, or narrative for that matter, but I'm attracted to iteration—the repetition of a process or an utterance, repeating the gesture until something else emerges. Most conceptual art has a specific formulation that unfolds through some kind of repetition in the work or in the execution itself. This "aesthetics of administration" (a term from Benjamin Buchloh) feels richer to me than creative subjectivity or expression: you set up a paradigm or hypothesis and then follow it through with some internal consistency.

Trying to be random, or receptive to chance, is obviously not something you can just let happen. You have to invite chance in. I began to keep paper with me all day and to note whatever came up. After about three lists the patterns were already formed. Like Cage, I found things that stuck in my head, the things I read or things people told me, and things that were happening around me. I pushed them away, hoping for something wilder. But then the random things had to be about me, and I'm not wild at all: everything came out clean and polished and even in complete sentences, as if to put a point on it. Like the English language, the complete sentence is stamped into my mind.

Peggy's declining health worked its way into my daily list more often than not. She stopped eating her dog food, so I'd cook things for her. When I wasn't traveling, she was at the heart of my daily life; when I was away, I thought about her. I knew that Peggy's death and the end of the project might coincide. Sydni Bender, whose cat had died of cancer, was full of advice about what to feed her. As I hit the last ten days, Sydni begged me not to let the last list end with Peggy's death. Everyone with cancer deserves hope, she said. She noticed that I skipped writing a list on occasional days. Was I manipulating the narrative or was I manipulating my life? I felt guilty that I was engineering the lists around Peggy's coming death, as though it was not just a narrative manipulation but might even contribute to Sydni's death, or at least her suffering. I tried to ignore the tone of her messages, and often left one-word answers. She was going through her next course of chemotherapy and somehow lost her internet connection, and then she stopped writing.

Sydni Bender died in 2011. Her Facebook page is still active a year later; people leave sentimental notes for her, testaments about her life, elegies for her death. If I were a guiltier person I would dedicate this book to her. In fact she did affect the book: so as not to hurt her, I wrote the final list as we were leaving to put Peggy to sleep, but I left out her actual death. It's the most conspicuous example of the ways in which many aspects of the list were against my will. Writing anything, much less a book, is always an act of will, but perhaps this one is less so.

This brings me back to Umberto Eco's sad old chestnut about making lists because we don't want to die. I prefer even clinical formalism to rage-against-the-dying-of-the-light poetics. If I'm fighting anything, it's my own divided will, and yours as well. You want me to make sense, and to tell you stories. You want more than words. Maybe you're a bigger coward than I am, and fear death even more. I traded one thing I didn't want, to finish this project, with another: the end of Peggy's life. Or you could say I traded my attention to her death for your attention to my list.

Los Angeles
2011

Postscript:

The problem with memoir is its unrelenting focus on the self, and memoir was often the category in which my book was placed. Despite my intentions to the contrary, *2500 Random Things About Me Too* was too much about me. It's a failure to the degree that I am not random. So I've embarked on a new project and it's all about you. Me was easy, but you are hard. Writing 2500 random things about you is like stuffing too many things through a small hole. I was big, but you seem…smaller. Psychoanalysis tells me that I am a subject, and you my object, but there is no subjectivity without an other, that thing which I am not. That thing is you.

One of the great inventions of the English language, you merges intimacy and detachment, the informal and the formal: the *du* from German and the *vous* of French, particular and universal. Behind my desire for you might lay my desire to desire—a way to stay alive—but perhaps behind that is my desire to be desired. You're a gift to me, and my objective gift in return is my recognition. As I work on listing things about you, you're constantly being displaced with someone else. You never stay still. It makes me wonder if I have more desire than you. Is it possible that I am filled with longing to such a degree that without it, I barely exist? And if this desire is for you, what does it say about me?

Los Angeles
2014

Material

Casements

Parapet

Tracer

Maneuvers

Recon

Surplus

08. Logistics

Redell Olsen / Dodie Bellamy / Chris Tysh / Divya
Victor / Alice Könitz / 2013

MIND THE GAP:
A PREFACE

Vanessa Place

The world is full of partial objects. In part, one could safely say the world is only partial objects. Or at least say that since 1915, the vicissitudes of the object have been as familiar as their tendency towards flotation, and that since 1975, we've been happy as shiny state quarters in our castrated understandings of the same. In the collection I'm now fronting, partial objects are proudly on parade: mouths, cunts, cuts of tongue, and the skin-surface of films/film-surface of skins. And while it would be terribly safe to say this all falls in the now-comfortable discursive register of the gap, the vacuous referent that puts the *de* in deconstruction, this itself is insufficiently partial, or hardly provisional enough. For just as *de* is "duh," the pieces before me obviously say, as the voice-over obviously says, "mind the gap." Put another way, the mind is here, dumbly on display as the partial object par excellence, that horribly skinny chasm between what may be and what, for all intents and purposes, *is*. Put another way, the mind as such is that *Ding* which cannot be said, but only literally minded. Of course, this is old Kantian hat, and yet, like any hat, once doffed, it's as easily forgotten. Luckily for us, meaning you, we have these four partial reminders, set, perhaps improbably, in a series entitled *Logistics*. Logistics, of course, is that branch of the military that addresses the support and deployment of its personnel: support meaning making sure there is proper equipment; deployment making sure there is proper movement, including evacuation and hospitalization, as needed. In business, logistics simply refers to minding the organizational details. The devil, as you know, is in the details.

Thus, the devilish deployment of scripture in Chris Tysh's "In the words of a djinn: an exercise in transcreation," in which the author speaks to and for the impossiblity of translation, which is also a partial trope, but rather than whinge and wail or pledge some partial fidelity, a monstrous infidelity is happily sworn. And, like the advice columns advise, infidelity is trickier, involving rules and big-picture promises, with no room for petite or grand jealousies. *I.e.*, when Tysh takes Genet, as Deleuze advises, and Jean might have liked, from behind, it is as an American, that is to say, without saying *bonjour*. What issues is a Frankenstein that is not frightening but frighteningly familiar. In the same way that truly new poetry can creep gently under the skin, then erupt, unbidden, in the same way that one's own American-ness comes unwilling from the heart, mind, and mouth, including the American-ness that wants to escape being American, but is forced to the fore by the foreign, this Genet can't help but yawp in the *langue du jour*. Is there a gap? Between now and then? To my mind, it reads more like an evacuation. As with soldiers in retreat and bowels in action. After all, what is history, what is literature, if not yesterday's tomorrow today? Prisoners in cells know as much, as do penned children: all that poetry is is the hash of time, what's marked *now* for later. Versus prose, of course, which presents itself in the puffed golden crust of *fait*. The plans one makes when one doesn't yet fully grok the enemy at hand. So Tysh properly slices our sailor-bait into seven-line stanzas (same number as the seas) and *Our Lady of the Flowers* becomes a fresh bouquet of thick and salty sensations that set us back into the slits of our orifices, with little to do but wait, watch, and try hard not to itch.

Children, being fundamentally Humean, often confuse itching and scratching. Similarly, Redell Olsen's filmic metamorphoses are itchy scratches and scratchy itches. Effect, that is, creating cause. In her "To Quill at a Film," Olsen plucks at the resultant scrim between images and words, pointing at that suture-point where iconiclasm becomes iconicism because each limns what ought, by rights, lies beyond each, but which are only illuminated in their negative lights. In other words, just as birds cannot be photographed for field guides, but must be drawn and colored—because photographs are too specific, reducing the generic creature to a singular bird, whereas illustrations are general, only typographical, amplifying a bird to Bird—Olsen indicates language operates as guide to and obfuscation of image, and image as key to and confusion of sound. Meanwhile, as the motion pictures say, her mind is ostensibly set in the gap between image/word, as if there should be a harmony, or as if harmony is anything more than a happy synchronicity. The *mise en abyme*, like the scratch, is now *mise en face*, put in place of the itch. By characterizing her practice of writing and "saying live" over/on extant film as the movement from a found relation to a poetic one, Olsen creates a kind of feeding tube running from room to room, which serves to hide the salami, so to speak, from the real logistical work at hand: showing that all poetic relations are fundamentally found. And the rest, as they say in Hollywood, is history.

Historical razzle-dazzle is the preferred mode of Divya Victor's glitterati *oratorio*: mouth after mouth after mouth, so many maws flapping throughout her "buccal biography" that Freud himself would have called for some face-saving, a bit of clamming up. There are no elegant mouths in this Cubo-Futurist *bios*, for whether in repose "crusted with Colgate edges" or "scrubbed with a gnashed *neem* twig," or moving "elated to teats" or messed with "mother's tampons," these orifices are pinkly feral, scribbled with rank desire. Rank is a good thing in the military, proving an easy guide to who ought be listened to. But Victor's mouths are moreover revealed as senseless as a footsoldier's soliloquy, "sweaty" being as illogical in the mind of the mouth as "minty" is to the mind's eye. What comes through these serial gapes then is not an oral fixation, but a scopophilic one: we see that we love to look inside, to watch the sponge of a fat rouge tongue and oogle the uvula's plump bounce and clutch. It's not a point we're after, just the constant in-and-out: we take in what exits and duly expunge a serrated self in fits of sound and excremental story. And, if I can sustain this slippery slide from one speculum to another, mouth-feel is just what Dodie Bellamy's "These Lips Which Are Not One" provides. By supplying a country cook's guide to her cunt-ups, Bellamy does Burroughs one better: if the phallus is the thing that cannot be shown (as it will be revealed as merely a penis), the cunt is the thing that can/must be constantly on display (as no matter how hard the gaze, the mystery, *comme l'origine du monde*, persists). Author is no substitute for authority.

These cunts prove as impermeable and reversible as raincoats: as Bellamy writes, once a text is cunted, it is "monstrous, unashamed," walking about like it wasn't showing its toothed seams, which, by happy harmonic chance, articulate the rough seems that the hybrid always suggests. If the difference between metamorphosis and hybridity is that the metamorphic text is entirely transformed, going from *esse* to *esse* with full faith and credit given each to each, the hybrid text is necessarily a messier proposition. The hybrid can neither relinquish nor fully regulate its constituent parts: the creature is a logistical failure to the exact degree it is a logistical success—for every deployment, there is something unaccounted for. And why not? If we can ditch the love of the gap for a moment, and just hold hands, can we not agree that we are, at best, ourselves only partial solutions, flapping wildly about, mouths hanging open, images flitting before our faces as monstrous sounds sound from our guts, mouths, and butts. It's the same old story, trying to fashion some sort of crummy coherence out of our various partial engage-ments. Including, as it hardly need be said, the conceit of the sentient self. But, as Deleuze would say, bugger me. Or, put another way, as artist Paul Chan has written: "If art has any insight into life today, it is that we have no other interior than the world."[1] Logistically speaking, in other words, I'm glad I'm a man.

---

1. Paul Chan, "Where Art Is and Where it Belongs," *The Return of Religion and Other Myths: A Critical Reader in Contemporary Art.* Eds. Maria Hlavajova, Sven Lütticken, and Jill Winder. (BAK: Rotterdam, NL, 2009) 67.

TO QUILL AT FILM

Redell Olsen

*(A Masque as it was Presented
on Five Film Poems
not necessarily shown here)*

"The power of poetry depends on its ability to maintain
continuity while achieving discontinuity, but it is difficult
to show precisely how this is done in particular cases."
– Veronica Forrest-Thomson

"One must beware of contrasting aesthetic refinement
and a certain crudeness, a certain instant effectiveness of
a realism which is satisfied just to present reality."
-– André Bazin

The Preface to the Reader

For so much as shows and spectacles of this nature are usually registered among the memorable acts of the time, being complements of state, both to show magnificence and to celebrate the feasts to our greatest respects, it is expected (according now to the custom) that I, being employed in the business, should publish a description and form of the work done.

Poetry shares with the pre-war classics of the American screen the luxury that artifice can be "invisible." Poems were broken down for one purpose, and it was not for scrap value to the munitions factories. What is the material or historical logic of a phrase or a word that has owned itself already and been sprayed with meaning as it passes through use like a star through a crowded room?

SONG OF TRANSFORMATION

REALISM: And it is not only to be found on the electronic pages of some galley walls in high-end financial districts.

STILL: In 2013 the silent word poem has peaked.

POESY: Liar. In 2013 the silence of the word "poetry" is at a peak.

REALISM: [Aeolian splutter]

POESY: The silent "word" poem is peaky with regret at what remains undone.

SONG OF TRANSFORMATION (AGAIN)

They enter singing.

Chorus: Keep talking at readings in the same old or get with the new movies that place voice and image in impossible relations to adjust to open. A shout out to the lyric harpies as deviate extends, which some would say are torches.

Boweth towards the state, craveth their stay.

Chorus: All is at sea in a sink of poetic justification, yet some justification of poetics remains or forms the gaps in splutter between the sound of word and image meeting in conversation.

Enter in pixels.

Film Poem #1: This film poem stands to one side as a voice and refuses to know it all or does the voice over in difficulty as a live one against the other found wanting.

POESY: What is read is an acknowledgement of loss and the beginnings of a film over writing.

Film Poem #2: Or, this film poem as the meniscus of words as images as words that film up at the surface of encounter.

Chorus: Souped up desktopkitchens at galley proof set to the live-edit place at playhead against body as confined that is a poetic language in resistance that spreads its distance from nowhere near the red carpet as dim prospect.

Enter as B-Movie or costume in pixelated form.

Enter in their forms with these words.

POESY: I drew a plan of the filming instrument. The writing drew within the field of the camera and the filming commenced. The hunting, filming, and capture of wild form. I drew a plan of the writing instrument as a poetics as a film for showing in live performance as a writing of day for night. Situations in which I might be expected to film writing occurred, and I was drawn to the archives and made them in the everyday. The bear was filming a commercial in the Western Isles when he swam off to take a partlet in the making of (a film) as a writing implement, or a piece of lace, or a feather. The filming of this is put last as pure speculation to give the camera time to catch up, or to open it to the viewing public for redistribution by other means. What is filmed over is where the curtain rises to disappear:

London Land Marks (2007): On a secondhand stall on Brick Lane, London, I chanced across a late 1950s 8mm black and white ciné film entitled 'London Landmarks' which was clearly aimed at the tourists visiting London. The first time that I tried to screen the film on an old ciné projector, the film caught fire as it went through the projector. I was left with long pieces of film that were apparently useless. I scanned what remained of these pieces of film reel onto a computer and compiled a series of still images that I later began to project in performance. These stills often contained multiple frames, as well as the edges of the original film stock which had words and letters already printed on them.

STILL: When your eyes have done their part.

> at times an attempt to break the covering
> of projective film writing in verse high
> energy discharge. The digital kinetics
> of the thing and feathers for coding quills
> collide as stills of no private-soul at
> any public wall and some as TALKIES,
> HAPPENINGS, or, a WRITING of the FILM
> over writing found across objects. FOUND
> fit for repurposing the READER of
> this showing DISLOCATES at opening,
> the viewer an object of interrupt to
> film at writing: *to cover with or as*
> *with a film.* Also, *to film over, to film*
> *up* or, *this incident should "film" well*

REALISM: After this low induction, by these succeeding degrees the chief masquers were advanced in their discovery.

The original film included pictures of famous landmarks in London such as Tower Bridge, Trafalgar Square, and Buckingham Palace, as well as more incidental images of a woman feeding pigeons, a London bus, and the crowds on Oxford Street. One section of the stills recovered in the scanning process showed a hand setting up a poster that detailed suggested topics for speeches that were to take place at Speaker's Corner in Hyde Park. This is a place in which open-air speaking, debate, and discussion are allowed apparently on any subject as long as the police consider the speeches lawful. In 2003 the park authorities had tried unsuccessfully to ban a demonstration against the war in Iraq that was to take place in the park.

I used the scanned images from the broken film as the basis for my own film poem and performance that made reference to the suggested subjects for public speeches at Hyde Park that had been listed on the poster in the film. My performance / reading was periodically interrupted with directions from a teach yourself Arabic audiotape which suggested a number of "basic expressions of survival."

ANTIMASQUE OF INTERTITLES

POESY: Boundaries at noise define but refusal of edges cannot limit actual noise of language.

Film Poem #1: A belief in velvet curtains curtails illusions of narrative but also offers a device for frame.

Chorus of Pixelated Forms: Speech bubble from the wise: "screen us from authenticity projectors set to auto-play."

Repeat.

STILL: Likewise, the elite despair felt up by so many has been dismantled and stowed: the uncritical shed.

STILL: What was "ideal" about that is now just a city with an underground that is subject to minor delays as passengers are advised to make alternative arrangements for grammatical transport to and from that this is called a work for your information as matter disrupts.

Enter as frame.

A Newe Booke Of Copies (2009): In this film poem for performance, I presented a film of a woman (myself) engaged in the action of making feathers into pens for writing. I followed directions for quill cutting as set out in Elizabethan writing manuals. The performance of the poem was delivered in relation to this footage as reading against and through the increasingly distorted noise of the knife on the cutting block as it shaped the feathers for writing.

untie feathers begin

hands take blade shave

keratin to cut of stem

How I always knew I had the sort of
face for production: to take WRITING
with a feather, to quill at film. We who
cannot leave it to film over or, as
we leave it FILMING while writing
so as it is necessary to take
to CUTTING towards an instrument
for writing as IMAGE. Some other
kind of Foley, filmy over writing
surfaces spread. One as film up of found
or as in the TRANSLATION of MATERIALS
across media and the whole distance
from there was this USE now USE changing
to this ONE. Here dislocated
and bent out of time parallels those placed
in contigual risk through new showings.
A coming soon LIVE ONE respliced
and interrupted by way of Neo-Benshi
commentary on documentary once
apparently certain. Now a new PRINT
with doubt MARKED as integral. For example:
"Say the subjects are long done. London land
is marked." This is not a guide book speaking.
In one a VOICE-OVER that refuses to
confirm what you know what it is to be
seeing and states itself as an alternative

The film poem draws on a number of sources and materials relating to penmanship, needlework, and their conflicting histories. I borrowed the title for the piece from an Elizabethan writing book also entitled *A Newe Booke of Copies* which was first published in 1574 and highlights rules and directions for correct handwriting in a variety of hands or styles.

direction to LOOKING. One that interposes
itself between the screen entered and left
as ongoing while in SHOWING risks
self-cancellation or excess of NOISE.
At insistence through repetition
of an ACTION that is restating by
deformation. Or, an impossible
book of the READY-MADE as a film
screening. A copyist interposed as
a moth in the self-projector by way
of PERFORMANCE. Irrupts as part of and
in part obstruction to the Matinee
Idol for war or for the sake of ornamental
SPRIGS & spots. Sure, you should not be without
a clean historical shirt and this cuts
one to the cloth of the body in making.

———————————

PLATE TWO

The   *Text Hand or*
great and monstrous ruffes
transgresseth law of most

It is also the first book of its kind to be printed in movable type and marks a shift in power from
the biblio-calligrapher to the printer. Medieval scribes, like embroiderers, are mostly lost to
anonymity. They usually did not sign their work. The individuality of the writer or seamstress
is caught or glimpsed in the flourish of the decorative pattern, in the margin or on the collar of a
garment. Unattributed illuminations and rough copies in whitework are re-sampled. The earliest
named and dated British sampler to have survived was by Jane Bostocke in 1598. Her sampler is
from a period of transition in the practical use of embroidery in the sixteenth century. Contemporary with this, the Elizabethan ruff is taken by many people to epitomize the high fashion of
this period. Ruffs were often covered in embroidery and seemed to have enacted an extremity of
ornamentation which marked the status of the wearer. Due to shortages of paper, damaged clothes
were recycled into the rags used to make pulp for paper.

REALISM: If joy had other figure.

If there is a narrative then it is redistributed as a screech lyre of the noise to quill cutting under written. Or, as an unsteady challenge to any self-presentation in mourning, cuts-in with difficulty extended so come the interval there are no sentimental ice creams to be had. One that is writing through loss at image cranks up the materials of penmanship and its matter in live presentation that if caught alight could disrupt the screening matter in its entirety. A refusal of all that hooklets us towards. A performance at the film of writing.

Bucolic Picnic (or, toile de jouy camouflage) (2009) is a film poem which incorporates texts with found footage from a number of sources that include: a documentary on the history and the making of Toile de Jouy fabric, the history of camouflage as a textile developed for use in the first world war, footage from a 1927 film version of Daniel Defoe's *Robinson Crusoe*, and amateur footage of people who make and use their own ghillie suits. The film poem has two epigraphs, the first from Gertrude Stein:

> *I very well remember at the beginning of the war being with Picasso on the boulevard Raspail when the first camouflaged truck passed. It was at night, we had heard of camouflage but we had not yet seen it and Picasso, amazed, looked at it and then cried out, yes it is we who made it, that is cubism.*

and the second from Defoe's *Robinson Crusoe*:

> *at low water I went on board, and though I thought I had rummaged the cabin so effectually that nothing more could be found, yet I discovered a locker with drawers in it, in one of which I found two or three razors, and one pair of large scissors [...]*

Still from *A Newe Booke of Copies* (2009-10)

NEW [SONG IN TRANSIT] POP

REALISM: What gives in "us" the community to mock it up?

STILL: The chosen aesthetic path of interference buffered self in "exquisite embarrassment."

POESY: Fess up to the realization that this writes through channels between stations.

REALISM: I left my hat on a blue seat with little squares.

FILM POEM: I get the picture. Still moving.

Enter in song.

FEELING OFF SEATS

POESY: No, in process surrender in process.

REALISM: No, luxury in chaos totes.

STILL: Too branded.

REALISM: One frame follows the next is an illusion we carry on like luggage that can be stowed in the lockers above our heads.

STILL: Accept no responsibility for how poetics is feeling belated these days.

POESY: Get that lyric out of my eye, I am trying to become reading watching or as a listening post sounds happens outwards as thinking projects as back-story.

REALISM: Noise of image at proof will fulfill the film poem that must properly ask if the technical revolution of *iMovie, Premiere, Photoshop* is in any sense an aesthetic revolution?

STILL: In other words, did the years from 1995 to 2013 actually witness the birth of a new one?

POESY: Or, enter as Jane Bostocke to try one's hand at writing a treatment for Elizabethan ruffs to rags pulped for paper. I could not tell her that she should have to become expert in the Secretary hand before taking this on.

Self-borders husk enters as film poem but does not conform to the directions given as the credits roll.

Now Showing!

Screen 1:

> A film over of London complete with Landmarks
> A film over of marks in the Land complete with London

Screen 2:

> A covering for war in the textiles of pastoral delight
> A covering for delight in the war of pastoral textiles

> Razzle-Dazzle in battle dress films up the boundary
> Boundaries at Razzle-Dazzle film up battles in dress

> Between text and textile a film overmade by collect
> By collection a film over between textile and text

The Lost Swimming Pool (2010) was a site-specific installation and collaboration with a chore-ographer, a researcher, sound designer, and an artist filmmaker. The installation took place in a disused swimming pool that had been remodeled as a lecture hall. The original swimming pool was still just visible and perfectly intact underneath the current floor. The project was conceived in part as an homage to Esther Williams who would have represented the U.S. as a swimmer in the 1940 Summer Games had they not been cancelled. It also drew on images of women's physical education contemporaneous with the founding of Bedford and Royal Holloway Colleges in London.

Screen 3:

> A covering in feathers or writing at the border of film
> Feathers or a writing to film up with borders covering
> A movement from quill to type films over with cutting
> Over at the film a movement types to cut with a quill

Screen 4:

> Not writing as refabrication of instructions in the archive
> Instructions as writing through the fabrication of archive
> sum writing as exploration of soluble properties writ
> writ sum as soluble exploration of property

Screen 5:

> An industrial process that films up the ornamentation
> An ornament to the industry of the film in that process
>
> Of work done by hand and of itself as a "natural" record
> Of a "natural" record of itself of work and done by hand
>
> In the mode of a machine that films up the natural breaks
> In the mode of a machine that films up breaks in "natural

The text for this film poem incorporated the written accounts of women who had used the pool from the 1940s to the late 1960s. The sound and images for the piece included recordings made from underwater footage of contemporary synchronized swimmers and samplings from 1930s swimming musicals. Apart from my voice, the voice of Esther Williams was also heard, as recorded in a 1996 interview in which she recalls auditioning for the 1940 San Francisco *Aquacade* during which the director and entrepreneur, Billy Rose, instructed her to swim "pretty" rather than "fast" to which Esther replied, "If I can swim fast then I can learn pretty."

Let us distinguish between two bored and often
opposing trends in poetics: those writers who put their
faith in words about the other place we call really here
and now, and those who put their faith in language
as a part of it to be writing as itself as in the film of
writing thinking between us. Of course these are not
necessarily mutually exclusive positions. By filming,
here I mean, very broadly speaking, the writing of what
represents as even as it is one itself and includes objects
long lost in an archive or car boot sale for that is matter
joining as meaning as some others will arriving and
so to remain. The writing and saying live, on and over
film of what is already existing but stills as reshaping in
terms of thinking over pages. This is the language of the
film poem and this is where the film was a found one
until used differently. This could all be reduced to two
categories: the relationship to the plasticity of language
and found images and the relationship to the resources
of the language as a film of syntax, which, after all,
is simply the ordering of words in time that might
go better somehow differently behaved. Not unlike
montage but less dressy. Before you leave the page,
look at the screen and take one thing off.

Certainly, as regards showings, history does not actually
show as wide a breach as might be expected between the
silent visual work and the poem. On the contrary, there

S P R I G S & spots (2011-12) is a film poem written in response to a silent film which was made
to document the Nottingham lace industry (*Lace*, 1930). The title refers to the most common
industrial designs for lace. The poem is performed live in relation to the film which is played in
slow motion and fragments into a grid as the piece progresses. The text is read live in relation to
the noise of Jacquard looms and percussion on toy piano.

is discernible evidence of a close relationship between
certain curators and writers if the work assaults neither
eye nor feeling. Words are the film between what was
said and seen and also the means of seeing that is
something burning in the projector called language.
This is worth filming in writing, or writing in filming,
and redistributes the slump of star-struck poetic reverie
to outtakes. Film of the film between words and images
interrupting as voice is over. Words acting out of love in
language almost. Feathers to quill at film, in rushes.

––––––––––––––––

The poem for the new voice-over appropriates material from: the history of the development of
lace manufacture as it moved from hand to machine, descriptions of paintings of lace-makers,
Renaissance accounts of lace, and 1950s advertisements for machines in domestic use. It has three
epigraphs:

> *The whole value of lace, as a possession, depends on the fact of its having beauty which has*
> *been the reward of industry and attention […] If they all chose to have lace too, if it ceases to*
> *be a prize, it becomes, does it not, only a cobweb?*
>
> – John Ruskin

> *And how will you bee able, Lady, with this frugalitie of speech, to giue the manifold (but*
> *necessarie) instructions, for that Bodies, these Sleeues, those Sirkts, this Cut, that Stitch,*
> *this Embroydery, that Lace, this Wire, those Knots, that Ruffe, those Roses, this Girdle, that*
> *Fanne, the tother Skarfe, these Gloues? ha ! what say you, Ladie.*
>
> – Ben Jonson

The third is from Ada Lovelace who was a mathematician who corresponded, and subsequently
collaborated with, the nineteenth century scientist and inventor, Charles Babbage. Babbage had
already designed the Difference Engine and the Analytical Engine and Ada's explanatory notes
clarified and extended his designs. Versions of these machines were subsequently taken up by
manufacturers of industrial lace and later recognised as early forms of computers:

> *Whenever from any point without a given line, you draw a line to any point in the given line,*
> *you have inflected a line upon a given line.*
>
> –Ada Lovelace

London
2013

THESE LIPS WHICH ARE NOT ONE

Dodie Bellamy

Cunt Norton is the big-budget sequel to the indie *Cunt-Ups*, which I published with Tender Buttons in 2001. I've merged the porno-erotic source text of my original cut-ups with poems harvested from the second edition of *The Norton Anthology of Poetry*. In *Cunt Norton*, I send *Cunt-Ups'* lovers to extravagant English and East Coast U.S. locales. They fuck and suck in dramatic landscapes, lightning flashing, on the earth and in bodies of water; they come spraying though rarefied air. I costume them in gowns by Edith Head, glamorize them with guest appearances by famous stars. No more Jeffrey Dahmer confessions and internet articles on the connection between sperm and ectoplasm; we're talking Shakespeare and Lord Byron, we're talking the big-time verse philosophers.

Published in 1975, the second edition of *The Norton* is the one I was exposed to as a young poet. In the anthology's preface, the editors rehearse the additions they made to the 1970 first edition: they doubled the amount of women—they're particularly proud of Anne Bradstreet, Emily Brontë, and Elizabeth Barrett Browning—and they added 34 additional modern poets (the youngest being Nikki Giovanni and Michael Ondaatje). They also diluted the volume's whiteness a bit. "Four new black poets amplify the presentation of that tradition," they write, implying that all black poetry hails from a single altern ("that") tradition. In the back cover copy, the 1344-page (including the index) collection is heralded "a magnificent bargain, with poems a penny each"—perhaps a reference to Joyce's *Pomes Penyeach*, though Joyce himself is not included in the anthology. My original plan for *Cunt Norton* was to focus solely on white male poets, but after reading *The Norton*'s preface, I was reminded that patriarchy—ditto its canon—has more moving parts than I had anticipated. Therefore, in acknowledgement of the 1975 edition's proud tokenism, I have cunted one white female poet and one black male poet.

To tart up this introduction, I'd planned to weave in a juicy quote from "These Lips Which Are Not One," an essay by Luce Irigaray that was really important to me as an antidote to the reverence for the literary canon I was taught at Indiana University. I discovered it in the early 80s when Irigaray's translator, Carolyn Burke, visited Kathleen Fraser's Feminist Poetics class at San Francisco State. When I started researching the essay online, I could find no reference to such a text, and I eventually concluded that my remembered title is an amalgamation of Irigaray's book *This Sex Which Is Not One* and her 1980 essay, "When Our Lips Speak Together." By citing a hybrid text that doesn't exist I invite you into the tangled world of *Cunt Norton*, through the veins of which misappropriation flows like donated blood that's been mistyped.

Burke's translation of Irigaray's "When Our Lips Speak Together" begins like this: "If we continue to speak the same language to each other, we will produce the same story." A bit later: "If we continue to speak this sameness, if we speak to each other as men have spoken for centuries, as they taught us to speak, we will fail each other. Again.... Words will pass through our bodies, above our heads, disappear, make us disappear." In *Cunt Norton*, I will not flee from an aesthetic designed to make me disappear; instead I take on these texts, in the spirit of the Buddhist tonglen practice, where instead of turning away from painful material, you embrace it. You breathe negativity into your body and breathe out light. This is my dream for *Cunt Norton*, that the text breathes out light, or something more feminist than light.

These patriarchal voices that threatened to erase me—of course I love them as well. To cunt a text is to adore it. As those bards of yore so well knew, desire—think Cupid's arrow—arrives from elsewhere. You can feel it coming on like the flu, suddenly there's this other—it doesn't matter if you've known them for 20 years—suddenly there's this energy and even if you say to yourself, not him, not her, you know there is no resisting, it's inevitable, this person—even if they're unaware of you, they take up residence in your psyche and there's no getting rid of them. You feel destroyed before it begins, yet compelled. Desire exhausts us, dissolves us. *Cunt Norton* will last as long as there are quadrants of desiring text. When those are spent, the book ends. Until then it will keep fusing with poem after poem, desperate and insatiable. The irrationality of uncontainable desire consumes the tight metrics of logocentrality. As the two texts thrust against one another a new rhythm is co-created, Shakespeare Frost Stevens Byron Whitman Wordsworth Milton Poe seasoning the act with loftiness, melancholia, hubris, Romantic kinkiness, nostalgia, a range of mysticisms, mourning, religiosity, and nature, nature, nature. Libidinous voices cry out in the night. We're never quite sure if the voices are one or two, if it/they are talking to one another—us—or it/themselves. This is as it should be.

On Facebook I asked friends if there were any poets in particular they would like to see cunted. Pazit said Shakespeare; Juan chose Gerard Manley Hopkins. Dorothy Trujillo Lusk wrote, "ooooh! do ME!…but I'm not there…do me anyways! oxox…" To "do" someone is to fuck them. I'd love to *do you*, Dorothy. Writing is a sexual act. Cunting forefronts that. Cunting is so exhilarating I have the fantasy of marketing Cunt-Ups Kits—a packet of pretorn porno-erotic quadrants and instructions. Here's how you do it:

Do not study the original *Cunt-Ups* before beginning this process. Each instance of cunting is a new encounter, not a reinscription. Each person who cunts will impart her unique DNA. (All persons who cunt are female, regardless of the gender they present in ordinary reality.)

Choose a poet and decide which poem(s) of his you want to "do." Find text(s) online and copy it/them into an MS Word document. Remove line breaks so you create a solid block of text. Format in 12-point Palatino font, line spacing set for 1.5 lines, left-justified. Set document margins at 1-inch, top and both sides, 1.6-inch on the bottom. This should give you 30 lines of text per page; you need exactly 30 lines of text per cunt-up. If your source poem does not yield 30 lines of text, add more poems to it until you get enough text.

Print out prose block. Fold in half, top to bottom, so you have 15 lines on each half. Rip in two (ripping against a ruler expedites the process and results in a nice, clean edge). Fold these two pieces in half, left to right, rip again. You should end up with four quadrants of equally distributed text. Choose two quadrants for your cunt-up. Randomly choose two quadrants of porno-erotic source text. For the top half of your page, combine a quadrant of poem with a quadrant of porno-erotic text so they line up perfectly, then tape them together. Left or right positioning is up to you. Repeat for bottom half of page. Then tape together top and bottom halves of page. You should end up with a prose block the same size and shape as your original prose block. Retype and rework until something interesting emerges.

Burroughs' instructions for cut-ups are so vague they're hard to follow. You can tell this guy never baked a cake from a recipe. Here's some non-Burroughsian fine points:

If a word is cut in half, you may finish it any way you like. E.g., "wo" expands to woman, worry, word, wonder, etc.

Words may be deleted; tenses and grammatical categories may switch. E.g., "because" (subordinating conjunction) becomes "becauses" (noun). Pronouns are totally up for grabs. Word order may not change; "hair beautiful" *cannot* become "beautiful hair." Though the practice is discouraged, extra words may be inserted, cautiously and sparingly, mostly for rhythmic purposes.

Irigaray: "Kiss me. Two lips kiss two lips, and openness is ours again. Our 'world.' Between us, the movement from inside to outside, from outside to inside, knows no limits [...]. Between us, the house has no walls, the clearing no enclosure, language no circularity. You kiss me, and the world enlarges until the horizon vanishes."

When you cunt a text, both texts are devoured, both are spit back up stunned by their new undulations, their hybridity an act of endurance and of disappearance, meanings evaporating behind them like a trail of smoke. Monstrous, unashamed, the new text mobius-strips itself, sprouts long silvery corkscrews of hair, walks barefoot over gravel, gold lunula glinting about its throat. Its lips they are not one.

San Francisco
2013

IN THE WORDS OF A DJINN: AN EXERCISE IN TRANSCREATION

Chris Tysh

To situate:

The new year is an infant. Behind us, the fiscal cliff, the Newtown rampage, Hurricane Sandy, the evil malfeasance of U.S. banks and the immensity of vulture capital, but also the Arab Spring and the OWS movement in their daring embodiment of emancipatory demands and dreams. To bring those into the witness box, to the *barre*, as the French say, is to think of writing as deeply inhabited within its historical circumstances. *Point à la barre.*

A new sentence is needed, a new stanza—"a poem to shatter the walls of my prison," as Jean Genet says with utter urgency. *Meditations in an Emergency*, indeed. My words stand on that narrow gangway, out to sea. Most recently, a new zone of interest has entered my writing: translation. I'm not talking about a classical exercise of translating, say, Baudelaire's *Les Fleurs du Mal* into English, as Keith Waldrop recently did, and sublimely, I might add. Instead, I extend the concept of literary translation toward what we might call a transcreation, or a transcultural dialogue. In *Molloy: The Flip Side*—the first leg of *Hotel des Archives*—I use the French language in which Beckett wrote his 1951 novel, *Molloy*, to find a contemporary American vernacular through which the hapless narrator speaks. The three-line stanza compresses Beckett's diegetic universe, sparse as it is, and allows me to link the two texts through the projection of a new, speaking subject—a funny, witty, old and disabled bum, going slowly nowhere. "Gotta check out soon / Be done with dying." The result is a poem that opens up the unendurable abyss of being, but whose zany, hobo lyrics keep a beat in a souped-up version of Beckett's existential masterpiece.

I confess:

I've been possessed by phantoms: from the ones I summoned from the death camps and crematoria in *Night Scales: A Fable for Klara K* to *Our Lady of the Flowers*, Jean Genet's 1943 disturbing elegy for social heterogeneity. Divine, Mignon-Dainty-Feet, and the young assassin, Our Lady, saintly figures in a forbidden realm of the senses—I snatch them up and cross time zones, native tongues as if someone was forever on the run, with fake papers, fake passport photo, yet such a resemblance...but also, or maybe foremost, an exuberance at leaving that fractious, spleeny self.

Relational poetics:

Nicolas Bourriaud's elaboration of altermodernity has been for me a useful framework, in particular, when he defines it as "putting translation, wandering and culture-crossings at the centre of art production":

> The altermodern goes against cultural standardization and massifi-cation on the one hand, against nationalisms and cultural relativism on the other, by positioning itself within the world of cultural gaps. The altermodern artist considers the past as a territory to explore, and navigates throughout history as well as all the planetary time zones. Altermodern is heterochronical.

That tactical move away from ground, origin and monologic truth functions, and instead, toward change, difference, deterritorialization, to use a Deleuzian vocab, is consonant with postmodernism's practice of appropriation, détour-nement, and literary piracy. We have the klepto-texts of Kathy Acker and the riotous cover of Dante by Susan Landers to light the way, just to name a few fellow travelers in these interchanges and switches.

I'm squatting, I'm OCCUPYing, I'm writing on the walls of Genet's prison-house. Cursive temple of felons:

A tag about *Martin the faggot,*
Bob the Queer and *Li'l Meadow*
The Swish

Bourriaud's planetary travel notwithstanding (I suppose hyperbole comes with the terrain), *Our Lady of the Flowers, Echoic* will not reside on Christopher Street nor on Castro. I've kept the legendary place names intact—Pigalle, Les Grands Boulevards, Place Blanche—and Divine cruises *au petit matin* in her tight sailor pants up and down the Parisian macadam.

As is the habit, Divine will hustle
On Place Blanche while Mignon
Takes in a show.

In the transfer from French to American, I strive to keep to the narrative arc of the novel while cutting and condensing the trajectory of the actants. In other words, I squeeze the bellows, as Dorothy Allison likes to say about her compositional method. The textual economy, always a desideratum in the lyric mode, here becomes an obligation not to chatter nor fall into the thick folds of the story, and yet retain the libidinal signifier, which, like a pool of blood, stains the whole poem. The seven-line stanza proves kinetic and plastic enough to perform such a contradictory demand.

Under the sheets I choose my nightly
Outlaw, caress his absent face
Then the body which resists at first
Opens up like a mirror armoire
That falls out of the wall and pins me
On the stained mat where I think
Of God and his angels come at last

In Genet, certain indelible images crush us, turning us inside out like a kid glove, sublime moments of inverted logic wherein the quintessentially debased, vile, and criminal is canonized, made holy, a savage god: Divine, crowning herself with a dental plate; Our Lady strangling the old man; Alberto showing the young Lou a mess of snakes. I lift the originals out of their glass frames and reposition them on my naked table, careful to let the cadences of the line bring out the crystallized word, grafting, suturing in tiny stitches.

>Only the men stand. Then D raises
>A strange strident laugh and sudden
>As a card trick rips out her dental plate
>Only to set it on her skull and with a
>Changed voice, lips eating dust, says,
>"Get this, ladies, I'm still a fucking queen."

To brush up against "the crystal of the sentence," as Zola writes, calls for a lexicon that ushers in the irrepressible prick of desire and moves around in a radical yet supple way. The camp vocabulary of the '40s—fairies, queens with their flower names and pearl tiaras, hustlers, pimps, and stool pigeons—weaves a lacy texture that is pure ensorcellment and revelation. To this local idiom that contours sexual otherness—"pants that cup his butt like a public bench"—I add the hard edge of contemporary American slang—smack, coke, cock, plow, spike, broad—the syllables laying waste to our stubborn fear of the other.

>With a crystal spike
>The room slides like a diamond
>On her index finger into gold
>Velvet and walnut-paneled walls
>"I feel it, Lou's hour has come,"
>She moans using the boy's old name
>Buried axe at the bottom of a pool

But at times I also can't help the irresistible charm of certain contemporary porn metaphors:

>But for Divine he's everything:
>Her joystick, little pony, love missile
>Jesus in his manger, baby brother
>An object of pure luxury that she decks
>Out with ribbons and flowers

If "each text is a machine with multiple reading heads for other texts," as Derrida claims in his 1979 essay, "Living On: Borderlines," a sort of hero sandwich which stacks a discourse on Blanchot and Shelley with a commentary on translation, then my text incorporation in *Our Lady of the Flowers, Echoic* both returns us to the first edge, the engendering border line and brings in a new graft that allows the living on, the survival under a new set of linguistic conditions. "Thus triumphant translation is neither the life nor the death of the text, only or already its living *on*, its life after life, its life after death," Derrida repeats. Ultimately, transcreation positions and permits this mutual, dialogic, participatory, relational traffic from one to the other.

More than anything, it is Jean Genet's keen, even aching sense of gender roles, and their corset of expectations, that has always struck me as immensely radicalized in his refusal of biological determinisms. Robert Glück's lapidary formulation in *Margery Kempe*, "gender is the extent to which we go in order to be loved," traces Divine, *né* Lou Culafroy, as the tragic embodiment of that desire.

In the final analysis, my writing practice has to do with the endlessly renewable pleasure of the text. Behind every encounter with a word, sign, or cultural frame, lies a field of possibility where the lyric turns to follow the naked body of its own song. Whatever our project happens to be at the moment, language ought to jimmy the lock of what is pushed into the night of knowing. From deep inside the walls of Fresnes prison, where Genet is incarcerated for theft, he writes a love poem dedicated to a young killer: "Le condamné à mort" will be our alarm.

> Amour viens sur ma bouche! Amour ouvre tes portes!
> Traverse les couloirs, descends, marche léger,
> Vole dans l'escalier, plus souple qu'un berger,
> Plus soutenu par l'air qu'un vol de feuilles mortes.
>
> Ô traverse les murs; s'il le faut marche au bord
> Des toits, des océans; couvre-toi de lumière,
> Use de la menace, use de la prière,
> Mais viens, ô ma frégate une heure avant ma mort.

Come to my lips, Love! Open the doors, Love!
Go down the corridors, tread softly,
Take the stairs flying, nimbler than a shepherd,
More buoyed by air than a flight of dead leaves.

Glide through the walls; and if you must, walk
The edge of roofs and oceans; wrap yourself in light,
Use threats, use prayers,
But come, o my raft, an hour before my death.

That "language leads into places I'd otherwise fear to go," as per Aaron Shurin's claim, reminds us that poetry's singular gift is to allow words to descend from their tagged and priced selves and spill, unbidden and profane, between the lines we're always just about to write.

Detroit
2013

Works Cited

Bourriaud, Nicolas. *Altermodern*. London: Tate, 2008.

Derrida, Jacques. "Living On: Border Lines." *Deconstruction and Criticism*. Ed. William Golding and Geoffrey H. Hartman. New York: Seabury, 1979. 62-142.

Genet, Jean. *Le condamné à mort et autres poèmes*. Paris: Gallimard, 1999.

Tysh, Chris. *Molloy: The Flip Side*. Buffalo, NY: BlazeVox, 2012.

Tysh, Chris. *Night Scales: A Fable for Klara K*. New York: United Artists, 2010.

A MOUTH TO MOUTH WITH YOUR MOUTH: A BUCCAL BIOGRAPHY

Divya Victor

a mouth sweaty with mutton
a mouth rushing with doves
a mouth with uneven peaks
a mouth headlined by a Marilyn mole
a mouth split open by a swinging swing
a mouth upside down brimmed by a drinking glass
a mouth rent by bicycle tires brittle with blood and sugar
a mouth crusted with Colgate edges
a mouth scrubbed with a gnashed neem twig
a mouth with a tongue forked in two by a fruit knife
a mouth gargling with glass marbles
a mouth with lips dearly departed
a mouth open face like a coffin or a tomato sandwich
a mouth gnarled by a dry chicken breast
a mouth with fennel interruptions
a mouth minty, clean, with pencil in between
a mouth coddled with curds and whey
a mouth so terse it snaps necks
a mouth licking the edge of a green glass bottle with a cork floater
a mouth curved in an umbra of a spit bubble
a mouth like a clod with a toad on it
a mouth groined by two hoary secrets
a mouth gummy purple with cream spinets when it opens to scold
a mouth with tender gums bled white with retreating edges
a mouth shaded by boney awnings

a mouth opening to incisors gutted by the primary-school gate
a mouth marbled grey and blue left too long in a lake
a mouth flung open and ringing from the belfry
a mouth puckered where the areola prickles
a mouth arched by the strain of a squat
a mouth green with split pea soup
a mouth so flopped like a fool's cap
a mouth pink as calamine and dull as the afternoon nap
a mouth like a gravy boat, empty with a greasy ring
a mouth hung open with a prolapsed grin
a mouth insistent in some crevice
a mouth foamy with Gillette
a mouth not quite near a gullet
a mouth replete with teeth
a mouth elated to teats
a mouth suckling metal railings near the dispensary waiting for ointments
a mouth kissing eucalyptus bark calling it a girl's name
a mouth chewing latex nipples
a mouth stuffed with rolled dough embalmed in palm margarine
a mouth smacked with a wooden ruler says every body remains at rest or
        moves with constant velocity in a straight line
a mouth smacked with a plastic hair brush says blessed are you among
        humans and bluster is the food in your home jesus
a mouth lined with chalk says if you have no daughters give them to your
        sons
a mouth two times six is twelve two times ten is twenty two is wrong
a mouth thick with eucharist take it and eat it and when you do
a mouth between slats looking for the loose guava
a mouth gloating with lemon jelly
a mouth agape on the flash light and drying
a mouth that rattles like 'a far away man shouting'
a mouth hurling into the hibiscus bush
a mouth quivering ave maria ave maria ave maria
a mouth licking bed frame, door knob, rosewood, lead
a mouth yellow and leathery as a jaundiced belt
a mouth sucking the errant thread
a mouth bleached the color of white-people band aids
a mouth mottled with comic book freckles

a mouth stuffed with gauze and harboring a grudge
a mouth blinking with hiccoughs
a mouth washed with boiled water and Vaselined for Christmas
a mouth caught sucking a deflated rubber balloon after the birthday party
a mouth found eating mother's tampons
a mouth caught arched with a Faber-Castell mustache
a mouth smug at Bob Saget's grainy, VHS crotch
a mouth cued to kiss for the camera
a mouth named Leticia not in that photograph
a mouth through the keyhole a sheet a flash of arm a mouth through a sheet
      a key hole
a mouth pressed against the creased fist pressed against
a mouth pressed against the creased fist
a mouth tracing the map of her stretch marks where the shirt skirts the skirt
a mouth eating grandmother's braid
a mouth eating out the soft egg
a mouth wafting out the Ambassador window
a mouth hung out to parch with the starched laundry
a mouth lolling about a mother's hemline
a mouth pressed on a Hello Kitty blue lacey knee
a mouth of the Chiclet full frontal
a mouth of gruel
a mouth of ash and sawdust
a mouth of stamps and salt licks
a mouth of the rolled 'zha'
a mouth of chlorine and egg yolks
a mouth five parts flesh four parts bone

Buffalo
2013

SYMBOL ON ISLAND

Alice Könitz

The company's symbol
on the island marks the
location of a hidden elevator
that leads to underground
laboratories in volcanic caves

Los Angeles
2013

appendices

A. Categorical Index

B. List of TrenchArt Titles

C. Note on Notes

A. CATEGORICAL INDEX

A non-comprehensive index of the TrenchArt essays arranged categorically.

Documentary Poetics

Ecopoetics

Ekphrasis/Reverse Ekphrasis

Essay Practices

Language Theories

B. LIST OF TRENCHART TITLES

A chronological list of the complete series of TrenchArt titles.

TrenchArt: Material (2005–06)
Dies: A Sentence | Vanessa Place
A Story of Witchery | Jennifer Calkins
Requiem | Teresa Carmody
Grammar of the Cage | Pam Ore
Material Series Visual Art: Stephanie Taylor

TrenchArt: Casements (2006–07)
Inch Aeons | Nuala Archer
in the plain turn of the body make a sentence | Sissy Boyd
Tribulations of a Westerner in the Western World | Vincent Dachy
+|'me'S-pace | Christine Wertheim
Casements Series Visual Art: Molly Corey, Lisa Darms, Tamzo, and Julie Thi
   Underhill

TrenchArt: Parapet (2007-08)
Chop Shop | Stephanie Taylor
Voice of Ice/Voix de Glace | Alta Ifland
God's Livestock Policy | Stan Apps
A Happy Man and Other Stories | Axel Thormählen
Parapet Series Visual Art: Danielle Adair

TrenchArt: Tracer (2008-09)
A Fixed, Formal Arrangement | Allison Carter
re:evolution | Kim Rosenfield
I Go To Some Hollow | Amina Cain
a | Sophie Robinson
Tracer Series Visual Art: Ken Ehrlich and Susan Simpson

TrenchArt: Maneuvers (2010)

Sonnet 56 | Paul Hoover
Not Blessed | Harold Abramowitz
The Evolutionary Revolution | Lily Hoang
The New Poetics | Mathew Timmons
Maneuvers Series Visual Art: VD Collective

TrenchArt: Recon (2011)

By Kelman Out of Pessoa | Doug Nufer
Negro marfil/Ivory Black | Myriam Moscona, translated by Jen Hofer
The Phonemes | Frances Richard
Tall, Slim, & Erect | Alex Forman
Recon Series Visual Art: Renée Petropoulos

TrenchArt: Surplus (2012)

2500 Random Things About Me Too| Matias Viegener
Lividity | Kim Rosenfield
The Memoirs of JonBenet by Kathy Acker | Michael du Plessis
Words of Love | Mark Rutkoski
For Want and Sound | Melissa Buzzeo
Surplus Series Visual Art: Klaus Killisch

TrenchArt: Logistics (2013)

Our Lady of the Flowers, Echoic | Chris Tysh
Cunt Norton | Dodie Bellamy
Things to Do With Your Mouth | Divya Victor
Film Poems | Redell Olsen
Logistics Series Visual Art: Alice Könitz

C. NOTE ON NOTES

As the writers in this volume use "notes," "works cited," "references," "endnotes," and "end- and bibliographical notes," to different purposes, we have maintained their preferred citation styles.

$$(p + r)^n$$

LES∮FIGUES
PRESS